3-3-79

The Art of Independent Investing:

**A HANDBOOK OF MATHEMATICS, FORMULAS
AND TECHNICAL TOOLS FOR SUCCESSFUL
MARKET ANALYSIS AND
STOCK SELECTION**

The Art of Independent Investing:

A HANDBOOK OF MATHEMATICS, FORMULAS AND TECHNICAL TOOLS FOR SUCCESSFUL MARKET ANALYSIS AND STOCK SELECTION

Claud E. Cleeton

PRENTICE-HALL, INC.
ENGLEWOOD CLIFFS, N.J.

Prentice-Hall International, Inc., *London*
Prentice-Hall of Australia, Pty. Ltd., *Sydney*
Prentice-Hall of Canada, Ltd., *Toronto*
Prentice-Hall of India Private Ltd., *New Delhi*
Prentice-Hall of Japan, Inc., *Tokyo*

Library of Congress Cataloging in Publication Data

Cleeton, Claud Edwin
  The art of independent investing.

  Bibliography: p.
  Includes index.
  1. Investment analysis--Handbooks, manuals, etc.
2: Investments--Handbooks, manuals, etc. I. Title.
HG4521.C513   332.6'78   76-9039
ISBN 0-13-047290-5

Printed in the United States of America

A Word from the Author

This book is written for the do-it-yourself stock market technician and is a handbook of procedures useful to the independent market analyst. It provides adequate mathematical background for the investor not trained in mathematics who wants to explore the methods used by the sophisticated market technician. Techniques are described to simplify calculations and procedures that make such studies practical as a part-time endeavor. Mathematical tables are included to complete the reference material needed for investors computing their own market indicators. 1949629

Many market books are available on market systems. Some by authors about their own systems and methods, and others of a general nature. Some systems work some of the time, but no system works all the time. An individual who finds a system which works for him most of the time is fortunate indeed. Reading the many stock market books can become confusing with all the various approaches described. Many market axioms which work some of the time appear under various descriptions leaving one with an uncertain feeling. Often they have a common basis and when viewed in the light of their true origin not only become plausible, but also become easier to interpret and thus more useful. A number of such *axioms* will be discussed and you are urged to develop methods of market study which will enable you to be comfortable in your appraisal of the stock market and which will provide you with the goals of success you establish for profits commensurate with the effort you choose to apply to those studies.

The book begins with fixed income investments, interest computations and a discussion of some of the money market instruments available to the investor looking for security of principal. This is followed by the alternative of investing in the stock market, with a discussion of stock price movements and methods of technical analysis for prediction of price movements.

The cyclic approach is presented as being fundamental to understanding and predicting market movements. A number of market indicators are related to the cyclic approach. Methods are described for doing your own analysis and forming your own indicators. Finally, analysis methods are applied to actual cases which indicate the quality of results one may expect to achieve.

In Chapter 16 the background mathematics is given, which serves as a review for those whose mathematical memories have become hazy; or for those not trained in the particular procedures, it serves to teach what is required to understand and perform the analysis presented in this book. This chapter may be read independently of the remainder of the book and should be read ahead of the mathematical discussions if you need a review.

No attempt is made to cover the entire stable of stock market systems and indicators, quite the contrary. Many indicators of market behavior have been developed which at times look like the last word; and some are religiously used by market analysts and advisors to make their predictions. Many, when examined over the years, have their bad times as well as good. Often, their proponents find it necessary to modify their system or interpretation in order to fit the circumstances better. This may make the record appear good but it leaves one with an uneasy feeling about the future. Many indicators are based on the same data and merely offer differing methods of presentation and interpretation.

This book keeps as close as possible to the basic data and how to use it in as direct a method as possible. Even though you use purely mechanical methods for making decisions, there is something added by devoting a little time each day, regardless of the market conditions and your present interest, to plotting a few charts, reviewing your results, and thinking about how and why the market and your selected stocks behave as they do. This book will provide you with the necessary background and simplified procedures to do this work with a minimum of effort. It contains timing and selection tools that make it possible for you to accomplish your financial objective independently.

My thanks goes to my wife, Mary Ellen, for editing, proofreading and assistance in typing.

Claud E. Cleeton

Contents

The Art of
Independent Investing:

A HANDBOOK OF MATHEMATICS, FORMULAS AND TECHNICAL TOOLS FOR SUCCESSFUL MARKET ANALYSIS AND STOCK SELECTION

1

Money Market Instruments

THE WAYS YOU MAY BE PAID FOR THE
USE OF YOUR MONEY

This chapter discusses some basic facts and observations relating to ways you can be paid for the use of your money. It might well cover the only type of investment a person of limited means would ever use, and should be considered by all investors as a part of their plans. The discussion is intended to aid you in defining your objectives and setting goals within the framework of your own situation.

A point is often made that gains are in proportion to the degree of risk one is willing to take. This is true only to a degree. The safest investment at any time is probably a fixed principal, government-insured, interest-bearing instrument. Such investments may earn an interest return greater than can be attained on investments of much greater risk. For example, in 1974 interest rates reached 10% on some guaranteed Federal Agency bonds available to investors of moderate means. The minimum investment amounts are usually $10,000 or $5,000 but some are as low as $1,000. At a given point in time there can be a wide variation in the rate of interest and also a wide variation in the restrictions related to such investments. If you decide to go this route, you should be aware of all these variations. Some investments may not be at all suited to your needs. The relative conditions may shift rapidly due to changes in the economic environment, government regulations or other conditions. What one might expect to be a most stable investment can, on a relative basis, undergo major fluctuations. Even these investments can not be bought and forgotten if you want to take advantage of your opportunities.

13

SAFETY

What is a safe, or low risk, investment? In one sense it is one where both the principal and interest are guaranteed. The best guarantor is normally considered to be the Federal Government, which of course backs the many U. S. Treasury bills, notes and bonds. Essentially as good are the Federal Agencies that guarantee deposits in commercial banks and savings institutions, namely, the Federal Deposit Insurance Corp. (FDIC) and the Federal Savings and Loan Insurance Corp. (FSLIC), whose insurance limit was raised in 1974 to $40,000 per account, although there are those who question whether these agencies could stand a massive crush of failures. There are a number of Federal Agencies that borrow money and have the guarantee of "the full faith and credit of the U. S. Government." Other Federal Agencies do not carry this stated guarantee, but there is an implication of government backing.

Banks and savings institutions are not compelled to be members of a Federal Insurance Corporation which commits them to government regulations on interest rates, etc. A non-federally insured institution frequently pays a higher interest rate. Some such institutions are state insured.

There is a further aspect of the low risk money instrument. Although your principal and rate of interest are guaranteed, there is frequently a large IF, that is, you must leave your money with the institution for a specified length of time, otherwise, should you need your money before this time is up, you may have to accept a lower rate of interest, or less than the full amount of principal. The familiar E bond is an example where maximum interest is received only when held to maturity. Savings and loan certificates have interest penalties if cashed in prior to maturity. Government and corporate notes and bonds, though redeemable at par (100%) at maturity, may be sold in the market prior to maturity at whatever price the buyer is willing to pay. This may be less than the principal amount you paid, or it could be more. In this case the shorter the time to maturity, the less the price is likely to vary and the more secure the investment. This comes about by realizing that the gain or loss on the sale, relative to the price paid, in effect modifies the yield on the investment. A bond having many years to maturity could sell well below par but yet not increase the yield very much when the gain is distributed over the years to maturity.

Corporate bonds are rated by Standard and Poor ranging from AAA, the highest, through AA, A, BBB, etc. to DDD, DD, and D. These last three are all in default. Moody's service and Fitch provide corresponding ratings.

SAVINGS BONDS

Nearly everyone is familiar with the Series E U.S. Savings bonds, in denominations starting at $25, which can be purchased at your bank or through a payroll deduction plan at most places where you work. They are sold at a 25% discount from face value and may be redeemed at various values prior to maturity. These were paying 6% compounded semiannually in 1974, *if held to maturity* of five years. However, if cashed before maturity, the interest return may be much less. For example, in 1974 they earned only 3.73% for the first six months, and only 4.5% if held only one year. In 1976 a 4-percent minimum was established.

These bonds illustrate a number of special conditions. They are easy to purchase and provide a disciplined savings when you are enrolled in a payroll deduction plan. They are sold and redeemed without a service charge. Interest may not be taxed until the bond is redeemed, which is an advantage if you expect your income to be less when the bonds mature such as after retirement. The Government has extended these bonds after maturity date at existing interest rates compounded semiannually. One may choose to report interest as it is earned if taxes would be lower. Such may be the case for minors who have little, if any, other income, resulting in the income being tax free. Interest on U. S. Government obligations are free of state and local taxes. This may result in the equivalent of up to a half of one percent additional interest for an average investor depending on your state income rate and income bracket.

These bonds may be redeemed at any time before maturity, after two months, if the money is needed. They can serve as a nest egg against emergencies, but, on the other hand, they do not pay full interest rate if not held to maturity. The rate increases with the time held. If forced to cash in some bonds, note the older bonds are earning at a much higher rate than the newer bonds, so cash in the latest ones. In order to achieve the maximum interest rate on these bonds, you are locked in for five years after purchase, so if you expect to need the money in less time some other form of investment may be preferable.

These bonds may be registered jointly with others, such as a minor or a beneficiary, and serve well for family gifts to children, grandchildren or other persons. If you are the donor, it is advisable not to be a joint owner unless you want to pay taxes on the interest.

Another type of savings bond, not quite as familiar as the Series E, is the Series H bond. Series E bonds may be converted to H bonds, or the H bonds may be purchased directly. They are not a discount bond and pay their interest as earned semiannually. There is also an interest reduction during the early years. Although earning 6% compounded semiannually when held for ten years, they earn only 5% the first year, 5.8% the next four years and 6.5% the remaining five years to their ten-year maturity. It may be useful to convert Series E bonds to Series H bonds when you retire in order to produce additional income on a recurring basis rather than cashing in your E bonds one at a time. However, remember that your return will be slightly less for the first five years if the bonds you convert are earning at their six percent or higher rate.

SAVINGS AND LOAN ASSOCIATIONS

Accounts in savings and loan associations and banks can be Federally insured up to $40,000 for each account but not all institutions are so insured. Federally-insured accounts are as safe as the U. S. Government. Various accounts can be set up to cover greater amounts in the same institution so there is no need to exceed the insured limit considering the number of different institutions available. Saving by mail is very easy. Accounts may be either the passbook or savings account type or may be the certificate or time account type. The interest rates vary considerably between types of accounts. The maximums as well as the withdrawal restrictions are Government controlled. The passbook type of account pays the lowest rate (typically 5¼%). A number of certificate types are usually available in which you commit your investment funds for a period of time ranging from three months to four or more years. They pay greater interest as the time increases, up to a point, such as 7.75% for six years. In either type, interest is normally compounded which increases the annual rate of return by fractions of a percent. Daily compounding became common place in the early 1970's and continuous compounding which provides the maximum rate of return is offered by many institutions. The associations are always pleased to provide you with specific information.

The passbook account, typically, has no significant restrictions. Any amount may be deposited or withdrawn on any day the office is open and in most associations interest is earned for each day the money is in the association. Such accounts are useful to earn some interest on funds temporarily in excess but which may be needed on short notice—a backup to a checking account.

Certificate accounts, though paying higher interest, have severe restrictions which may make them completely unsuited for your specific situation. You should investigate before going this route. Points to consider are illustrated by the following typical restrictions. Some interest penalty is applied if the certificate must be cashed before maturity. First, the rate of interest is reduced to the then current passbook rate, and second, you may completely lose the interest for a period up to three months. These regulations have been changed from time to time. There have been times when the restrictions were less severe for shorter-term certificates. On the other hand, one can lock in the higher interest rate if the funds can be left to maturity. This would be useful if you expect interest rates to decrease materially in the near future.

Certificates normally are issued for a minimum of $1,000 and up to five or ten thousand dollars for the longer terms. If interested, check available associations. They customarily advertise their rates and restrictions. Not all are federally insured; some are state insured. Uninsured associations usually pay higher rates. No service charge is involved for any of the transactions. The availability of certificates depends upon their need for your money and the general interest rates.

NEGOTIABLE CERTIFICATES OF DEPOSIT

Commercial banks provide similar account arrangements but are restricted to paying rates one-fourth of one percent less than savings institutions to the small depositor. If, however, you are fortunate enough to have $100,000 or more to invest, restrictions, other than the minimum, are off and instruments known as *CD*'s (Negotiable Certificates of Deposit) may be purchased for periods of one month or longer and often pay much higher interest. They reached up to 12% and more in 1974.

TREASURY BILLS

Each week the U. S. Treasury auctions bills maturing in 13 and 26 weeks, and auctions once a month those maturing for longer periods up to a year. These are often referred to as *T bills*. They are sold at a discount and the small investor can purchase at an average price determined by the week's auction. They may be purchased through a stock broker, your bank, or directly through a Federal Reserve Bank. You should expect to pay a service charge unless purchasing directly. This charge reduces the effective yield and can be significant when paid four times a year for repurchasing the 13-week bills. The Treasury establishes a minimum purchase which has been $10,000 face value. The service charge may not increase in proportion to the amount involved. You may be able to purchase a $15,000 bill for the same service charge as a $10,000 bill, so there may be an advantage in collecting your funds to be available at one time. The results of Monday's auction appear in Tuesday's newspapers. Settlement date and maturity dates are on Thursday. Costs are given on the basis of percent of maturity value. For example, if the average auction price is quoted as 97.912 for the 13-week bill, then a $10,000 bill would cost $9,791.20 plus the service charge of say $15 or $9,806.20 total. When the bill matures you receive $10,000 or $193.80 more than it cost which is the interest for one-fourth of a year. If rolled over (reinvested) at the same rate, you would receive four times this amount in a year, or $775.20 on an investment of $9,806.20, which corresponds to a simple annual interest rate of 775.20 divided by 9,806.20, or 7.9%. In addition, you receive interest quarterly which may be invested for additional interest. Besides the sale price of the Monday auction, the newspaper will also quote an interest rate, in fact, usually two rates. One is the yield quotation (see "Treasury Bill Yields" in Chapter 2) and the other an effective coupon rate but neither will take into account the service charge you may have to pay. I suggest you make your own interest computation. The significance of this suggestion is illustrated by assuming no service charge in the example above in which case you would compute a rate of 8.5% instead of 7.9%. A higher service charge would make this difference even greater. It is usually advantageous to purchase 26-week bills for then you pay only two service charges a year. In addition, at times their basic yield may be greater. Buying one-year bills may or may not be advantageous. Frequently their interest rates are lower but there is only one service charge a year. The shorter maturities price is easier to predict since there is a new auction each week and in between the financial newspapers report on the trend of resale yields. However, one must always contend with actions of the Federal Reserve Board which controls short-term money rates by various methods such as purchases or sales to put more money in or take it out of the banking system.

FEDERAL AGENCY INSTRUMENTS

There are several Federal Agencies that borrow money by selling notes or bonds having maturities ranging from six months to several years. Many of these are secured by "the full faith and credit of the U. S. Government", others are not Government guaranteed. Many require a minimum purchase of $10,000 but some do not. Most are issued at par ($1,000 per bond), but some are sold like T bills as a discount note. The interest of many is exempt from state and local income tax, but some are not. If interested in the details, check with your bank or broker.

These issues are traded over the counter, and bid and asked prices with yield to maturity are quoted daily in *The Wall Street Journal* for the most active agencies. They offer security second only to U. S. Treasury issues. Depending upon money needs, these agencies sell new issues at frequent intervals, sometimes as often as once a month. The offering is announced a few days before the auction, but the coupon rate may not be announced until the day previous to the auction.

Federal agencies whose notes and bonds have a market active enough to be quoted daily in *The Wall Street Journal* are: Federal National Mortgage Association (FNMA), Government National Mortgage Association (GNMA), Federal Home Loan Bank (FHLB), Bank for Cooperatives, Federal Land Banks, Federal Intermediate Credit Bank (FIC Bank), and United States Postal Service.

Frequently you can save money by buying new issues rather than purchasing in the resale market because the commission charge may be lower and the interest rate a little higher. Most enjoy an active market so you can get your money out, if needed, before maturity.

COMMERCIAL PAPER

Commercial paper is an IOU issued by a corporation to raise short-term working capital. The maturities range from one day to nine months. Standard and Poor, and Moody's Investor Service rate the paper of corporations, ranging through four grades with three breakdowns in each, the highest being known as A-1 or Prime-1. Besides the corporate rating, the paper may be supported by a bank line of credit known as two name paper.

The greater risk of Commercial Paper commands a higher interest rate than most other money instruments we have described. The small investors interested in this degree of risk to obtain higher income might be advised to put their money in a Money Market Fund, described below, where one obtains diversification and selection.

MONEY MARKET FUNDS

In the early 1970's, a type of mutual fund sprung up which offers the average investor benefits of the high yields obtained by the more affluent investor, having $100,000 sums for investment, in the unregulated CD's and other securities with high yield when purchased in large amounts. These funds[1] invest in short-term money market instruments such as Treasury bills, CD's, high-grade Commercial Paper, etc. They all have the objective of obtaining high yield on secure liquid investments. Their procedures differ in some respects and one may appeal to your needs better than another. If interested, you should write them for their descriptive material and application blanks. Although these funds retain some of the income for expenses, you will probably find the yield to you is greater than you could obtain if restricted to smaller purchases.

FLOATING INTEREST RATE NOTES

The floating interest rate note came to life in 1974 with the issue of the 15-year notes of Citicorp, a bank holding corporation. The pattern was established for many other bank holding companies and some other corporations. Two features are important in these issues. One is an interest rate that is determined every six months as one percent above the average *coupon* rate of the U. S. Treasury 13-week bills for the three weeks prior to the interest period. The other is that after two years they are redeemable at par at any 6-month interest date, upon proper notice. There are some floating rate issues with somewhat different features such as a lower limit on interest rate, other float spreads and not being redeemable until maturity. The waiting period of two years for company redemption was forced by the government and savings institutions on these inital issues, but to compensate, the interest rate of 9.7% which was called for during the initial period was guaranteed for one year. Government regulations may come into the picture and affect future issues. The major issues are traded on the stock exchange and their prices tend to fluctuate with the short-term money rates.

GINNIE MAE PASS-THROUGHS

The Government National Mortgage Association (GNMA) is a wholly-owned U. S. Government corporation which has certain responsibilities in mortgage purchasing functions. They issue various types of

---

[1]The Reserve Fund, 810 Seventh Avenue, New York, N. Y. 10019, lead the way and was followed by Money Market Management, Inc., State Street Bank and Trust Co., P. O. Box 1912, Boston MA. 02105; Dreyfus Liquid Assets, Inc., The Bank of New York, P. O. Box 11039, Church Street Station, New York, N. Y. 10249; and Fidelity Daily Income Trust, c/o FMR Service Corp., P. O. Box 193, Boston, MA. 02101. These have now been followed by many others.

securities of which one, the *Ginnie Mae Pass-Through*, is unique and has some features that may be of particular interest to certain investors. This security allows you to participate in the mortgage market with the U. S. Government fully guaranteeing prompt payment of both interest and principal. The payments are made monthly and could therefore serve to provide a cash flow much like an annuity which may be especially desirable during retirement years. The monthly repayment of principal gives these securities a characteristic ranging from a very short to a long-term bond. They may be purchased through your broker or bank and are very liquid, there being a secondary market maintained by dealers in Government Securities. The interest rate tends to follow longer-term corporate bond rates and may provide a greater yield than other forms of fully insured instruments.

The pass-through security is originated by a mortgage banker making up a pool of similar mortgages, all of which are FHA or VA insured and carry the same interest rate, then obtaining the approval of GNMA, after which a GNMA certificate may be issued and sold. The mortgage banker services the investment by collecting interest and principal and making payments monthly to the purchaser with a statement of what portion is interest, regular principal, and prepayment of principal, and the amount of principal remaining. The certificate identifies and describes the mortgage pool and is issued in registered form only. The minimum certificate is originally for $25,000, but as principal is paid off its value and cost decrease.

There are many mortgage pools in existence carrying various interest rates. The mortgage banker normally retains one-half of one percent for servicing the pool. That is, if the mortgages in the pool were 9%, you could expect to receive an 8 ½% return. This rate is used to identify typical mortgage pools for price quotation in the press. *The Wall Street Journal* lists a spread of such rates daily in terms of bid and asked prices and yield. These pass-throughs may sell at a discount if the going interest rate is above the original rate, which identifies the security, in order to bring the yield up to the market rate. They may sell at a premium if the original rate is above the market rate. The papers quote a yield to maturity which gives a measure of the true investment return. While quotations may be given for pass-throughs ranging from 6 ½% to 9%, the asking price, on which the yield is computed, will vary to make all these issues yield about the same.

There are several different ways to compute the yield. The mortgage when first made may be for 30 years, typical for one- to four-family dwellings, but experience is that prepayments result in an average life of about 12 years. Yields are computed for both a 30-year life and an average 12-

year life, but if only one is given it is the 12-year life. Because you receive interest monthly, rather than at 6-month intervals as is customary for corporate bonds, you have the use of this interest early which could be reinvested immediately upon receipt. This makes the pass-through worth a little more than a corresponding bond. Sometimes a bond-equivalent yield is quoted. This yield assumes reinvestment at the yield of the pass-through which amounts to adding about 0.05 for a 5% rate to 0.17 for a 9% rate. In your own case you may not be able to invest small sums at the higher rates. A more realistic figure might be obtained by assuming you deposited your monthly interest in a passbook savings account. You should also consider that you receive each month a payment of principal which reduces your investment and you may not be able to reinvest these amounts in as high a rate as obtained on the pass-through. If you need this money for living expenses, then the repayment becomes an advantage. The exact amount of prepayment can never be predicted so you can not do better than take some average return percentage as a measure of the investment value.

The security we have been discussing is more precisely known as the *modified pass-through* which means the prompt payment of both interest and principal is fully guaranteed by the Government and is the most common type. We have referred to the one- to four-family dwelling pool which is the most common, but there are pass-throughs for mobile homes with mortgages of 12 to 15 years and having an average life of 5 or 7 years; multifamily mortgages of 40 years maximum with an average life of 20 years; construction pools; hospitals; and others.

Your first payment is received 15 days after the first month and following payments by the 15th of each month. The last payment is due 45 days after the termination of the last mortgage in the pool. This could be up to 30 years but when the pool becomes small it can be terminated by mutual agreement. Of course you can terminate your participation at any time by selling your certificate in the secondary market.

Summary

There are many ways of investing your money in fixed asset instruments such as U. S. Government issues, Federal Agency bonds and notes, corporate bonds, commercial paper, and money market mutual funds. New types of money market instruments may appear at any time. The object of this chapter was to discuss enough of the various types and characteristics to illustrate the variations one encounters and why it is necessary to understand what is available and their own peculiarities. Further, the yields may vary rapidly. For example, 13-week T bills were yielding less than 4% in mid 1972 and were over 8% a year later. The large CD's went from about 4% to over 10% in this same period. On the other hand, high grade corporate bonds varied less than one percentage point during the same period, ranging between about 8.5 to 9.5% yield. In 1972, savings and loan passbook accounts paid 5% and would have been a better investment than T bills or CD's. In 1974, passbook yields were only 5¼% and the long-term savings certificates only 7½%, but T bill yields ranged to a coupon rate of 10% or more and the large CD's reached yields of over 12%, but again they fell to nearly half this yield in a six-months period.

You will have to make your own selection at the time of investment, for changed conditions can completely reverse the relative standings in a relatively short time. Investigation before investing is essential, even for the commonly considered simple investments, if you want to maximize your yield, and having obtained the background information and understanding of these types of investments will enable you to ferret out and discover the investment most suitable to your needs. Many writers point out that the decrease in the value of the dollar is not recovered by the interest received on fixed income securities and if you go this route you are actually losing money. Nevertheless, there are times when your alternatives may be even worse. It is better to lose purchasing power at only a 5% rate, for example, than at a 10% or 15% rate. You can use these types of investments during a bear movement in the stock market (if not inclined to operate on the short side); for surplus funds during periods when waiting for the right time to purchase other investments; and for nest-egg insurance to protect against emergencies.

Such investments can be divided simply into short-term and long-term issues, where time refers to the time remaining until the issue matures. The 13-week T bills are commonly used as a reference point for the short-term money market interest rate. They reflect a sensitive interest rate measure. Notes and/or bonds maturing within a few years are normally considered short term, the shorter the time to maturity the more stable the price since price variation would produce a greater effect on the effective yield to maturity. That is, the effective yield is the interest coupon which is paid, usually semiannually, plus the appreciation from present price to the redemption price prorated over the remaining years to maturity, assuming the present price is below redemption value. This increases the effective yield. This price difference decreases as the maturity date approaches. At times the current price may be above the redemption price having the effect of decreasing the effective yield.

Considerations one must make on choosing issues are: effective yield after service charges; the probability that interest rates will go up which would indicate the shorter-term instruments so funds may be reinvested at

the expected higher rate; possibility of interest rates going down and buying longer-term issues to lock in the higher yield; other uses for funds at
some anticipated future time; and the risk factor if branching out into
some higher risk investment. If waiting to employ funds in the stock
market, reference should be made to market timing techniques. For the
less sophisticated investor the solution may well be one of the money
market funds which provides good yields but allows withdrawal on re-
quest.

2

The Mathematics of Interest Income

DIFFERENT WAYS INTEREST IS COMPUTED AND THE FORMULAS YOU NEED TO INSURE THE GREATEST YIELD

Almost everyone is confronted with interest charges as payments throughout most of his adult life. The concept of simple interest learned in school is normally easy to apply, but interest computation and its true significance may be quite complex. The truth-in-lending laws became necessary to protect consumers from paying interest charges they did not understand.

We want to look at interest payments from the investor's point of view in order to evaluate and compare different possible investments of your money in interest-bearing instruments. Such investments may appeal to the investor because of security of the principal; at times they offer a good return compared to other investments; they may be used as a "nest egg" of available assets easily liquidated in case of emergencies. This chapter discusses the mathematics of interest income.

SIMPLE AND COMPOUND INTEREST

Simple interest is what a borrower pays for the use of your money. It is expressed as a percent of the principal (or rate) paid on an annual basis. *Compound interest* is the amount earned if each interest payment is added to the principal and reinvested at the same rate. Table 2-1 illustrates the growth power of annual compounding. Even greater earnings accrue if the compounding is done at more frequent intervals. It has become commonplace for banks and savings and loan associations to compound daily or even to offer continuous compounding. Table 2-2 shows the effect of compounding at more frequent intervals.

The compound interest formula giving the Compound Amount (S) for a Principal Amount (P) compounded t times per year at a rate of i percent for n years is

$$S = P(1 + i/t)^{tn} \qquad\qquad (2\text{-}1)$$

For example, $1,000 compounded quarterly at 6% will be worth three years hence: $1,000(1 + 0.06/4)^{4 \cdot 3} = $1,000(1.015)^{12} = $1,195.62$. This calculation can be made by hand using logarithms (see"Logarithms" in Chapter 16), with the aid of a slide rule, by use of the small electronic computers (the ease depending upon the sophistication of the function keys and/or memory), or using compound interest tables that are available in many mathematical handbooks.

For another way of looking at the effect of compounding, note in the example above that the interest earned in three years was $195.62 or an average of $65.21 per year resulting in 0.06521 (6.5%) average interest rate per year. Similarly, compounding quarterly for 10 years at 6% results in an average interest rate of $[(1.015)^{40} - 1] \div 10$ or 8.14%. If investments could be made at high interest rates with guaranteed compounding at that rate for a long period of time, the growth would be very great. Unfortunately such investments are not available in general. One can purchase money market mutual funds, restricted to interest-bearing instruments, that compound earnings on a daily basis but the rate varies with money market conditions and there will be times when the interest rate drops to low values. Series E savings bonds are an example of a bond with guaranteed semiannual compounding at their prevailing rate which is regulated by the Government and does not change rapidly. During the inital period the redemption value is predetermined so that the rate of interest starts out low and increases to a maximum at maturity. The extended periods are however essentially uniform.

The Series E bonds have always been sold at a discount of 25% and mature in a number of years which sets the interest rate compounded semiannually. The time to maturity has been decreased from time to time from the initial ten years to provide higher yield. A bond purchased in January 1974 and later earns at a rate of 6% compounded semiannually. This rate is certain for at least five years with considerable possibility of being extended at as good a rate. Should they continue at the 6% rate for

Table 2-1

Value of $1,000 after n years, compounded annually at rate of interest i. Values rounded to nearest dollar. $1,000 $(1 + i)^n$.

n	Rate i				
Years	.04(4%)	.05(5%)	.06(6%)	.07(7%)	.08(8%)
1	$1,040	$1,050	$1,060	$1,070	$1,080
2	1,082	1,103	1,124	1,145	1,166
3	1,125	1,158	1,191	1,225	1,260
4	1,170	1,216	1,262	1,311	1,360
5	1,217	1,276	1,338	1,403	1,469
10	1,480	1,629	1,791	1,967	2,159
15	1,801	2,079	2,397	2,759	3,172
20	2,191	2,653	3,207	3,870	4,661
30	3,243	4,322	5,743	7,612	10,063
40	4,801	7,040	10,286	14,974	21,725
50	7,107	11,467	18,420	29,457	46,902

Table 2-2

Amount of interest earned in one year on $10,000 at indicated nominal rate compounded at different periods. Continuous compounding is calculated for a 360-day year but posted for 365 days. Values are rounded to nearest dollar.

Compounding Period	Nominal Rate of Interest				
	4%	5%	6%	7½%	8%
Annual	$400	$500	$600	$750	$800
Semiannual	404	506	609	764	816
Quarterly	406	509	614	771	824
Daily	408	513	618	779	833
Continuous	414	520	627	790	844

20 years, a $100 bond, for which you paid $75, would be worth $244 for an average interest rate of 8.45% per year. Savings institutions offer time certificates which guarantee an interest rate for a number of years. They have been offered for up to six-year terms at rates, which when compounded daily, yield over 8% per year. When the institution does not need money and when interest rates are lower, the available certificates may not offer as good a value.

The generally used method of computing interest for periods less than a year is on the basis of a 360-day year of 12 months of 30 days each.

The U. S. Government uses the 365-day year for most calculations (but not for Treasury bill yields). The 360-day year leads to simplifications. For example, the interest on one dollar at 6% is one cent ($0.01) for 60 days. With this as a starting point, simple interest for any length of time on any amount at any rate may be arrived at simply by multiplying by the proper factors in succession.

The trend of savings institutions to daily and continuous compounding is of interest. To compute continuous compounding, the compound interest formula may be written as a series using the binomial expansion

$$(1+x)^n = 1+nx+\frac{n(n-1)x^2}{2!}+\frac{n(n-1)(n-2)x^3}{3!}+\ldots$$

Let $x = i/t$ where i is the interest rate and t the number of times compounded per year, then in one year the Compound Amount (S) = $P(1 + i/t)^t$ from Equation (2-1). For continuous compounding, t approaches infinity and the expression in parentheses can be expanded as a binomial to give for an initial amount P = 1

$$S=1+t(i/t)+\frac{t(t-1)}{2!}(i/t)^2+\frac{t(t-1)(t-2)}{3!}(i/t)^3+\ldots$$

Since t becomes very large, $t-1$ does not differ from t, etc., allowing us to simplify the formula to

$$S = 1 + i + i^2/2 + i^3/6 + \ldots \tag{2-2}$$

As an example, the computation for $7\frac{1}{2}\%$ compounded continuously for one year is $S = 1 + 0.075 + 0.0028125 + 0.000070312 + \ldots$ which equals 1.0778828 or the equivalent yearly rate is 7.788%. If this rate is posted daily on the basis of a 360-day year, but for 365 days, the effective rate becomes 7.9% obtained by multiplying by the fraction 365/360. This was the highest rate allowed under Government regulations for savings accounts prior to late December, 1974.

DISCOUNT BONDS

The Series E bond is one example of a type of discount bond or money instrument. Its unique characteristic is that it sells for a value less than the redemption value and the difference is the interest earned during the holding period. Treasury bills are another illustration. Coupon type bonds pay interest at stated intervals, commonly twice a year. They may also sell at a discount, or at a premium. The difference between the purchase cost and the redemption value represents plus or minus earnings which must be taken into account in calculating the effective interest return (yield).

If one dollar ($1.00) earns interest at 6%, it will be worth $1.06 at the end of one year at simple interest, or one can say a sum of $1.06 a year from now has a present value of $1.00. Again, a $100 (maturity value) savings bond has a present value of $75 at the time of its purchase. In general, rearranging the compound interest formula and calling the Principal the Present Value and the Compound Amount the Future Value we have:

$$\text{Present Value (P)} = \text{Future Value (S)} \div (1+i/t)^{tn} \qquad (2\text{-}3)$$

This formula allows one to compute the present value of a bond for an assumed compound interest rate. For example, a $1,000 bond maturing in five years, if yielding 6% interest compounded semiannually, would have a present value of $P = \$1,000 \div (1 + 0.06/2)^{2 \cdot 5} = \$744.09$.

TREASURY BILL YIELDS

Treasury bills represent a special case of yield computation. The Treasury computes the 13-week (91-days) and the 26-week (182-days) bill yields on the basis of a 360-day year and the redemption value as the cost of the investment. At one time the results of the Monday auction were:

	13-Week	26-Week
Average price (yield)	98.018 (7.841%)	95.954 (8.003%)
Coupon equivalent	8.11%	8.46%

The yield of 7.841% for the 13-week bills is found by dividing the interest (100 - 98.018 = 1.982) by 100 to obtain the percent gain, then divide by 91 (days) to obtain the interest for one day, and multiply by 360 to give the yield on the 360-day year. That is,

$$\frac{100-98.018}{100} \cdot \frac{360}{91} = 0.078408 \text{ (rounded to 7.841\%)}$$

The bills are normally quoted on the yield basis for both an asked and a bid discount yield price. They are identified by a month and day maturity date. If you want to determine what you could sell them for (bid) or would have to pay (asked) in the resale market, the above computation would be rearranged as follows:

$$\text{Price} = 100 - \frac{100 \text{ (Days to maturity) (yield)}}{360} \qquad \text{(2-4)}$$

The yield basis does not fairly state the actual yield in terms normally used. It uses the redemption value as cost of the investment instead of the discounted amount and shortens the year to 360 days. A coupon equivalent yield is published when the bills are auctioned each Monday but is not used in the resale market quotes. The coupon equivalent yield is computed in the normal interest computational manner. In the example above it is

$$\frac{100-98.018}{98.018} \cdot \frac{365}{91} = 0.081105 \text{ (rounded to 8.11\%)}$$

YIELD TO MATURITY

Corporate bonds are quoted as a percent of principal. That is, a $1,000 par value bond selling at $895 would be quoted as 89½. Fractions are in units of eighths of a point. Treasury bonds are quoted in thirty-seconds of a point. A $1,000 bond quoted at 72.23 means a price of 72 and 23/32 percent of 100. Treasury bonds, notes and Government agency instruments are quoted on a yield to maturity basis as well as their bid and asked prices. The quoted yield is computed on the asked side of the quote. Any bond paying interest (a coupon) and selling below redemption value (par) provides a yield made up of the coupon and the gain between present value and redemption value. If selling above par, then the yield to maturity is reduced below the coupon rate.

A $1,000 bond with a coupon rate of 6% pays $60 a year interest. This rate is called its *nominal yield*. If this bond were priced at $800, the *current yield* would be 60/800 or 7.5%. However, if this bond matures in 10 years, you would receive $1,000 at that time or $200 more than you would have to pay for it now. This extra money averages $20 a year additional income. You do not receive it until the bond is redeemed, or if sold before maturity you might expect to receive a price which has appreciated $20 per year since the original purchase if market interest rates at time of sale are the same as when purchased. On this basis the value of your investment is $800 at the beginning of the first year of your holding, $820 at the beginning of your second year, and so on to $980 at the beginning of your tenth year. An approximate *yield to maturity* can be calculated using the average annual income (in this example 60 + 20 = \$80) and an average annual investment of (800 + 980) /2 = \$890, giving the yield to maturity of 80/890 = 8.99%, which is more representative of the true value of the investment. Most bonds are purchased at the quoted price plus accrued interest from the last interest payment date to the day of purchase. This makes your initial cost somewhat higher since you don't recover this accrued interest until the next coupon date. This will slightly modify the actual yield.

CALLABLE BONDS

Some bonds are issued with the option of the issuer to redeem the bonds at some future date, prior to maturity, at a call price which is usually somewhat of a premium over par. Computation of yield must take this factor into account. If the bond is purchased below the call price, it is reasonable to assume the bond will go to maturity, but if purchased above the call price, one should assume the bond will be called at the earliest call date.

Some bonds are issued with a feature requiring the issuer to call a certain number each year. If such bonds can be purchased at a discount under the call price, you have a chance of gaining an amount which may be considerably in excess of the coupon interest, if your bond is called.

CONVERTIBLE BONDS

Some bonds are issued with the provision that the bond owner may exchange it for a specified number of shares of common stock of the company. Such bonds will always sell for as much as the value of common stock into which they may be converted. When stock prices increase, the bond price likewise increases. However, when stock prices fall the bond price may not fall as rapidly, since the bond provides a fixed interest income and its price will be determined more by the current yield obtained than by the movement of the common stock.

A conversion price of the underlying common stock may be given, which means the value of each share of the common stock on the basis of the bond being worth \$1,000. This price may be compared with the actual quoted price of the stock to determine whether the bond is selling at a premium or not. Another figure is given which is the factor that multiplied by the price of the common gives the conversion value of the bond, this factor being the number of shares into which one bond could be con-

verted. This number may be an even number of shares when the bond is
originally issued but more often becomes fractional as it is adjusted for
stock splits and stock dividends. The conversion value may also change at
some predetermined time in the future as specified in the offering.

RISK

Corporate bonds are rated by Standard and Poor's, Moody's
Investor's Service and Fitch as highest grade (triple A), high grade, etc., to
speculative, and the interest rate reflects these ratings. Since the market
places its rating on these issues, the degree of risk may be determined as
follows. Consider the yield of issues of the U. S. Treasury as reflecting the
cost of borrowing money. Then the excess yield of corporate issues, of
comparable maturity and features, over the Treasury issue represents the
premium paid for risk. One must account for factors not present in both
issues. For example, Treasury issues are exempt from state income taxes,
municipal bonds are exempt from Federal income tax, some corporate
bonds have convertible features, some are subject to call, and some
Treasury issues have a special feature of being redeemable at par for payment of estate taxes. This last feature may be more pronounced as time
goes on because the Treasury no longer issues bonds with this provision.
Securities eligible for purchase by savings banks, trustees and life insurance companies tend to have a lower yield due to this artifical market.
The liquidity also exerts some influence. In spite of these variations you
get an approximate measure of risk.

TAX-EXEMPT BONDS

There are many bonds whose interest is exempt from Federal income
tax. They yield less than a corresponding fully taxed bond. How much this
is worth to you depends upon your own tax bracket. The formula for
computing the equivalent yield of a fully taxed bond is:

$$\text{Equivalent Yield } (y_{te}) = \frac{\text{Tax exempt bond yield}}{100\% - \text{Tax bracket}\%} \qquad \text{(2-5)}$$

For example, if your highest tax bracket is 45%, a tax-exempt yield of 6%
is equivalent to 6% ÷ (100% − 45%) = 10.9%. In addition, the issue may
also be exempt from state and local income tax which would make it even
more attractive. If purchased at a discount, the yield to maturity includes
the capital gain but this gain is taxable.

For detailed information on money instruments and interest computations, see References (1) and (2) listed in Appendix F.

YOUR OWN PENSION PLAN

Self-employed persons can establish their own pension plan and defer the income tax on the amount contributed each year and also defer the tax on the income on these contributions until the person receives the funds upon retirement. After retirement the individual's tax bracket may be lower and thus the tax bite less, but more important is that you retain dollars for many years which you would otherwise turn over to the tax collector, which can produce additional income for you. This can build up a truly significant amount, even with a modest annual contribution. The tax you are deferring is at the rate of your highest tax bracket. You may also be able to defer state income taxes as well. Check your state income tax laws on this.

Congress enacted the Self-Employed Individual's Tax Retirement Act known as HR-10 in 1962, often referred to as the *Keogh Act* or *Plan*. In 1974 Congress passed the Pension Reform Act-Employment Retirement Income Security Act of 1974 (Public Law 93-406) which increased the benefits and expanded the coverage. Under the revised Keogh Act the self-employed individual can contribute each year up to $7,500 or 15% of *earned* income, whichever is smaller, into this tax-deferred plan. Others not participating in Keogh or other plans are permitted under the newer law to establish an *Individual Retirement Account* (IRA) to which contributions up to $1,500 or 15% of earned income may be contributed each year, and which has the same tax deferred status.

It is not the purpose of this book to advise on establishing such retirement plans. Additional information can be obtained from publications of the IRS, tax services and their publications, other writers on the subject, and professionals in tax law. Information is also available from saving associations, insurance companies, mutual funds, and others interested in investing your funds, but they tend to give emphasis to their own plans. The purpose here is to provide the calculations and illustrate what can be accomplished for various assumed situations.

Table 2-3 shows how a contribution of $1,000 made at the end of each year, earning interest compounded annually, will grow over the years. For example, the fund grows in 40 years when compounded at interest of 6% to over $154,000 of which only $40,000 was contributed by you and of this you would have retained only $24,000 if your tax bracket averaged 40%. Forty years corresponds to an individual working from age 25 to retirement at 65. If you contribute more each year, the total increases in direct proportion. For example, if you contribute $1,500 each year, the 6% interest rate would produce $232,143, or if you contribute the maximum under the Keogh plan of $7,500 each year, it would total $1,160,715.

If you want to make the computation yourself, the formula is

$$\text{Sum after } n \text{ years} = \text{Yearly contribution}[(1+i)^n - 1] \div i \qquad (2\text{-}7)$$

where i is the annual interest rate and n the number of years. As an example, $1,000 contributed yearly with interest at 6% compounded annually will in four years amount to $1,000 $[(1 + 0.06)^4 - 1] \div 0.06 = \$4,374.62$. For large values of n you can use logarithms. Using a calculator with y^x operation key, you may compute directly, or if only a squaring function is available it is still very easy. For example, for n = 23 years, break up as follows the quantity

$$(1+i)^{23} = (1+i)^{16}(1+i)^4(1+i)^2(1+i)$$

where the factors can be obtained by repeating the squaring function.

Table 2-3

The amount accumulated at the end of n years for an annual contribution of $1,000 invested in a tax-deferred pension account at an interest rate i compounded annually. $1,000 $[(1 + i)^n - 1] \div i$.

At End of Year	Amount Contributed	Total Amount, at Interest Rate i, Compounded Annually					
		.05(5%)	.06(6%)	.07(7%)	.08(8%)	.09(9%)	.10(10%)
1	$ 1,000	$ 1,000	$ 1,000	$ 1,000	$ 1,000	$ 1,000	$ 1,000
2	2,000	2,050	2,060	2,070	2,080	2,090	2,100
3	3,000	3,153	3,184	3,215	3,246	3,278	3,310
4	4,000	4,310	4,375	4,440	4,506	4,573	4,641
5	5,000	5,526	5,637	5,751	5,867	5,985	6,105
10	10,000	12,578	13,181	13,816	14,487	15,193	15,937
15	15,000	21,579	23,276	25,129	27,152	29,361	31,772
20	20,000	33,066	36,786	40,995	45,762	51,160	57,275
25	25,000	47,727	54,865	63,249	73,106	84,701	98,347
30	30,000	66,439	79,058	94,461	113,283	136,308	164,494
35	35,000	90,320	111,435	138,237	172,317	215,711	271,024
40	40,000	120,800	154,762	199,635	259,056	337,882	442,593
45	45,000	159,700	212,744	285,749	386,506	525,859	718,905
50	50,000	209,348	290,336	406,529	573,770	815,084	1,163,909

If you likewise have a memory function, you can store intermediate powers and/or products. With more frequent compounding, n can become extremely large. For daily or continuous compounding it is simpler to find the equivalent annual interest rate, then make the calculation on a yearly compound rate using the equivalent value. That is, 5% compounded daily is equivalent to 5.13% calculated on a 360-day year. Table 2-4 gives the equivalent annual rate for various nominal interest rates when compounded daily and continuously. These values are for a 360-day year which is usual for saving institutions. Some pay this rate for 365 days which increases the effective rate by the ratio $365/360 = 1.0139$.

Table 2-4   1949629

Equivalent annual rate of interest when a nominal rate i is compounded daily or continuously for a 360-day year.

Interest Rate (i)%	Equivalent Annual Rate (%)	
	Daily Compounding	Continuous Compounding
5.00	5.12643	5.12708
5.25	5.38975	5.39022
5.50	5.65335	5.65402
5.75	5.91798	5.91848
6.00	6.18290	6.18360
6.25	6.44883	6.44938
6.50	6.71507	6.71583
6.75	6.98233	6.98294
7.00	7.24995	7.25072
7.25	7.51816	7.51916
7.50	7.78747	7.78828
7.75	8.05703	8.05807
8.00	8.32768	8.32853
8.50	8.87060	8.87149
9.00	9.41621	9.41715
9.50	9.96419	9.96554
10.00	10.51527	10.51667

Daily compounding is common with saving institutions. Many investment plans will reinvest earnings which provides the advantage of more frequent compounding. Table 2-5 gives the result for daily compounding corresponding to Table 2-3. The advantage of even a small increase in effective interest rate mounts up as the years increase. For example, daily compounding at 6% rather than annual compounding increases the amount of interest earned in 40 years for the $1,000 a year contribution by $7,299.

Conservative investment in interest-bearing instruments can produce very significant sums. The importance of interest rate is illustrated by comparing the sums under the different rates. For example, increasing the rate to 7% from 6% will in 40 years earn enough additional interest to more than cover all of the contributions made during the 40 years. Even small increases in interest are significant. If you can achieve a 10% rate you can retire after 40 years with well over a half-million of interest alone with the $1,500 yearly contribution allowed under the IRA.

Table 2-5

The amount accumulated at the end of n years for an annual contribution of $1,000 invested in a tax-deferred pension account at an interest rate i compounded daily. Equivalent rate of Table 2-4 is used.

At End of Year	Amount Con- tributed	Total Amount, at Interest Rate i, Compounded Daily					
		.05(5%)	.06(6%)	.07(7%)	.08(8%)	.09(9%)	.10(10%)
1	$ 1,000	$ 1,000	$ 1,000	$ 1,000	$ 1,000	$ 1,000	$ 1,000
2	2,000	2,051	2,062	2,072	2,083	2,094	2,105
3	3,000	3,156	3,189	3,223	3,257	3,291	3,327
4	4,000	4,318	4,387	4,456	4,528	4,601	4,676
5	5,000	5,540	5,658	5,779	5,905	6,034	6,168
10	10,000	12,652	13,295	13,981	14,714	15,497	16,337
15	15,000	21,785	23,603	25,618	27,855	30,339	33,100
20	20,000	33,511	37,517	42,132	47,457	53,613	60,737
25	25,000	48,568	56,299	65,565	76,700	90,112	106,298
30	30,000	67,899	81,650	98,817	120,322	147,350	181,409
35	35,000	92,721	115,870	146,002	185,396	237,112	305,236
40	40,000	124,592	162,061	212,958	282,470	377,880	509,375
45	45,000	165,514	224,409	307,969	427,281	598,635	845,916
50	50,000	218,057	308,567	442,790	643,304	944,828	1,400,733

Tables 2-3 and 2-5 are for the situation where you wait until the end of the year to make your annual contribution. If you made a deposit each pay period in a savings account as a part of the plan, which pays daily interest at say 5%, then for 26 payments a year you would have earned approximately $25 interest at the end of the first year per $1,000 annual contribution. This amount earns compound interest for 40 years. Likewise, in the second year you have another $25 interest, and so on. At the end of forty years, following a 5% plan, this amounts to an increase of $3,000. If at the end of each year you transfer your savings to a higher interest rate investment, for example from a passbook account to a certificate, even greater increases are obtained. For example, if a 7% certificate is purchased, in 40 years with daily compounding your investment is worth over $5,300 more than if you waited to year end to make your contribution. Further, you can build up additional amounts by taking every opportunity to increase your interest. If you can move your funds to a higher interest rate, do it as soon as possible. Even though it seems like pennies at the time, the effect of compounding over long periods of time is truly like magic. You may select a money market fund which accepts minimum deposits of $100, etc. You can change from one form of investment to another when it is to your advantage. No allowance has been made for service charges which may, in fact, not exist in many situations, but if commissions or other charges are assessed their effect should be carefully considered.

You may say, "Why should I tie my money up in such a plan? I will pay my taxes and not have that hanging over my head when I retire, and pick good investments with what is left." Table 2-6 illustrates the effect of paying your taxes as income is received for various tax brackets. Even if you are in a very low bracket (22%), a 6% investment return, tax-deferred, gives you $67,581 more at the end of 40 years, but of course you will have to pay taxes on this as it returns to you. If this pension is your main source of income, received in a form of an annuity over your remaining life, your tax will be applied after exemptions at the lower rates which can average much less than the highest bracket at the time the contributions were made. You have some choice as to how you receive it, but in any case, if you had only been in the 22% bracket for 40 years, you could hardly expect to average more than this rate on your retirement, probably less. But at 22% you still have $52,713 more than if you paid the taxes as money was earned, or considerably more than the total of the contributions. Of course if your yearly contributions are greater and/or your tax bracket higher, the differences are all the greater.

Table 2-7 shows what you can earn on the deferred taxes you would otherwise have to pay for each $1,000 of earned income contributed to the plan. This is like an interest-free loan from the tax collector, and you only have to pay back a percentage no greater than your tax bracket during your retirement.

If you want to make a calculation for your own income bracket (T) and assumed rate of interest (i) where you pay tax on the income as earned and on the interest received on the remainder invested at fixed income, the formula is

$$\text{Amount at end of } n \text{ years} = \text{Before tax yearly Contribution} \; \{[1+(1-T)i]^n-1\}\div i \quad \text{(2-8)}$$

Table 2-6

Amount accumulated in *n* years after paying taxes on earnings and interest, as earned, with remainder invested at 6% compounded annually, for before tax earnings of $1,000 each year for various tax brackets.

At End of Year	Earnings Before Taxes	Tax Bracket 22%	32%	42%	50%	60%
1	$ 1,000	$ 780	$ 680	$ 580	$ 500	$ 400
2	2,000	1,597	1,388	1,180	1,015	810
3	3,000	2,451	2,124	1,801	1,545	1,229
4	4,000	3,346	2,891	2,444	2,092	1,659
5	5,000	4,283	3,689	3,109	2,655	2,098
10	10,000	9,665	8,194	6,798	5,732	4,461
15	15,000	16,432	13,697	11,175	9,299	7,121
20	20,000	24,936	20,418	16,369	13,435	10,116
25	25,000	35,626	28,626	22,531	18,230	13,488
30	30,000	49,063	38,651	29,843	23,788	17,284
35	35,000	65,952	50,895	38,519	30,231	21,558
40	40,000	87,181	65,850	48,813	37,701	26,371

Table 2-7

If $1,000 is contributed each year to a tax-deferred plan, that portion which would have been paid in income tax would earn the amount shown here when invested at 6% compounded daily.

At End of Year	Tax Bracket 22%	32%	42%	50%	60%
1	$ 220	$ 320	$ 420	$ 500	$ 600
2	454	660	866	1,031	1,237
3	702	1,020	1,339	1,595	1,913
4	965	1,404	1,843	2,194	2,632
5	1,245	1,811	2,376	2,829	3,395
10	2,925	4,254	5,584	6,648	7,977
15	5,193	7,553	9,913	11,802	14,162
20	8,254	12,005	15,757	18,759	22,510
25	12,386	18,016	23,646	28,150	33,779
30	17,963	26,128	34,293	40,825	48,990
35	25,491	37,078	48,665	57,935	69,522
40	35,653	51,860	68,066	81,031	97,237

For example, for each $1,000 earned on which you pay 42% income tax, if that remaining after taxes is invested at 6% and taxes are paid on this interest as earned you would have after 5 years

$$\$1,000\{[1+(1-0.42)0.06]^5-1\}\div0.06=\$3,108.98$$

A person with good earnings may feel, "What's the use, I make good money so why worry about retirement?" But take the case of a person in the 42% bracket, if paying taxes as income is earned, investing at 6% produces only a little more than the earnings before taxes. But if the tax is deferred, one could have over three times the earnings used for contributions and if the taxes after retirement were still as great as 42%, one would still have doubled one's money in 40 years at 6%. Again if higher interest rates are achieved, the gains are greater.

You may think, "What is the use for me to become involved in such a plan? I only intend to work a few years, or I will eventually work for someone with a good pension plan that will take care of me." The fact is it is these early years that are most important. Table 2-8 shows what you can achieve with a few years' contributions, while young, that are left to multiply over the years. For example, a one-time contribution of $1,000 will grow to $9,704 in 40 years when invested tax-deferred at 6%. It is the early years that make the greatest contribution.

Table 2-8

Amount accumulated at end of 25 to 40 years for each $1,000 contributed to a tax deferred pension plan for one to ten years and invested at interest of 6% compounded annually.

No. of Years Contributed	Amount Contributed	Amount Accumulated at end of Year for 6% Compounded Annually			
		25 Years	30 Years	35 Years	40 Years
1	$ 1,000	$ 4,049	$ 5,418	$ 7,251	$ 9,704
2	2,000	7,869	10,530	14,092	18,858
3	3,000	11,473	15,352	20,545	27,494
4	4,000	14,872	19,902	26,633	35,641
5	5,000	18,079	24,194	32,377	43,327
6	6,000	21,105	28,243	37,795	50,578
7	7,000	23,959	32,062	42,907	57,419
8	8,000	26,652	35,666	47,729	63,872
9	9,000	29,192	39,065	52,278	69,960
10	10,000	31,589	42,273	56,570	75,704

If you want to calculate for values other than given in Table 2-8, first use Equation (2-7) to compute the amount to the end of your working period during which time you make annual contributions. Then next using the sum thus determined as the amount in Equation (2-1) for the *additional* years the funds remain at compound interest.

Sums accumulated under these deferred tax plans can be paid out in various ways. Under normal conditions you must reach the age of 59 ½ before any withdrawal and you must start by age 70 ½. The funds may be paid out in a lump sum or under some type of annuity. Funds remaining continue to earn tax-deferred income.

In Chapter 1, we discussed various interest-bearing investments, all of which are applicable to your pension plan as well as other investment vehicles. You can have a diversified plan, and can move from one type of investment to another to maximize income and maintain safety. One vehicle, which we did not discuss before because it is specifically designed for these plans and can not be used for other investments, is the United States Retirement Plan Bond for the Keogh Plan and the U. S. Individual Retirement Bond for the IRA plan. They may be purchased over-the-counter or by mail from Federal Reserve Banks and Branches and the Office of the Treasurer of the United States, Washington, D. C. They are described in Treasury Department Circular, Public Debt Series-No. 1-63 and amendments thereto for the Keogh plan and No. 1-75 for the IRA plan. They are available in denominations of $50, $100, and $500 for both plans and also $1,000 for the Keogh, at face amount price, and earn interest compounded semiannually until redeemed. When first available in 1963 the interest rate was 3.75%, but later issues have carried higher rates reaching a rate of 6% in 1974. Since U. S. Government bond interest is exempt from state and local taxes, the effective interest rate may be as much as 6 ½% depending on your state tax bracket. These bonds give you a chance to *lock in* your interest rate for the life of the plan. However, *you* aren't locked in for you may *roll over* these bonds into another plan, under proper conditions, if it becomes advantageous to do so. These bonds, being available in small denominations, having no commission charges, and easy to obtain, offer an excellent starter program for a small wage earner.

ANNUITY FORMULA

If you receive a fixed number of dollars at periodic intervals for a specified number of years, this is called an *annuity*. An annuity may be established by paying a single sum, called the premium, or by making a series of payments over a number of years. The pension plan discussed in the previous section is one example of the accumulation of funds which upon retirement may be paid back to you in the form of an annuity. These funds not only are increased by their earnings while the accumulation was taking place, but the funds remaining for future annuity payments continue to earn for you. The amount earned each year will decrease because the principal decreases by an amount required to make up your annuity payment. This payment may be largely met by earnings in the beginning when the principal amount is large but as time goes on a larger portion is taken from the principal.

There are plans, such as issued by insurance companies, which agree to pay you an annuity for life, combination of lives, or other possible arrangements. These plans are based upon life expectancies and assumed earnings on the money they hold. If you want to calculate an annuity (A) per payment period for a specified number of payments (n) and interest rate (i) for the principal amount (P) at the start of the annuity payments, the formula is

$$A = P \frac{i}{1-(1+i)^{-n}}$$

For example, if your pension fund had built up to $100,000 at retirement and you elected to take out uniform annual payments for ten years while earning at a 6% annual rate on the funds not withdrawn, you would receive

$$A = \$100,000 \ \frac{0.06}{1-(1+0.06)^{-10}} = \$13,586.80 \text{ per year}$$

If you desired monthly payments under the same conditions, they would be

$$A = \$100,000 \ \frac{0.06/12}{1-(1+0.06/12)^{-120}} = \$1,110.21 \text{ per month}$$

If you are investing in a Ginnie Mae pass-through as described in Chapter 1, pages 20-22, you may be interested in determining the amount you would receive each month which includes interest and repayment of principal. The annuity formula above applies. Any prepayments of the loan would of course be added. As an example, if you purchased a $25,000 pass-through made up of 30-year mortgages at an 8½% rate, the monthly mortgage payment would be

$$\$25,000 \ \frac{0.085/12}{1-(1+0.085/12)^{-360}} = \$192.23$$

Of this amount, the first payment includes interest at 8½% on the $25,000 amounting to $177.08 which leaves $15.15 to apply to the reduction of principal. The mortgage banker usually receives one-half of one percent out of the 8½% interest charge for servicing the pool. This would be $177.08(0.5%)/(8.5%) = $10.42. You would then receive $192.23−$10.42 or $181.81 the first month. As the loan is paid off the interest charges decrease which in turn reduces the service charge giving you a little more per month as time goes on. The difference is not great even after many years for it is due only to the reduction of the service charge which is small to begin with. You may, however, receive substantial additional amounts on an irregular basis in the form of prepayments.

Summary

Interest which you can receive for the use of your money is computed in many ways. If you are to gain the greatest benefits, you need to understand what the real results are for the various conditions and choose those which are most advantageous at the particular time. You can make your own computations using the formulas given in this chapter or you can make comparisons using the Tables.

Compounding is very powerful when continued over long periods of time. A conservative investment plan which has a stable earnings rate can be more productive than a plan whose results oscillate between good times and bad.

The tax-deferred pension plans not only allow you to defer tax on a portion of your income each year until retirement, but in reality allow you to use otherwise unavailable tax dollars for investment. The results, when the plan is started at an early age, are phenomenal. Remember your contributions receive tax-deferred treatment at the rate of your top tax bracket but when your investment is returned to you on retirement, if you have little if any other income, some may be applied against exemptions and the remainder taxed at the lowest rates upward. Anyone who is eligible should participate in such a plan to the maximum of his ability.

3

The Stock Market

PRICES AND HOW THEY MOVE

The commonly thought of alternative to fixed-income, stable-principal investing is the stock market where one hopes to realize capital gains in addition to dividends. To be successful, you must buy low and sell high, but this is only a relative matter. The question really is will the stock go up after you buy it and move far enough to pay commissions and make you a profit within a time period commensurate with your objectives. The problem becomes one of prediction—prediction of the price movement of the specific stock of interest. If operating on the short side, the question is will the stock decrease sufficiently in price to make a profit. In this case, remember you have to pay dividends on the borrowed stock and your risk is greater.

STOCK PRICE MOVEMENTS

There are many market indicators which purport to measure the condition of the market and to give guidance in determining buying and selling times. We must say something at this point about the relation between a market average movement and the price movement of a specific stock. While the market average is some sort of a composite representation of the individual stocks making up the average, this gives no assurance that any one stock, included or not included in the average, has moved or will move in the same direction as the average. To examine this relationship, charts of the individual stock prices plotted against time are needed.

These can be purchased on a subscription basis[1] or may be constructed from data found in the financial section of your newspaper. If using your daily newspaper, you need the edition that gives *closing* daily prices rather than a midday edition. It is desirable that the daily high and low prices also be given. In any case, you are encouraged to maintain some price charts of selected stocks. The exercise provides an insight into price movement which it is difficult to obtain otherwise. Daily plots are preferable as some very interesting movements are not apparent on weekly or longer time plots and further this keeps you in touch with the market on a daily basis.

STOCK CHARTS

High-low-close charts plotted on semi-logarithmic paper are useful for measuring rate of trend and are available from chart services at a nominal price. A service giving weekly price ranges of a thousand or so stocks, and distributed monthly, gives ample information for selecting a few stocks to follow more closely. These services provide other information about each individual company which is useful in evaluating the company performance and its potential. Your own plotting may be on ordinary cross-section paper with linear scales (see Figure 3-1 as an example). The drug or variety store product is satisfactory but there are differences. Select a clean printed paper, with not overly heavy lines, and closely ruled such as five lines to the centimeter. Try to keep the same type in stock for you will want to make comparisons and there are sometimes small differences in the line spacing. Daily plots should show the date by marking the date of the first market day of each week on the horizontal axis. Plot market days only, even though there will be some 4-day weeks. The price axis (vertical scale) should be marked with a convenient scale. Using five lines per centimeter, convenient scales are: one small division per eighth point for stocks priced at about ten or less; one small division per quarter point for stocks priced between 10 and 50; and one small division per point for those priced 50 and above.

MARKET AVERAGE PLOT

You should also plot some stock average such as the Dow Jones 30 Industrials. This average, although of only 30 blue chip stocks, is easily

---

[1]Look through the advertisements in *Barron's* a weekly financial newspaper available at newsstands or your public library, procure samples and select one you prefer.

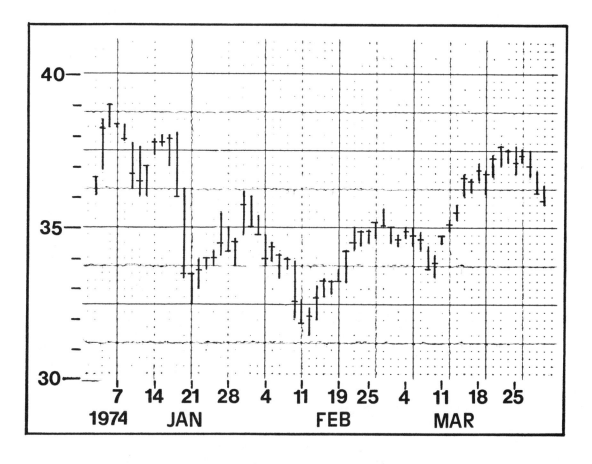

Figure 3-1. This chart of Crown Zellerbach is an example of charts you may want to keep on selected stocks to show how the price moves on a day-by-day basis.

available and serves most purposes. If used, a scale of one small division per two points using the long direction of the 8 x 10 inch paper is compatible with the scales suggested for the stocks and does not run off the paper too often. You may want to maintain, in addition to the high-low-close plot, a line chart of the average of the daily high and low. This may be on a chart with other curves to be described later.

RELATIVE STRENGTH

Procure a sheet of transparent plastic on which you can mark with a pencil. Rubbing the surface with steel wool will provide a suitable surface.

Now trace the line graph for your DJIA plot on this plastic and mark the date so you can overlay your stock charts and bring the dates into register. By moving the overlay up and down, fit the curve to your stock chart and note the relative trends. You will see that many stocks move with the average, particularly on a day to day basis. Compare the reaction lows and look for a low on the average which is lower than the previous low and see whether the stock may show the opposite, that is, the corresponding second low is higher than the previous one, thus indicating the stock is doing better than the average. The opposite situation will show up stocks performing worse than the average. The lows may agree in direction but the relative difference in the average may differ markedly from the difference in the stock chart thus giving an indication of relative strength. Experiment further with this overlay to compare your stock with the market average. Look for corresponding oscillations. Does your stock have a longer trend that is different from the longer trends in the average? Use the overlay to compare stocks, finding which one is the strongest, etc. Move the overlay back and forth along the time axis and look for similar movements. Does your stock lead or lag the market average, or does it tend to move in coincidence? These observations will be useful to assist in timing purchases and sales in conjunction with other techniques described later.

CYCLIC MOVEMENTS

If you examine a book of stock charts or charts you plot yourself, you will note that many stock prices rise and fall in a somewhat regular fashion. The same is true of market averages. That is, stock prices tend to move in cycles over a period of time.

A periodic motion is one which describes the same path cycle after cycle such as the plot of $y = A \sin x$. If x is an angle measured in degrees and is plotted on a horizontal axis, A is some constant value and y is plotted on the vertical axis, we form the graph as illustrated in Figure 3-2a. We observe that the curve traces out the same shape every 360°. It rises to a value A and falls to a value $-A$. A is called its amplitude. The distance between two corresponding points such as (a) and (b) of the curve is called its *period*. Cyclic motions are similar but differ in that the distances between corresponding points of the curve vary from cycle to cycle as illustrated in Figure 3-2b in the lengths (c) to (d) and (d) to (e); in the maximum amplitude varying from cycle to cycle; and in distortions in the smooth flow of the curve. The length of the cycle may be measured between alternate points of zero amplitude as shown in the figure,

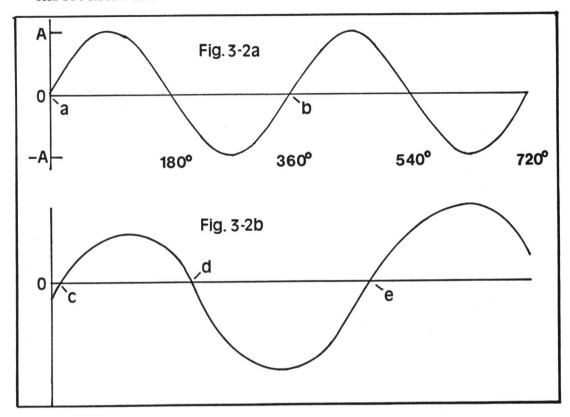

Figure 3-2. A pure sine wave function, curve (a), repeats itself precisely every 360°, and is therefore said to be periodic. Curve (b) is similar in shape but does not repeat itself. It is referred to as a cyclic wave or motion.

between successive points of minimum amplitude, or between successive points of maximum amplitude.

A study of stock price movements discloses these cyclic motions, which are often complicated by the superimposition of different cycle lengths and amplitudes. In the sine wave curve of Figure 3-2a the starting point, or the point in time on the horizontal axis where the curve crosses zero on the y axis going positive, designates the phase of the wave. Two waves may have the same period but differ in phase.

Approaching this concept from a synthesis point of view, Figure 3-3 shows two sine wave plots (a) and (b) having different periods and amplitudes. The individual amplitudes are added with proper regard to sign and plotted as curve (c). Think of this composite plot (c) in terms of stock price movement. It has major swings resulting from the component

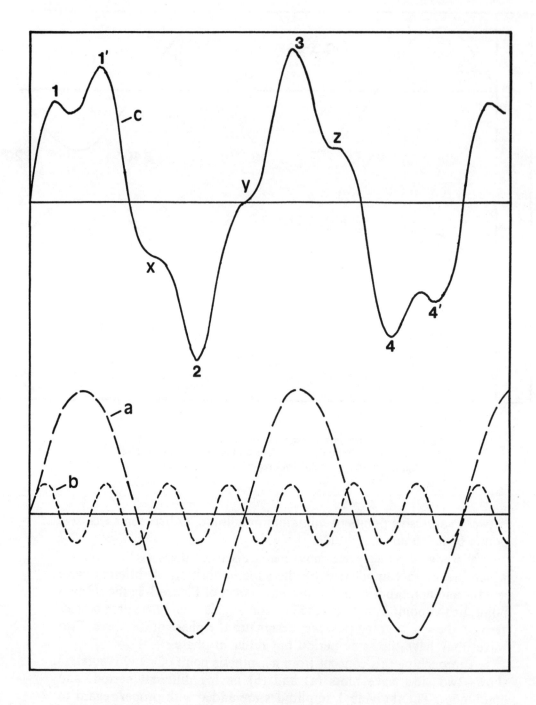

Figure 3-3. Curve (c) is the sum of the two sine waves below and is similar to some stock price movements. Note that the peaks and the depressions may shift along the horizontal axis.

(a), but note the peaks and depressions do not occur at exactly the same time as in curve (a), in particular 1 and 4. Does 4′ remind you of "testing the previous bottom" (4)? Are regions x, y and z consolidations? Note the added push given by the small wave (b) when it has a peak near the peak of (a) such as point 3. Now this is a simple situation indeed—the two components are pure sine waves of constant amplitude and fixed period. If they were merely cyclic in shape, and more components present, it is easy to imagine how they might well represent a market price movement.

As a more complex example, Figure 3-4 is the plot of

$$y = 12 \sin x + 4 \sin 3x + 2 \sin 6x + \sin 24x + 0.04x$$

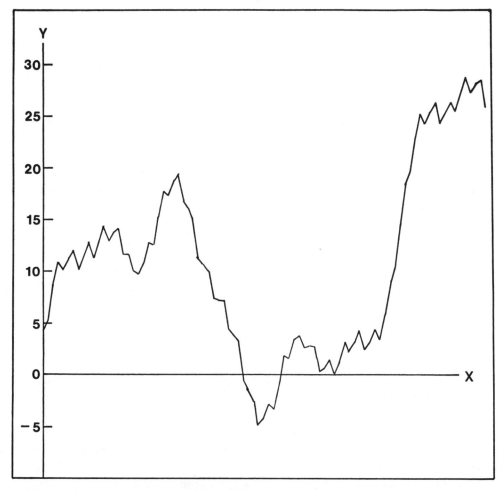

Figure 3-4. Plot of the equation
$y = 12 \sin x + 4 \sin 3x + 2 \sin 6x + \sin 24x + 0.04$
Note the resemblance of this curve to a stock chart such as the DJI Average.

The last term represents a steady upward trend added to the four periodic sine wave terms. The periods are in the ratio of 1 to 1/3 to 1/6 to 1/24. They may be thought of in time as representing 18 months, 6 months, 3 months and 3 ¼ weeks, periods often found in stock market movements. The plot is not unlike a stock market chart.

It does not seem far-fetched to attempt to find cyclic motions in stock market averages and in plots of individual stocks. If it is possible to identify these individual cycles, then they become a powerful aid in prediction of the future price movement. Although the cyclic movement is not periodic, in which case predictions would be exact, the change in the cyclic components is not abrupt but relatively smooth and continuous thus permitting extrapolating for predicting the future.

The cyclic analysis of stocks was first extensively described by Hurst (Reference 3, Appendix F). He developed the technique of enclosing the conventional high-low-close plot in a constant price (vertical scale) envelope. This is illustrated in Figure 3-5. These envelopes are most easily drawn using a pair of dividers to measure off a constant vertical distance. Extend one side of the envelope at a time to the next major price reversal, using the dividers to sketch in the envelope between reversals. It is surprising how easy this becomes and how much clearer the cyclic motion appears.

The example chosen is, of course, a good one. Not all stocks behave this well, nor will any one stock necessarily follow a good cyclic pattern at all times. However, the point is that many stocks do behave in a good cyclic manner enough of the time to take care of any amount you want to invest, so scan your charts until you find a well-behaved stock you like. Did you notice the cyclic movement of Crown Zellerbach in Figure 3-1? Go back and visualize the prices enclosed by Hurst envelopes and note how the two prominent cycles now stand out. If trading on the long side, the upswing expected must be great enough to pay commissions and make a reasonable profit. While profits can be made when these trading cycles move up and down within an essentially horizontal channel, it is preferable to find a stock moving in an upward trending channel. Avoid any stock moving in a down trend; these are for the short-side trades.

Many market technicians have found trend lines and channels to be a most useful tool in timing of buy and sell actions. Reference 4 (Appendix F) describes these together with a very complete presentation of chart reading. Hurst has extended the straight line trend channel concept to curvilinear channels which result in improved timing and a prediction capability founded upon the more basic movement of stock prices. More will be said in later chapters about the basic cyclic movements and old market concepts.

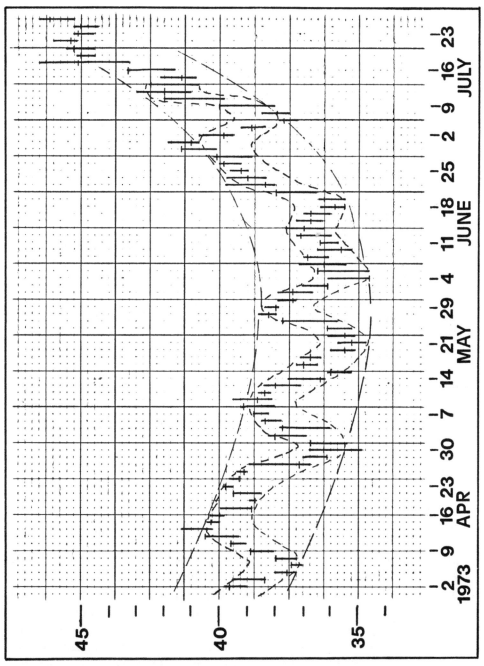

Figure 3-5. The stock of Citicorp exhibits a well-formed cyclic pattern. The prices oscillate with a cycle of about three weeks within a long sweeping cycle. The movement is made clear by enclosing the price swings in "Hurst Envelopes."

MARKET INDICATORS

Many market indicators have been derived to determine the state of the market and generate buy and sell signals. In evaluating these indicators it is important to determine whether they merely measure today's position or whether they predict the future. What good is it to know we had a bull market after the peak is reached unless we can also know that the peak has been reached. Many indicators do provide the present direction of price movement but merely looking at the past prices tells you this direction without any manipulation. True, market trends tend to continue for a time in the same direction, and investing with the trend can be profitable. When the trend reverses, it takes time to be convinced and a lot of money can be lost in the meantime.

One needs a market indicator which tells in advance either where in price or when in time, or both, the price reversal is going to occur. The cyclic analysis enables such a prediction. There are indicators which have given a degree of success in the past which, if carefully analyzed, may be seen to be based upon a cyclic market movement. Going directly to the cyclic analysis provides a better picture and simplies the interpretation. In addition, there are a number of market axioms which may be seen to be grounded in the cyclic movement. A future chapter will take up a number of these one by one.

Having an analysis system which enables price prediction does not insure high profits unless properly used. As previously pointed out, the price movement is not periodic and therefore is only approximate. Small changes in cycle shape will result in greater and greater deviations as time elapses and so require periodic updating. Thus the overall prediction is generally better for short times into the future than long-term predictions. This leads to the conclusion that short-term profits are easier to achieve than long-term profits. This reference is to the cyclic periods, not short- and long-term capital gains. Although short-term trading is commonly termed speculation versus holding purchases for long periods as investment, it is postulated that intelligent short-term trading can be safer in preserving capital as well as offering greater profits. The long-term investor rides up and down the cycles with only a nominal appreciation at best. The short-term trader can pick predictable price swings with small profits over short periods of time, stand aside when the cycle is against the desired trend, then re-enter when the timing is right and attain successive small profits several times a year which add up to a high annualized rate. Table 3-1 gives the result of realizing a profit of i percent for N times. For example, if you can make a clear profit of 10% on your investment and reinvest the proceeds, including the profits, for another 10% gain, etc. for ten successive times, you multiply your initial investment by 2.6. The oftener you turn over your investment at a moderate gain, the greater the total profit potential.

Table 3-1

If you make a profit of $i\%$ n successive times, investing all the profits each time, your original investment will be multiplied by the factor given here.

n	i=2%	3%	5%	7%	10%	15%	20%	50%	100%
1	1.02	1.03	1.05	1.07	1.10	1.15	1.20	1.50	2.00
3	1.06	1.09	1.16	1.23	1.33	1.52	1.73	3.38	8.00
5	1.10	1.16	1.28	1.40	1.61	2.01	2.49	7.59	32.0
7	1.15	1.23	1.41	1.61	1.95	2.66	3.58	17.1	128
10	1.22	1.34	1.63	1.97	2.59	4.05	6.19	57.7	1024
15	1.35	1.56	2.08	2.76	4.18	8.14	15.4	438	
20	1.49	1.81	2.65	3.87	6.73	16.4	38.3	3325	
25	1.64	2.09	3.39	5.43	10.8	33.9	95.4		
30	1.81	2.43	4.32	7.61	17.4	66.2	237		
40	2.21	3.26	7.04	15.0	45.3	268			
50	2.69	4.38	11.5	29.5	117				

It is reasonable to assume that one takes a greater risk when operating in the stock market than when investing in fixed income securities as discussed in previous chapters. For this increased risk, one expects to achieve greater profits. If you are inclined to worry about such risks, there are some mutual funds that have a plan with an insurance company which insures your investment against loss of principal over some extended period of time. These plans have certain limitations such as a minimum investment, leaving dividends and capital gains in the fund, etc. The cost is nominal and you can cancel and reinsure if large profits accrue to be sure of your gains. If interested get information from your broker or one of the funds.[2] Following this course is conservative and at the worst prevents loss of your initial investment without income from it, but the plan does not lend itself to trying for the above average profits you may be able to achieve if on your own.

---

[2]You may obtain information from Insured Mutual Funds. Write IMF Services, Inc., 294 Washington Street, Boston, Mass. 02108

Summary

Market averages and many individual stock prices move in a cyclic manner. These form patterns which tend to repeat and thus allow you to judge the direction they are most likely to follow in the near future. The patterns of various stocks may be compared with each other and with a market average to estimate their relative strength. Predictions are naturally more reliable for the short term than if extended far into the future. This leads to the conclusion that short-term trading can be more informed than long-term investment and thus can lead to greater profits. A small gain on each trade, if repeated at frequent intervals, can produce extraordinary results.

4

Pinpointing the Underlying
Trends with Moving Averages

The day-by-day variations of stock prices, or other data, often give a random appearance when presented as a graph of price versus time. Averaging the price values can be used to reduce these variations and bring out longer-term trends which are more significant. The average of the daily high and low values of a stock price, or a stock average [1] may be used to provide a single value representative of the day. This value may then be used in calculating averages for longer time periods.

FINDING THE MOVING AVERAGE

A 10-day average, for example, is found merely by adding the values for ten successive days and dividing the sum by ten. Using ten time units (days or weeks) is convenient since the division is accomplished by simply moving the decimal point one place to the left in the sum. Other periods are commonly used such as 30-days, 60-days, 200-days, 39-weeks, 12-months, etc. The time over which the average is found is called the *span* of the average. The sum is always divided by the number of items summed to give the average value of the items. This average value then represents the value at a time midway between the first date and the last date of the time span making up the items averaged. If an odd number of items is

---

[1] The term stock average refers to some combination of the individual price values of a specified number of stocks at a specified time. There are various ways to combine the prices which may be different from the simple procedure discussed in this chapter.

averaged, then this midpoint falls on the middle day. If an even number of items, such as ten, is averaged, the midpoint falls between the fifth and sixth days.

A *moving average* is a series of averages computed for the same span length at successive times. It is conveniently calculated by first finding the average for one span of items, then finding the next average in time by adding the value of the next item in time to the sum previously found and subtracting the oldest item in time from this sum and dividing by the number of items. This process is continued as each new item becomes available. The moving average may be plotted along with the price plots to show the smoothed trend of the price value. Stock prices may be either the high-low range (for the day, week, etc.) or the average of this high and low range. The moving average value must be plotted one-half span earlier in time than the time of the last item used in calculating the average[2] to statistically center the moving average so as to register with the price movement.

An aid to calculation is to tabulate the items to be averaged in a column on narrow-ruled note paper (wide-ruled paper may be used with two entries per space), then use a card cut so as to cover a number of lines one less than the number in the span. When in place, all numbers used in computing the sum are covered except the new number to be added and the old number to be subtracted.

A SYSTEM OF MOVING AVERAGES

Oftentimes one desires to form several moving averages of different spans. The longer the span used, the greater the amount of smoothing one obtains. For example, a 10-day moving average eliminates (smooths) variations of a day-by-day nature. A span of 100-days eliminates these short variations and others on up to times corresponding to the span length. More will be said about this later. Usually there is considerable variation permitted for selecting the span durations. In stock market analysis, selected spans of 10-, 30-, and 60-days, and 3-, 9-, 12-, and 18-months are often desirable. For example, I have found useful the following combination: 10-day, 30-day, 60-day, 3-month, 9-month, 27-month and 54-month. The days are market days, not calendar days, thus 10-days is two weeks when there are no holidays present and 60-days is very nearly

---

[2]Many stock market charts show a moving average plotted at the same point in time as the last item used in the computation. This method does not properly show a smoothed price curve but is used for certain theories of price prediction. See Chapter 6, "Moving Averages."

3-months. Now for a labor-saving technique. The 10-day moving average is the only one calculated directly. The 30-day average may be found by adding together the three sums of three successive blocks of ten days to obtain the sum for 30-days, then dividing by 30 for the 30-day moving average. Simpler yet is merely adding the three 10-day averages at points in time ten days apart, then dividing by three. An aid may be constructed from a strip of cardboard marked to identify the three lines, each separated by ten days, on which the three 10-day average values are found that are to be added and averaged by dividing by three to get the 30-day moving average. Use narrow-ruled paper to avoid running off the page too frequently. When spanning two pages, the old page may be placed in register above the new to give a continuous column. It is important that the lines be equally spaced and fill every line on each sheet. The 60-day moving average is found in a similar manner from two 30-day values. Since the average value changes at a slower rate than the individual items, you will observe that only the last, or last and next to last, figures usually change from one sum to the next, so you do not need to go through the complete mental process of the addition but proceed to write down the sum after adding the right-hand column or possibly two columns.

Since 60 market days are very nearly three months, they can be considered the same for practical purposes. A plot of the daily value of the average of the high and low of some market average, such as the Dow Jones Industrial Average, with the 10-, 30- and 60-day moving averages has been found useful for analyzing short-term movements of the stock market. Figure 4-1 illustrates such a plot. The Monday date of each week is noted on the horizontal time scale and only market days are plotted. The 10-day average (dotted curve) lags the market by half a span (5 days) where the values are plotted between the fifth and sixth days prior to the current date. The 30-day points are plotted between the 15th and 16th prior days and the 60-day average between the 30th and 31st prior days. The increased smoothing of the longer spans is noted. The curves are not always separated as distinctly as shown here. If short-term variations are not present in the data, the curves may actually be essentially superimposed. Spans longer than 60-days are better displayed on charts plotted with weekly rather than daily data.

When plotting data on a weekly entry chart, the price average used may be either the average of the high and low for the week, the Friday close value, or a vertical bar showing the range for the week. It is convenient to construct the plot by marking the time axis in weekly intervals with the first Friday of each month noted. Assume the 60-day value to be identical with a three-month value and transfer this end-of-week value of the 60-day average to a tabulation by weeks and call it a three-month

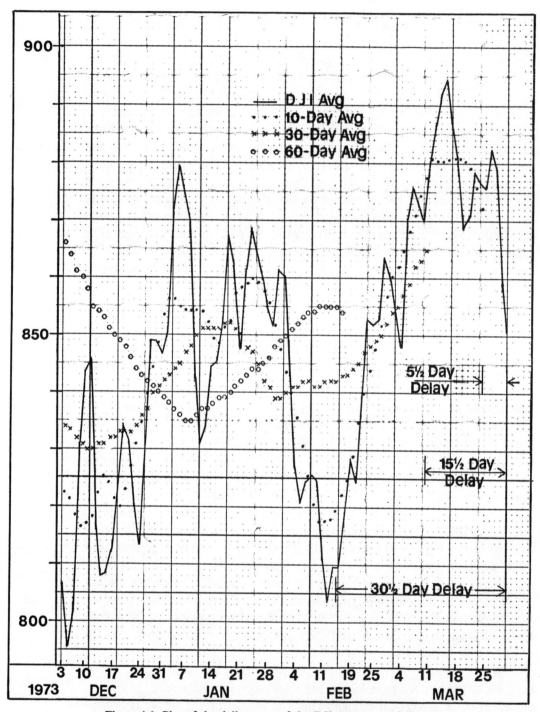

Figure 4-1. Plot of the daily mean of the DJI Average and three centered moving averages of the DJIA. Note the greater smoothing of the longer span averages, and their greater delay.

average. It is convenient to combine three 3-month values to form a 9-month moving average. For this purpose, three 13-week blocks are combined. The plot is made on the 20th week previous to the last week used in the calculation. A 27-month average may be found from three 9-month values, and a 54-month average from two 27-month values. Since the longer-span averages change very slowly compared to weekly entries, one may further condense the data by making a third tabulation using intervals of say three or four weeks for calculations of the 27- and 54-month averages. Figure 4-2 shows a portion of the calculation tables used for this system of moving averages. There are many more spans that could be calculated within the basic system just described and are sometimes found to be useful in analysis. One can allow for additional columns on each tabulation sheet to be used for such additional spans as may be found desirable at any given time but which do not normally need to be calculated on a continuous basis. It is convenient to number the tabulation sheet and time axis with day or week numbers, as the case may be, as well as the calendar date. This aids in avoiding confusion between charts and in studying time relationships. When these numbers become large, start over from zero.

Use of the moving average to imply market trends and cyclic behavior of stock prices will be treated in Chapter 7. For such purposes the calculated point is plotted one-half span prior to the date of calculation. In other words the result is delayed by a half span in time and the greater the smoothing (longer span), the greater the delay. Curve fitting, Chapter 8, is a method of getting around some of the disadvantages of long delays. Other uses of moving averages either ignore the delays, when small, or use them in a manner not directly apparent.

One may approximate the moving average in the delay region by merely extending it by eye to follow the trend of the data, or you can make a mathematical approximation. This is done by dropping the oldest data point and finding the average for the shortened span. This is repeated point by point and the average of the successively shortened spans is plotted at their respective centers to move the approximation forward in time to form what is known as a *truncated* moving average.

THE MODIFIED MOVING AVERAGE

One disadvantage of the moving average is known as the *drop-off* error. In forming a 10-day moving average, if there is an unusually large difference between the value of the item subtracted (oldest day) and the average value, there will be a sharp jump in the newly computed value.

Daily Entry Table

Date Yr Mo Day	Week No	Day No	DJIA Hi-Lo Avg	10-Day Avg	Σ	Avg	30-Day Σ	Avg	60-Day Σ	Avg
74 Feb 5			820.9	851.75			2554	851	1691	846
6			824.4	847.30			2555	852	1688	844
7		155	826.7	843.50			2555	852	1686	843
8	433		824.7	839.98			2552	851	1684	842
11			811.3	835.64			2549	850	1682	841
12			803.7	830.84			2544	848	1679	840
13			809.6	825.66			2540	847	1677	839
14		160	809.4	820.56			2534	845	1675	838
15	434		816.9	817.52			2527	842	1673	837
19			828.6	817.62			2523	841	1672	836
20			824.5	817.98			2518	839	1671	835

Weekly Entry—as of Friday

Date Yr Mo Day	Week No	3-Mo (60-Day)	Σ	Avg	9-Mo Σ	Avg	Σ	Avg	Σ	Avg
74 Feb 1	432	849			2675	892				
8		842			2669	890				
15		837			2666	889				
22	435	836			2658	886				

Monthly Entry—Every Fourth Week

Date Yr Mo Day	Week No	9-Mo Avg	Σ	Avg	27-Mo Σ	Avg	Σ	Avg	54-Mo Σ	Avg
74 Feb 1	432	892			2781	927			1745	873
Mar 1	436	885			2746	915			1746	873
29	440	882			2719	906			1745	873

Figure 4-2 Examples of tabulation sheets used in computing and recording a system of moving averages.

This jump results from the oldest data which is the least significant item of the ten items of the sum and thus produces a misleading distortion of the smoothed curve. One practice is to watch for such drop-off distortions and avoid misleading conclusions. Another method of calculating the moving average may be used to reduce such jumps. Instead of subtracting the oldest item, the average value is subtracted. This has the effect of avoiding large drop-off errors, gives a curve more responsive to the new day added, and provides a correction of calculation errors. With respect to the latter, if one makes an error in summing the items, a permanent bias is produced in the standard moving average calculations. The calculations should be checked periodically to avoid building up such a bias. The modified moving average is self-correcting and errors will disappear in due course.

The calculation is further simplified with certain span intervals. For example, the 10-day modified moving average may be shown to be computed as follows: subtract yesterday's average value from today's new number, divide by ten and add to yesterday's average value to find today's average value. If negative numbers are used, signs must be properly observed.

The modified moving average is particularly useful in forming certain market indicators. For short spans, such as 10-days, it may be plotted without a delay. I, for example, plot the 10-day upside and downside NYSE volumes and an overbought-oversold index in this manner.

This modified moving average should not be used when it is to be mathematically related to the price values, for example, in filtering and curve fitting to be described in later chapters.

Summary

Moving averages are employed to smooth out minor variations in market prices. When used to represent prices they must be centered to give a true picture. The longer the span of data which is averaged, the smoother the result and the more the short-period variations are eliminated, but at a cost of greater delay in being able to compute the average. One does not always want to eliminate all the shorter cycles and so may desire to compute several moving averages whose spans differ. A system of moving averages built upon one short actual computation provides these several spans with very little computational effort.

A modified moving average can be used for certain purposes which avoids some of the distortions of the ordinary moving average but it should not be used to represent price data which is later to be used as a smoothed price for other calculations.

5

How to Express Curve
Shapes Mathematically

It is often desirable to represent stock prices, market averages, or market indicators by a mathematical curve. It is therefore useful to have an understanding of the mathematics involved. If we have the closing price of a stock market average for each market day, we can plot a chart showing how these prices move with time. We may desire to draw a line through these points to represent the trend of the price. This can be done by hand, or we can use methods described in Chapter 8 to calculate a curve of some specified form which best fits all these points. In this chapter we will describe the mathematical representation of various curves which are found useful in market studies. If you do not have a mathematical background, it would be well to read Chapter 16 at this point.

THE STRAIGHT LINE

On a graph where values of x are plotted on the horizontal axis, called the *abscissa* in mathematical language (or simply the x-axis), and values of y are plotted on the vertical axis, called the *ordinate* (or the y-axis), a straight line is represented by the algebraic equation

$$y = a + bx \qquad (5\text{-}1)$$

Examples of this "curve" and other points discussed in this section are shown in Figure 5-1a. When the value of x is zero, $y = a$. This is the point

63

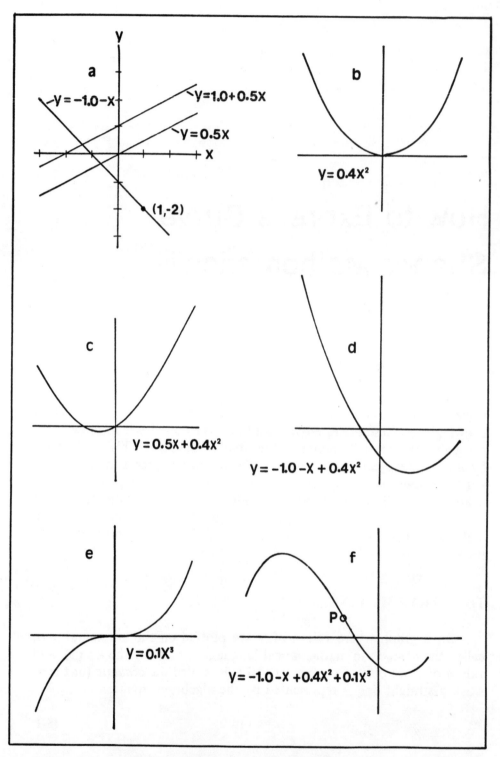

Figure 5-1. Examples of various basic curves which can be represented by a simple algebraic equation.

where the line crosses the y-axis and is known as the *y-intercept*. When y = 0, a + bx = 0 and x = − a/b, this being the *x-intercept*. If these two intercept points are plotted on the graph and connected by a straight line, which may be extended in both directions, the curve is plotted which is represented by Equation (5-1). One may choose any two convenient values of x and substitute them in the equation to find the corresponding values of y. These pairs may be plotted to also determine the location of the straight line. This may be preferable in order to spread the points far enough apart to permit drawing the line accurately. Pairs of corresponding points are designated by corresponding subscripts on the variables x and y thus: (x_1,y_1), (x_5,y_5) or in general (x_n,y_n).

The values of a and b are constants for any given equation and are what determines the equation. The number a is known as the *constant term*. The factor b is known as the *coefficient* of x. These definitions are carried on to other equations we will discuss. When a = 0, the straight line passes through the point (x_0,y_0) or the origin of the graph. The value of a may be either positive or negative. Changing its value shifts the straight line upward or downward parallel to itself. The value of b may also be positive or negative. When positive the line slopes upward from left to right when the graph plots increasing values of x to the right, as is conventional. If b is negative, the line slopes downward from left to right.

Algebraic equations of this type and others to be described in following sections are called *polynomials*, meaning an expression of two or more terms. The straight-line type is called a *linear equation*, or sometimes called a *polynomial of degree one*, or first degree, because the variable x appears only as the first power of x.

SECOND-DEGREE EQUATION

The polynomial involving x squared and any lower powers is called a *quadratic*, or a second-degree equation. Its general form is

$$y = a + bx + cx^2 \tag{5-2}$$

Comparing this equation with Equation (5-1), we see it differs only by adding the term cx^2. This term always has the sign of the coefficient c since x^2 is always positive for negative values of x as well as for positive values. This term is symmetrical about x = 0 as shown in Figure 5-1b where $y = 0.4x^2$ is plotted. If c had been negative, the "U-shaped" curve would have been inverted, opening downward. The addition of the constant term *a* would displace the curve in the vertical or *y* direction. Including the first-degree term, *bx* will distort the symmetrical "U-shape" pulling one side down while pushing the other side up (see Figure 5-1c). Note the minimum no longer occurs at x = 0 and the *y* value is slightly negative at the minimum. This shift in minimum is important to remember. Suppose we have a stock chart where the price has declined, reverses and increases in a "U-shaped" pattern. This price pattern may be represented by a second-degree equation. We may think of it as consisting of two components, one being the cx^2 term which represents the effect of the decline, reversal and recovery, and the other which represents an overall upward price trend. The trend may be or may not be present and may be either an uptrend or a downtrend. If the trend is present, it will shift the actual minimum to the left if upward and to the right if downward. The shift of a minimum is always in the direction of the lower value of the trend. If instead, the price is passing through a peak, the actual peak is shifted toward the higher value of the trend. You may want to check this by plotting the equations $y = 0.5x - 0.4x^2$ and $y = -0.5x - 0.4x^2$. The complete Equation (5-2) is illustrated in Figure 5-1d.

THIRD-DEGREE EQUATION

The polynomial having x^3 as the highest power of *x* is called a *cubic*. We have seen that the first-degree equation represents a straight line—no curves. The second-degree equation is curved in one direction, having one reversal in direction and it may be concave upward or downward. The third-degree equation has two reversals of direction and may be described as S-shaped when the S is laid on its side. The general equation is formed by adding a term dx^3 to give

$$y = a + bx + cx^2 + dx^3 \qquad (5\text{-}3)$$

The term dx^3 is illustrated in Figure 5-1e, and the complete expression is illustrated by Figure 5-1f. This curve is symmetrical about the point P. The cubic equation may represent a price movement containing a maximum and a minimum. Both the *a* and cx^2 terms may be zero and equation

$$y = bx + dx^3 \qquad (5\text{-}4)$$

will still exhibit the same shape. This equation is merely symmetrical about the origin.

PERIODIC-WAVE EQUATIONS

The simple plot of y = sin x has already been discussed in Chapter 3. In more general terms a periodic wave may be expressed as the sum of a cosine and a sine wave, that is,

$$y = A \cos \omega t + B \sin \omega t \tag{5-5}$$

The trigonometric functions repeat themselves every 360 degrees, that is, they go through one cycle or one period every 360°. In many scientific computations it is convenient to measure angles in radians. There are 2π [1] radians in 360°, or one radian equals approximately 57.3°. For our purposes, we will measure angles in degrees and tenths thereof for convenience in taking products. One cycle or period is completed each time ωt goes through 2π radians or 360°. Thus, if the length in time of one period is T, the time for one cycle, or period, is $T = 2\pi/\omega$ if ω is in radians, or $T = 360°/\omega$ if ω is measured in degrees per unit of time.[2]

In stock market analysis, the time will be measured in days (or weeks, etc.) and the period T will be measured in the same units. Although the periodic-wave equation may be expressed in terms of T, it is more convenient to make the computations in terms of frequency, then determine the period for analysis and plotting. Having the frequency ω in degrees per day, the period T in days will be $360/\omega$.

The general Equation (5-5) expressed as the sum of a cosine and sine function can be expressed as a sine function alone of the form

$$y = C \sin(\omega t + \phi) \tag{5-6}$$

Equation (5-6) may be expanded by using a trigonometric identity, giving

$$y = C \sin(\omega t + \phi) = C \cos \omega t \sin \phi + C \sin \omega t \cos \phi \tag{5-7}$$

Comparing Equations (5-5) and (5-7), the right hand sides are similar in form and are identical if, $A = C \sin \phi$ and $B = C \cos \phi$. It follows, since the sum of the squares of the sine and cosine of an angle equals unity, that $A^2 + B^2 = C^2(\sin^2\phi + \cos^2\phi) = C^2$ and also, $A/B = (C \sin \phi) / (C \cos \phi = \tan \phi$.

---

[1]The symbol π is the Greek letter Pi and is a constant equal approximately to 3.1416. If you possess a minicomputer, it may have a π operation key, if not, you can obtain π to a seven-place accuracy by dividing 355 by 113.

[2]The symbol ω is the Greek letter Omega.

The angle ϕ is called the *phase angle*[3] and measures the displacement between corresponding points of sin ωt and sin ($\omega t + \phi$). See Figure 5-2 for illustration of these relationships.

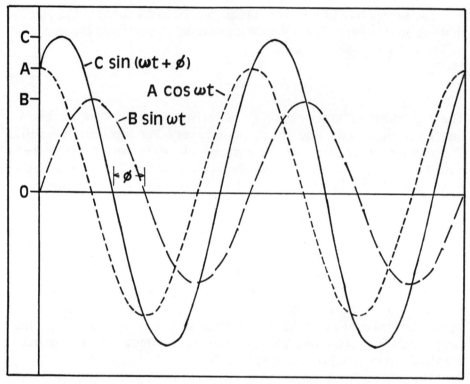

Figure 5-2. The sum of a sine wave and a cosine wave is a sine wave displaced to the left, by a phase angle ϕ, relative to the original sine wave.

Any sine wave involves three unknowns—frequency (ω), amplitude (C) and phase (ϕ). If the equation is in the form of Equation (5-5), the unknowns are ω, A and B. In going to the form of Equation (5-6), C may be either the positive or negative square root of $A^2 + B^2$. Also since ϕ is the angle whose tangent is A/B (that is, $\tan^{-1}\phi = A/B$), ϕ may be in any quadrant. If ϕ is taken to be in the first quadrant when A and B are of the same sign and in the second quadrant when of opposite sign, then C will have the sign of A. This may be verified by letting t = 0 in Equations (5-5) and 5-7) resulting in y = A = C sin ϕ, but sin ϕ is positive for both the first and second quadrants.

---

[3]The symbol ϕ is the Greek letter Phi.

SUMS OF PERIODIC WAVES

We have seen that adding a sine and a cosine wave of the same frequency results in a sine wave. The addition of two (or more) sine waves having different phases likewise results in a sine wave.

If two sine waves, having slightly different periods, are added, at one time their peaks will occur nearly at the same time giving an enhanced amplitude and are said to be in phase. As time goes on they will gradually get out of phase and will at some other time, when one is at its positive maximum and the other near its greatest amplitude in the negative direction, essentially cancel each other if their original amplitudes were equal, or they are said to *destructively interfere* with each other.

Figure 5-3 illustrates the effect of adding two wave motions, each having unit amplitude and one having a period of 10 days, the other 12 days. The two equations are

$$y_1 = \sin\,(360/10)t = \sin 36t \text{ and } y_2 = \sin\,(360/12)t = \sin 30t$$

The sum of y_1 and y_2, plotted as the upper curve of Figure 5-3 clearly shows the in-phase enhanced portion near $t = 3$ and the out-of-phase region near $t = 30$ where the resulting amplitude is very small.

It is interesting to note the spacing of the maxima and minima. As the two waves get out of phase, the spacings decrease. Also, note that if the minima were projected ahead by a 11-day spacing through the interference region, a minimum would be expected at $t = 8, 19, 30$ and 41. However, at $t = 41$ a maximum occurs, which amounts to a phase reversal in going through the destructive interference region.

In stock market cyclic analysis one often extracts waves resembling the upper curve of Figure 5-3. As the amplitude of a cyclic pattern decreases, the apparent period decreases, and when the pattern again builds up in amplitude the phase appears to have reversed. Such a pattern can therefore be thought of as the result of two components having slightly different periods. Of course, the amplitudes need not be equal which will add its own distortions.

Consider two sine waves, one of frequency ω_1 and the other ω_2 which is slightly smaller than ω_1 and each having unit amplitude. The sum of these two waves is then given by

$$y = \sin\,\omega_1 t + \sin\,\omega_2 t \qquad\qquad \textbf{(5-8)}$$

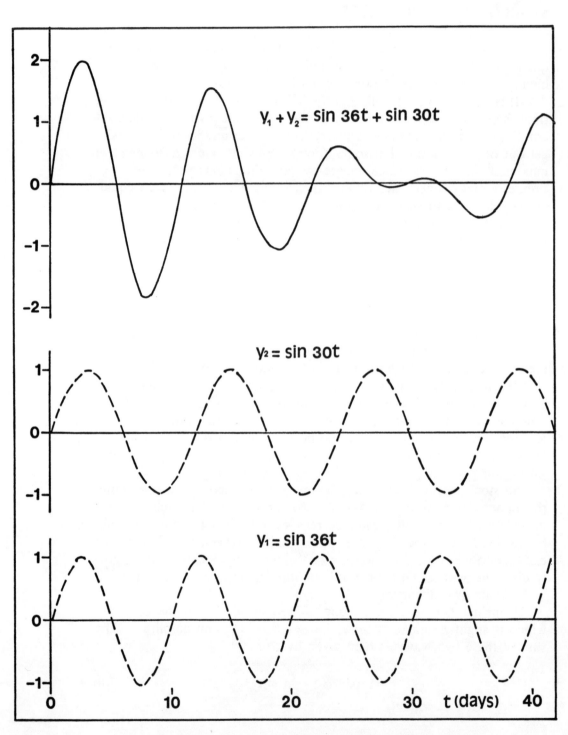

Figure 5-3. The sum of two sine waves of slightly different period.

By using a trigonometric identity this sum can be expressed as

$$y = 2 \cos \frac{\omega_1 - \omega_2}{2}t \, \sin \frac{\omega_1 + \omega_2}{2}t \qquad (5\text{-}9)$$

This can be thought of as a sine wave having a frequency that is the average of ω_1 and ω_2 modified by a variable amplitude of

$$2 \cos \frac{\omega_1 - \omega_2}{2}t$$

This amplitude varies from -2 to $+2$ at a low rate corresponding to a frequency which is one half the difference of the two frequencies.

If we take the derivative of Equation (5-8) with respect to t,

$$\frac{d}{dt}(\sin \omega_1 t + \sin \omega_2 t) = \omega_1 \cos \omega_1 t + \omega_2 \cos \omega_2 t \qquad (5\text{-}10)$$

it will be zero at points of the maxima and minima of Equation (5-8). Figure 5-4 is a plot of Equation (5-10) when it is the derivative of the equation plotted in Figure 5-3, namely $y = \sin 36t + \sin 30t$, the derivative being $36 \cos 36t + 30 \cos 30t$. Since we are only interested in the points where this derivative is zero, we will divide it by 30 and plot the equation $y = 1.2 \cos 36t + \cos 30t$.

The zero crossings can be easily read from the plot. Since the sine wave frequency of Equation (5-9) is the average of ω_1 and ω_2 or for this example $(36 + 30) \div 2$ or 33, the period would be $360°/33$ or approximately $10.9°$. Comparing the zero crossing points of Figure 5-4 with the ·maximum and minimum of the upper curve of Figure 5-3 we can mark the points of maxima and minima as indicated below the derivative curve. For the small values of t these spacings are very close to the average period but as we move into the destructive interference region the spacings decrease, then widen out as the enhanced region appears. Equally spaced intervals are marked by x's on Figure 5-4 equal to the period of 10.9, starting out at the first minimum at $t = 8$. Note that the fifth x corresponds to a *maximum* at $t = 52$. This illustrates the phase reversal in going through the interference region. Referring to Equation (5-9), this reversal is due to the cosine term reversing sign which occurs at $t = 30$ or where

$$\cos \frac{\omega_1 - \omega_2}{2}t = \cos \frac{36 - 30}{2}30 = \cos 90°$$

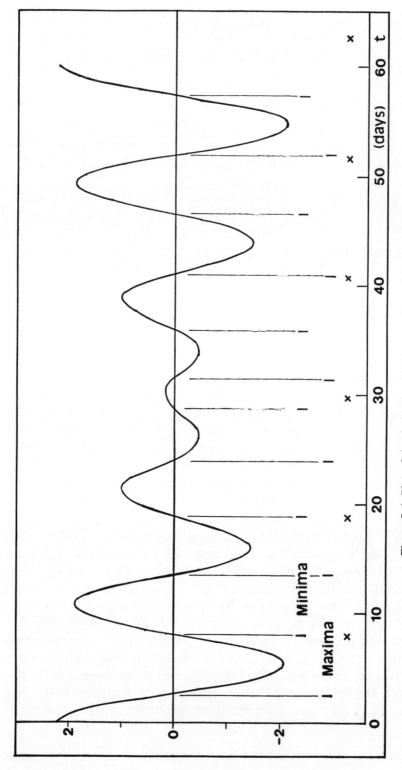

Figure 5-4. Plot of the derivative of the sum of two sine waves of slightly different frequencies. The points of zero amplitude are the maxima and minima of the combined sine waves and show how their spacings vary when going through the interference region.

72

Note that the period of the sum of the two sine waves is accurately given when measured between alternate points of zero amplitude of the plot in Figure 5-3, except for the phase reversal at t = 30. Here an extra point of zero amplitude occurs resulting in the phase reversal of the basic pattern. The appearance in this region takes different forms. In Figure 5-3 the two component sine waves go through zero amplitude at this point and are moving in precisely opposite directions which produces the symmetrical cross-over patterns of phase reversal. The two frequencies could be phased so that one sine wave is at its maximum amplitude when the other is at its minimum. In this case, the sum curve moves to zero and reverses in direction to produce the phase reversal. This gives the appearance of a double bottom or double top whose amplitude is less than the preceding or succeeding peaks. For other phase relations and for different amplitudes of the two component sine waves, the pattern is distorted

Summary

Simple algebraic equations combine to form curves resembling plots of stock market prices. When curves are added, the reversal points of the combined curve are usually shifted to the right or left of the reversal points in the original waves. Also the spacing of the reversal points, originally uniform, are likely to be different. This is important in analyzing stock market data to estimate the period of significant cycles. Two periodic waves of slightly different frequencies combine to produce a beat frequency giving the appearance of a cyclic wave changing in amplitude from twice the amplitude of one wave to essentially zero at the point of destructive interference. The apparent period varies with amplitude and the phase reverses when going through the point of minimum amplitude. Stock market prices exhibit the same type of overall movement.

6

Cyclic Thinking

AIDS IN DIAGNOSING TURNING POINTS AND PREDICTING TRENDS

TECHNICAL REACTIONS

When prices have moved in one direction for a time and with little or no excuse they reverse, it is called a *technical reaction*. There are short reactions, a day or so, and longer reactions. When the market has moved in one direction for a time, one hears that a correction is due.

A better way of looking at these movements is the cyclic approach. Take any daily high-low plot such as the DJI Average in *The Wall Street Journal* and mark each date where the low for the day was less than the low to either side of it. You will find these points spaced about equally in time, see Figure 6-1 where they average about five days. They may run longer or slightly shorter at other times. These marks measure the length of the shortest significant cycle. Likewise, one may look for high points and further note the relative duration of the up and down moves of the cycle. Viewed in this manner one can predict when reactions are likely to take place and even project succeeding minor highs and lows. Although deviations in the spacings of the lows of plus or minus one or two days occurs, the probability of continuing the pattern is high.

Further, more pronounced cycles may be picked off the same chart by finding the low area which is lower than the low areas to either side, such as one of about 24 days marked on Figure 6-1. Still it is a technical reaction, but how much more informative is the cyclic picture. The prices are shown enclosed in a "Hurst envelope" of 70 Dow points; note how well the movement is contained; further they were contained in this

75

envelope for months previous to the plot. This brings out a further advantage of the cyclic viewpoint. Since the prices tend to move to the envelope boundaries, one can predict the extent of the move, and since the approximate period is known, one can predict the time of the move.

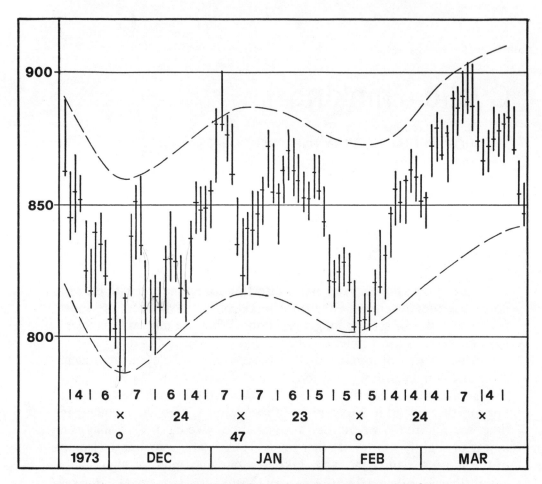

Figure 6-1. The daily chart of the DJI Average shows a low about every five days, and low areas spaced by about 24 days.

TREND CHANNELS

Trend channels have long been used to predict stock price turns. The channels are formed by drawing a pair of parallel straight lines. In a down market connect the peaks of prices on a high-low chart, then draw a parallel line passing through the first significant low point. This channel tends to enclose the price movement. In an up market, start by connecting the low points, then draw a parallel line through the first significant high point. This picture is similar to the "Hurst envelopes" except the channels are bounded by straight lines. The cyclic envelope better fits the price movement and provides more information when length of cycles are apparent, for then one can predict where turns are expected. Also a better choice of envelope (or channel) width can be made by working over a full cycle or more, rather than a small section which appears to be nearly a straight trend and which occurs, merely due to the geometry of the situation, during the nearly constant trend section midwway between reversal areas. Trend channel signals are given by breaking out of the channel. Better prices can be predicted by thinking in terms of cycles. Study Figure 6-2 which illustrates these comments. Note that the longer cycle of Bethlehem Steel, shown on the plot, differs considerably from that of Western Air Lines, but nevertheless the short cycles marked by the daily lows occur about the same time for both.

FAILING TO EXCEED

A price peak which fails to exceed the previous high has long been an indication of weakness; likewise a reaction low that fails to exceed the previous low signifies strength.

When viewed from the cyclic viewpoint it is obvious that these conditions arise when a cycle is rounding over and it is a bit late for the best prices. More often, the prices turn on a high (or low) created by a shorter cycle occurring in phase with the longer cycle you are watching and by the time you are certain the movement is going to fail to exceed, prices are well on their way in the new direction.

Conversely, a peak which exceeds the past peak indicates continued strength and a low which breaks the previous low indicates continued weakness. This is fully consistent with the cyclic viewpoint. Refer to Figure 6-2 for examples of these comments.

PULL BACKS

It is noted that breakouts from trend lines often pull back to the trend line before proceeding in the breakout direction, and worse, sometimes become a false breakout. This movement is the effect of a short cycle on a longer-term movement and an analysis of the basic movement is more revealing than depending upon some frequently observed effect.

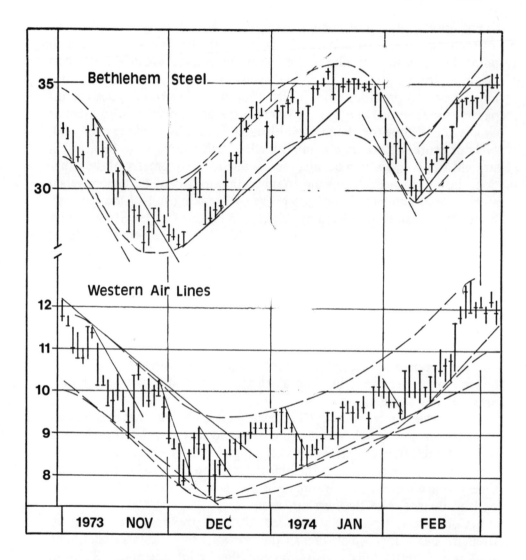

Figure 6-2. Comparison of the use of "Hurst Envelopes" with trend channels and trend lines.

MARKET LEGS

Many market systems describe market movements in terms of legs or phases. There are minor legs and major legs, primary phases and secondary phases, etc. These descriptions are akin to a cyclic description but in general they fail to appreciate the possibility of extracting the individual cyclic movements, projecting them into the future, and then combining for market prediction on both the price and time scales.

HEAD AND SHOULDERS FORMATIONS

Draw a positive half sine wave curve, then superimpose on it a shorter cycle of smaller amplitude, so that it has one peak near the peak of the first curve, and a preceding peak and succeeding peak positioned on the sides of the half sine wave. Stand back and view a beautiful *head and shoulders pattern*. Slight sidewise shifts will provide sloping necklines of your choice. Double shoulders appear if more of the short cycles are added on, provided they are not pushed too far down the sides of the half sine wave. These short cycles may be present but tend to be swamped by the steep slopes of the sine wave when down from near the peak. Waiting for breakthrough of the neckline will not give the best selling price.

DOUBLE TOPS AND BOTTOMS

Superposition of a short cycle on a longer cycle so that the minimum of the short cycle coincides with the maximum of the longer cycle produces a *double top*. The reverse produces a *double bottom*.

TRIANGLES

When a series of short cycles of decreasing amplitude such as Figure 6-3a is superimposed on a much longer cyclic movement, various well known patterns are developed. Figure 6-3b illustrates the well known *ascending triangle* where the longer cycle is sweeping upward. It is obvious that the damping out of the short wave motion allows the trend to continue its upward direction. Figure 6-3c illustrates the *descending triangle*. When Figure 6-3a is superimposed on an essentially flat movement, it forms a symmetrical triangle where chartists make no prediction, obviously because the flat main trend may be either a top, a bottom or a consolidation. However, knowledge of the position in the longer-term cycle provides the necessary information for reliable predictions. Other patterns such as flags, wedges, diamonds, etc. can be formed by assuming the proper combination of short and long cyclic movements.

BROADENING TOPS

The broadening top formation is considered bearish. Such a formation can be formed by two or more cycles moving into phase to reach a maximum when the individual peaks coincide. The longer cycle turns

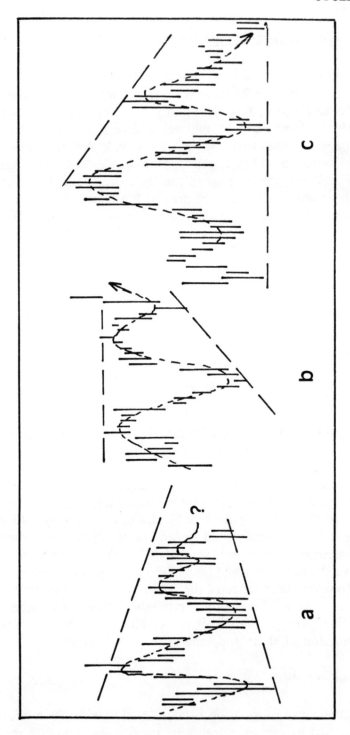

Figure 6-3. Illustration of formation of triangles when a damped cyclic oscillation is superimposed on (a) a horizontal trend, (b) an uptrend and (c) a downtrend.

down and the other cycles move out of phase resulting in a trend to lower prices.

MOVING AVERAGES

Many chartists plot a moving average of the market average and/or individual stocks. Short and long spans are used. A 30-week span corresponding to 200 calendar days is common. These are not plotted with the half-span delay necessary to provide a smoothed price presentation, but instead each computed value is plotted on the day of the last data point. The trend of this moving average is of no direct help. It shows the trend one-half span earlier, as may be observed by moving it backward in time by one-half span, but the prices have moved on giving more up to date information on their trend.

Some market technicians make a number of observations with respect to what the coincident plotting shows. In a 200-day rising moving average, the stock is bullish as long as it remains above the moving average. This merely means the stock is still moving upward in its cycle or has not rounded over its cyclic top enough to penetrate the average. A similar statement may be made about the bearish appearance of a stock remaining below its downtrending average. An upward penetration through a rising moving average is considered very bullish. This is an indication of a shorter cycle having bottomed out and rising along with a rising longer cycle. A similar observation may be made on the bearish indication of a downward penetration of a falling moving average.

Frequently two span lengths are plotted such as the 13-week and the 39-week moving averages shown with the DJI Average in the upper part of Figure 6-4. Conclusions are drawn based on whether the two spans are converging, diverging or crossing over, and how they move relative to the price curve. You can get lots of interpretations from the people who use these charts. On the other hand, look at the lower part of Figure 6-4 where the same data is plotted. The difference is that the moving averages are centered. Note the 39-week moving average shows the smoothed, rounding, intermediate top of the DJIA. The 13-week curve oscillates about the longer average due to a 40-week cycle producing crossovers at approximately 20-week intervals. There are shorter cycles which show up in the price curve crossing over the shorter-span average. These cyclic movements are not brought out in the upper plot. Taking the cyclic approach gives much better timing of the turning points as well as enabling prediction of when the next turn should occur from an extension of the cyclic period.

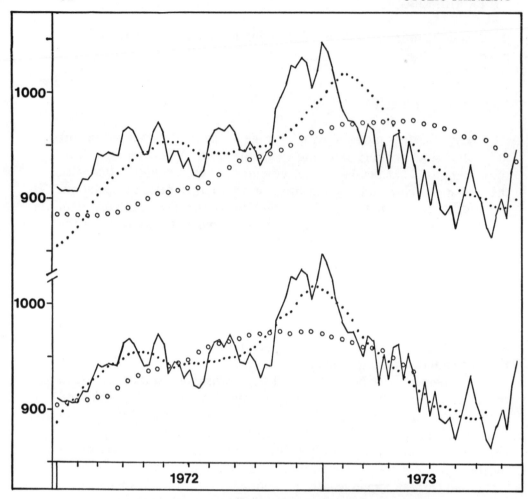

Figure 6-4. The DJI Average and its 13-week and 39-week moving averages plotted at a common date (upper curve) compared with the same data where the moving averages are centered (lower curve).

Summary

Chart formations which have stood the test of time are a result of interactions between price cycles. Not only does the cyclic approach explain the formations but thinking cycles leads to easier and more accurate interpretation. The old concept of technical formations frequently leaves you watching and waiting to see if the formation is in fact going to be completed, but thinking in terms of cycles allows you to tell ahead of time whether the formation will occur.

7

Filtering

HOW TO USE MOVING AVERAGES TO ANALYZE CYCLIC MOVEMENTS

We have seen how the statistically-centered moving average may be used to smooth stock price movements. At times these plotted averages appear to have the shape of a sine wave function. Such averages can be used to extract cyclic waves in stock price movements.

THE MOVING AVERAGE AS A FILTER

If we have a single periodic wave that repeats every T days, then a moving average having a span of T days will give a constant value, or will completely eliminate (smooth) the varying motion. If the periodic wave is shorter in period, smoothing is still very nearly complete and if only a little longer is still substantial, but, if very much longer, there is essentially no smoothing.

The moving average is a filter which separates a range of frequencies (or periods) into two groups. It tends to eliminate those frequencies having a period equal to or less than its span while passing unaffected those having periods substantially longer than its span. To the degree that it passes the shorter periods and reduces the amplitudes of the longer periods it gives a distorted output but only with respect to amplitude; there is no time displacement (phase distortion). The error curve of Appendix A gives the ratio of the unfiltered input amplitude to the filtered output (y-axis) for frequencies from zero to large values. The equation for this curve is given in Appendix 4 of Reference 3. Instead of plotting the period on the x-axis, points are marked on the curve giving the period of the periodic wave in terms of the span N of the moving average. Note that when the period equals the span the amplitude ratio is zero indicating perfect filtering. When the period is 2N, the ratio is 0.64 or the data wave motion is reduced to 64% of its actual amplitude. For periods slightly shorter than the span, note the ratio is negative. This means that the output amplitude is opposite in sign to the input amplitude, that is, when the price movement rises positive, the moving average will decrease negatively and the output is said to be 180° out of phase with the input. When the period is one-half the span, filtering is perfect again and so on as the periods become shorter. Note the maximum error for periods shorter than the span N is about 23% in amplitude. The amplitude errors given by this curve are important to consider if moving averages are used for price analysis. The above comments are illustrated in Figure 7-1 which shows the filtering effect of three moving averages, having different spans, on a periodic motion having a period of 12 units. The moving average of exact-

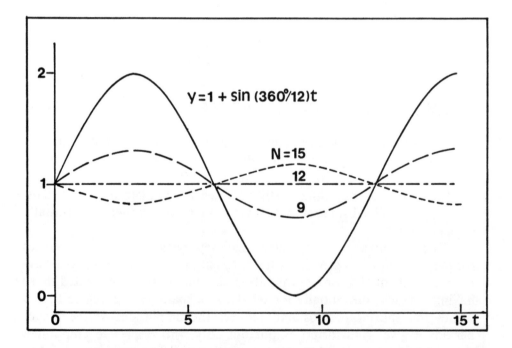

Figure 7-1. A sine wave centered about the value y = 1 has been "smoothed" by moving averages of different span lengths. With a span length equal to the period of the sine wave, the average is a constant value one. When the span is less than the period, the amplitude is reduced but not to zero and when the span is longer than the period not only is the amplitude reduced but is 180° out of phase.

ly 12 units gives a constant output of one. The span of 9 units gives an in-phase output but of reduced amplitude corresponding to $(12/9)N = (4/3)N$ or about 30% as may be seen by reference to Appendix A. The average of span 15 gives an out-of-phase output with an amplitude of $-(12/15)N = -(4/5)N$ or about -18%.

Note that when the amplitude of the input is zero, the output will likewise be zero, so that there will be no amplitude error at these points. This permits locating the zero crossing points by plotting two moving averages differing slightly in span length which will cross each other at these zero points. The distance between these points is one-half the period of the periodic wave.

ANALYZING A MARKET AVERAGE

Figure 7-2 is a weekly plot of data around the 1973 high. The DJI Average is represented by a heavy solid line, the centered 13-week as a dotted line (. . .) and the 39-week (x x x) moving averages are also plotted. The 39-week average is relatively smooth forming a rounding top of the major cycle. The 13-week average is seen to oscillate about the longer-span average. Each average has some small roughness due to short-term market fluctuations. Both averages may be smoothed by eye, if you desire, to give a continuous line. The difference between the price values of these two averages is plotted in the lower part of the chart. This is most easily done by measuring off the separation with a pair of dividers. When this is done and the points connected to form a smooth curve a cyclic wave is ob-tained which goes through zero amplitude at about 21-week intervals. This implies a cyclic wave with a period of 42 weeks.

Since the 39-week span length is very nearly equal the indicated 42-week cycle, there should be almost perfect filtering out of this cycle by the 39-week span. On the other hand the cycle period is about 3¼ times as long as the 13-week span so the shorter moving average does not reduce the amplitude very much. Referring to the error curve (Appendix A) we see about 85% of the amplitude is present. In this simple case we could as-sume the amplitude is in fact greater by a factor $1/0.85 = 1.18$.

CORRECTION FOR AMPLITUDE ERRORS

In more complex cases where both moving averages have an ap-preciable amplitude error one can also make a correction. We first es-timate the cyclic period by taking twice the time difference between points where the two averages cross each other. Call the amplitude of the cyclic

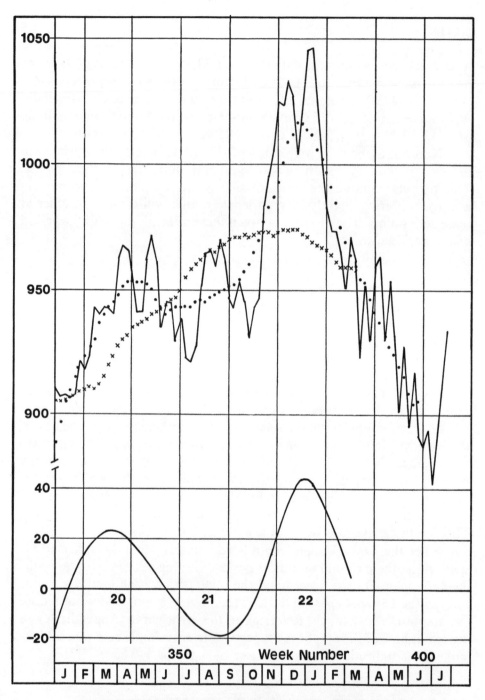

Figure 7-2. Moving averages of 13-week and 39-week spans are applied to the price of the DJIA from January 1972 through July 1973. The 13-week average oscillates about the longer span average. The price differences are found to extract the cyclic movement shown in the lower curve.

wave A, then look up the amplitude ratio for each span length in Appendix A and apply these ratios to A. The difference between the two plotted curves at maximum amplitude (or midway between two successive crossing points) will be the difference between the two fractional amplitudes and thus A can be determined. For example, if the first moving average had a value of 890 and the second 915 at the midpoint between their crossings, and the first had an amplitude of 0.5A and the second 0.7A as determined from Appendix A, then $915 - 890 = 25 = 0.7A - 0.5A$ or $0.2A = 25$ giving $A = 125$ as the amplitude of the cyclic component. The same calculation may be made at other points of the curve to give the y value for those points to form a complete cyclic curve of approximately the correct amplitude. This procedure words better at some times than at other times. There should not be a cyclic period between the spans of the two averages used. The amplitude of the cyclic motion should be significant so that the averages cross at a relatively sharp angle. It is useful to find the longer periods first, then detrend the data by subtracting the long-trend curve from the data points. Using the detrended data one can proceed as above to find the next component, etc. For general cyclic observations one may work with the original data points and estimate the cycles from properly selected pairs of moving averages.

DEALING WITH THE DELAY

The delay, particularly with the longer spans, is a problem in any filtering method. Moving averages are no worse than any other method. The longest span controls when extracting a cycle by taking differences between two spans. One can shorten the longer span at times to reduce this delay. Also two or more averages may be projected to an intersection point which is useful for estimating the cycle length. The amplitude of the cycle at its previous extreme may be used to project the cycle forward or if several periods of the cycle have been obtained and its amplitude shows a magnitude trend change, this factor may be taken into account in projecting the cycle. Truncation may be useful in extending the moving average (see the discussion at truncation on page 59 in Chapter 4). Curve fitting techniques discussed in the next chapter aid in overcoming some of this delay difficulty.

THE OUT-OF-PHASE PROBLEM

Figure 7-3 illustrates the distortion in a moving average when the amplitude error is negative. The 30-day (x x x) and 60-day (o o o) moving

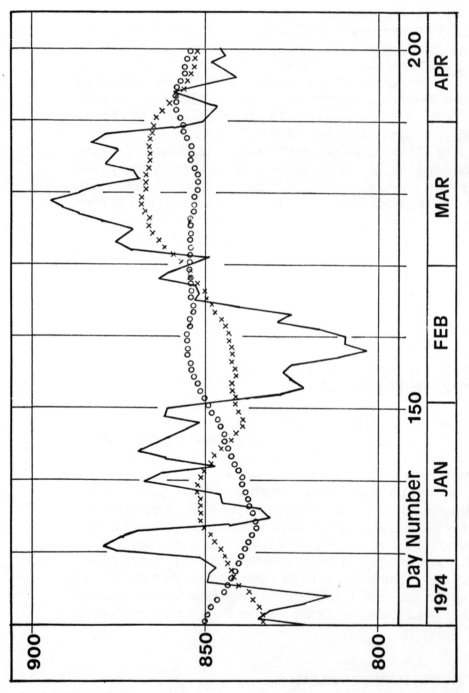

Figure 7-3. The 30-day and 60-day moving averages crisscross to show a cyclic component in the DJI Average. The period of the cyclic component is such that large amplitude errors are introduced in the moving average and further the 60-day average is moving out of phase with the price data.

averages crisscross to indicate half periods of 19, 24 and 25 days. Since the 30-day average is shorter in span than the indicated period, the output amplitude is in phase with the data but reduced to 20 percent to 40 percent of its full value. However, the 60-day average is a little longer than the indicated period so not only is the magnitude of the output amplitude reduced, but also it is opposite in phase, that is, negative with respect to the input data. This is apparent by an observation of the chart. Note the plot between days numbered 145 to 170. The DJI Average shows a clean negative lobe, but the 60-day moving average actually rises during this time. For a period of about 40 days, the error curve (Appendix A) indicates an amplitude response of minus 22%, or the maximum out-of-phase response. The other two lobes which show up in this chart exhibit a similar distortion. The 60-day average does not show a good smoothed curve through this region and even is distorted in a direction opposite to the movement of the data. Careful observation of the charts you may plot will reveal these errors and you may want to draw a smooth curve by eye through such regions when constructing a longer trend. You can also try longer data spans.

If you want to extract the cyclic component, you can proceed as described in "Correction for Amplitude Errors" in this chapter. Taking each half period at a time, one can solve for the maximum amplitude. In the first lobe 0.4A $-(-)$0.22A equals 15 Dow points. The corrected amplitude A = 24. In a similar manner the second lobe has an amplitude of 33 and the third 38.

Summary

The moving average serves as a simple filter to smooth market price data. It suppresses completely the movements whose period is equal to the length of the data span used to form the average, suppresses periods that are any integral fraction of the span, and reduces the amplitude of any movements whose period is less than the span. Movements whose periods are longer than the span always show up, but the amplitude is reduced unless the ratio is large. For example, if the period is twice the span length, about 64% of the amplitude is passed.

For periods less than the span length, the output of the moving average may be 180° out of phase with the data. This distortion shows up in the charts and can be corrected.

Cyclic components can be extracted by using two or more moving averages whose spans are different and therefore pass a different percentage of the amplitude which results in the averages crossing over each other at points of zero amplitude. The time distance between these crossover points represents a half period of the desired cyclic component. If doing a complete analysis, it is best to find the longer periods first, then detrend the data and proceed with the next shorter-period component, etc.

8

Equations for Curve Fitting

TOOLS FOR FORECASTING WHERE THE MARKET IS GOING—AND WHEN

We have seen in the previous chapter how moving averages may be used to smooth price data. The data thus smoothed will exhibit trends and oscillations which may be desirable to express in terms of a mathematical equation. If the equation or equations closely represent the data, they may be extended into the future as a representation of what may be expected. Not only is the moving average restricted to the time where data exists but its most recent plotted point is delayed a half span behind the current data. As greater smoothing is attempted by using longer moving average spans, this delay is so great that the smoothed curve has little value in projecting probable direction of movement for times in the future. Oftentimes the general direction of the data is apparent and a reasonable trend can be projected through this data, thus providing an approximation to a mathematically-obtained smoothed curve.

A line drawn through a set of data points to represent their average value may take various forms. The simplest is a straight line and may be appropriate for data trending uniformly up or down, or even sidewise. At other times the data may curve concave upward or concave downward, then again the data may oscillate, that is form an "S" shape curve or a sine-wave-like curve. In general, the data may follow some combination of these simple forms.

LEAST SQUARES CURVE FITTING

Oftentimes we desire to make the best possible fit of a specified mathematical equation to a set of data points. The accepted criterion is to find the constants of the equation which makes the sum of the squares of the deviation of the data points from the curve a minimum.

As a simple example, suppose we want to draw the best straight line through a set of data points whose y values are given for the various values of x. We know that a straight line can be represented by the equation

$$y = a + bx \qquad \text{(8-1)}$$

where for each value of x there is a corresponding value of y, and there is a value of a and b which will give the best fit to the data by the least squares criterion. If Equation (8-1) is multiplied by x to give

$$yx = ax + bx^2 \qquad \text{(8-2)}$$

a second equation is obtained involving the unknowns a and b. If we have a set of data points (y_1 to y_n) corresponding to equally-spaced values of x ranging from x_1 to x_n, we can set up two sets of equations as follows:

$$y_1 = a + bx_1 \qquad\qquad y_1x_1 = ax_1 + bx_1^2$$

$$y_2 = a + bx_2 \qquad\qquad y_2x_2 = ax_2 + bx_2^2$$

$$\vdots \qquad\qquad\qquad\qquad \vdots$$

$$y_N = a + bx_N \qquad\qquad y_Nx_N = ax_N + bx_N^2$$

If corresponding terms are added, we obtain

$$\Sigma y = Na + b\,\Sigma x \qquad \text{(8-3)}$$

$$\Sigma yx = a\,\Sigma x + b\,\Sigma x^2 \qquad \text{(8-4)}$$

where the symbol $\Sigma y = y_1 + y_2 + \ldots + y_N$, etc. Equations (8-3) and (8-4) are called the *normal equations* and they may be solved for a and b to substitute in Equation (8-1) giving the desired equation of the straight line. The number of data points may be very large and it is not necessary to use all of them in fitting equations to stock prices. A moving average smoothing may be applied to the data points with a span long enough to smooth the data between the sampling points of the data. The N data points used in the least squares fit may then be the values of the moving average at equally-spaced points along the time axis.

Equations of higher degree may be used depending upon what appears to be the shape of the data curve. A second-degree equation giving a curved line may be fitted by finding three normal equations and solving for the three unknown constants. The procedure is the same as for the straight-line fit except a third equation is found by multiplying the first by x^2. The three normal equations then are:

$$\Sigma y = Na + b\Sigma x + c\Sigma x^2$$

$$\Sigma yx = a\Sigma x + b\Sigma x^2 + c\Sigma x^3$$

$$\Sigma yx^2 = a\Sigma x^2 + b\Sigma x^3 + c\Sigma x^4$$

The process may be expanded to equations of higher degree by merely forming additional normal equations using higher powers of x.

The location of $x = 0$ is arbitrary, so if zero is taken at the center of the data span and data points are taken at equal intervals from $-x$ to $+x$, the sums involving odd powers of x will be zero ($a\Sigma x = 0$, $c\Sigma x^3 = 0$, etc.). This materially reduces the calculation effort. For example, the normal equations for a third-degree curve reduce to:

$$\Sigma y = Na + c\Sigma x^2$$

$$\Sigma xy = b\Sigma x^2 + d\Sigma x^4$$

$$\Sigma x^2 y = a\Sigma x^2 + c\Sigma x^4$$

$$\Sigma x^3 y = b\Sigma x^4 + d\Sigma x^6$$

In this case note that there are two sets of two equations in two unknowns each to solve.

The third-degree equation has an "S" (laid on its side) shape. That is, for large negative values of x, y is large and decreases rapidly until it reverses direction, then reverses direction a second time and continues to large values of y in the opposite direction. The inital value of y may be either positive or negative depending on the signs of the constants of the equation. In the mid portion, the "S" part, it resembles one cycle of a sine wave. It is sometimes useful to fit a third-degree curve to the data to obtain the central portion, then convert to a sine wave equation for a better fit near the ends and for projecting into the future.

As already seen, placing $x = 0$ at the center of the data span eliminates the sums of all terms in odd powers of x. Further labor may be saved by using the Table (Appendix B) which gives the sums of the even powers of x for data points of 5 to 43. Always renumber the time scale axis so that values are $-n$, $-(n-1)$, ..., -1, 0, 1, ..., $(n-1)$, n so as to use the smallest possible values in order to reduce the magnitude of the numbers used in the computation.

EXAMPLES OF LEAST SQUARES FIT

In Figure 8-1, the average of the daily high and low of the DJI Average is plotted for December 1973 through March 1974 (solid line). Viewing this plot, one sees an overall uptrend of the data and it appears that a straight line trending upward would give the long-term trend of this price movement. On a shorter-term basis, the data shows an oscillating character, first trending upward, reversing and going down only to reverse again to again trend upward. This is characteristic of a third-degree equation.

Taking $x = 0$ at the date of January 24, 1974 and letting each integral interval of x equal five market days, a new time scale is established covering the range of -7 to $+7$. Table 8-1 (page 97) is made up to give the values used in making least squares fits. The y values, column (2) are read off the smoothed curve of the centered 10-day moving average plotted on Figure 8-1 as a dotted line.

First let us find the equation of a straight line for the computed value y' given by $y' = a + bx$ which best fits the smoothed price curve. Only columns (1), (2) and (3) of Table 8-1 are required. The sum of x^2 terms is found from Appendix B. The normal equations are:

$$\Sigma y = Na + b \Sigma x \qquad \text{(8-5)}$$

$$\Sigma xy = a \Sigma x + b \Sigma x^2 \qquad \text{(8-6)}$$

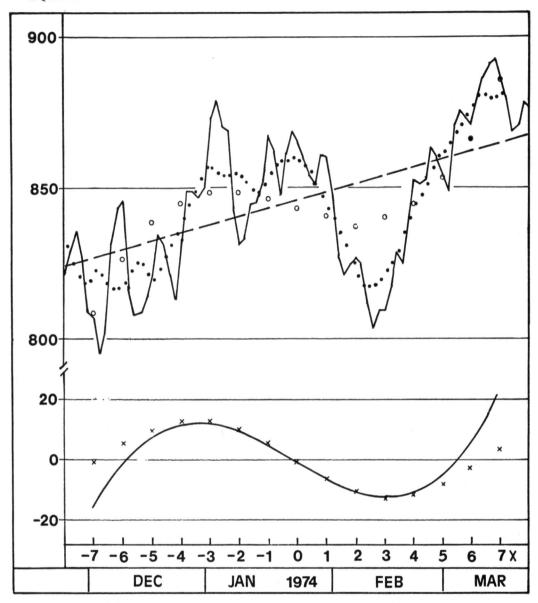

Figure 8-1. Upper chart shows the daily mean of the DJI Average (solid line) and its 10-day moving average (dotted line) with a straight line (dashed) least squares fit to the moving average. Below is the least squares fit of a cubic equation to the moving average detrended by the straight line. The points marked (x) denote a corresponding sine wave equation derived from the cubic equation. The sum of the cubic and linear equations is designated by o's in the upper plot.

Since the sum of the odd powers of x equals zero, the equations to solve for a and b are: $12,675 = 15a$ and $801 = 280b$. From these, $a = 845$ and $b = 2.8607142$[1] and the equation for the desired straight line is

$$y' = 845 + 2.86x \qquad (8\text{-}7)$$

This is plotted on Figure 8-1 as the dashed line. It is only necessary to compute two points in order to draw the line. When $x = 0$, $y' = 845$ and when $x = \pm 7$, $y' = 845 \pm 20$.

Although the straight line appears to give a good long-term fit, there may be some curvature present. We can explore this by making a second-degree equation fit. Thus, the normal equations, with odd powers of x eliminated are:

$$\Sigma y = Na \qquad\qquad + c\,\Sigma\,x^2 \qquad (8\text{-}8)$$

$$\Sigma\,xy = \qquad\quad b\,\Sigma\,x^2 \qquad\qquad (8\text{-}9)$$

$$\Sigma x^2 y = a\,\Sigma\,x^2 \qquad + c\,\Sigma\,x^4 \qquad (8\text{-}10)$$

Immediately we obtain $b = 2.8607142$ from Equation (8-9) which is the same as Equation (8-6). Equations (8-8) and (8-10) are solved simultaneously to give $a = 843.53846$ and $c = 0.0782966$. We see when $x = 0$, the curve passes only 1 ½ points below the plot for the straight line. Also c is quite small and can only contribute ± 3.8 points at the extreme values of x. Thus, the second-degree equation does not differ importantly from the straight line in this example.

The third-degree equation $y''' = a + bx + cx^2 + dx^3$ is plotted on Figure 8-1 as circles. Its solution will be carried out to illustrate further the solution of the more complex equation and use of the Gauss reduction in solving simultaneous equations. The normal equations are:

$$\Sigma y = Na \qquad\qquad + c\,\Sigma x^2$$

$$\Sigma yx = \qquad\quad b\,\Sigma\,x^2 \qquad\qquad + d\,\Sigma\,x^4$$

$$\Sigma yx^2 = a\,\Sigma\,x^2 \qquad\quad + c\,\Sigma x^4$$

$$\Sigma yx^3 = \qquad\quad b\,\Sigma\,x^4 \qquad\qquad + d\,\Sigma\,x^6$$

---

[1] It is unnecessary to carry out the calculation to eight places as shown here. This number resulted from use of an 8-place hand held computer. If using hand methods, round off the values to about one place more than the plotting capability.

Table 8-1

Data and calculations used in making least squares fits to the 10-day moving average of the DJI Average charted in Figure 8-1.

(1)	(2)	(3)	(4)	(5)	(6)
x	y	xy	x^2y	x^3y	y'''
−7	823	−5,761	40,327	−282,289	808.6
−6	818	−4,908	29,448	−176,688	826.5
−5	821	−4,105	20,525	−102,625	838.4
−4	837	−3,348	13,392	−53,568	845.3
−3	857	−2,571	7,713	−23,139	848.2
−2	854	−1,708	3,416	−6,832	848.2
−1	854	−854	854	−854	846.3
0	860	0	0	0	843.5
1	845	845	845	845	840.9
2	824	1,648	3,296	6,592	839.5
3	821	2,463	7,389	22,167	840.3
4	843	3,372	13,488	53,952	844.3
5	861	4,305	21,525	107,625	853.4
6	876	5,256	31,536	189,216	866.2
7	881	6,167	43,169	302,183	886.1
Σ 0	12,675	801	236,923	36,585	

Substituting the values from Table 8-1 and Appendix B, the equations to be solved are:

$$15a + 280c = 12,675 \qquad 280b + 9,352d = 801$$
$$\text{and}$$
$$280a + 9,352c = 236,923 \qquad 9,352b + 369,640d = 36,585$$

where the right-and left-hand sides have been reversed and equations paired with each pair of unknown constants. Writing the numerical coefficients in vertical columns, the first pair of equations give the first vertical set of two groups below. Next divide the first group by the first member of the group (15)

15	1
280	18.666667
12,675	845
280	0
9,352	14.733333
236,923	1.15357

to give the first group of the second column, then divide the second group by its first member (280) and subtract the corresponding value of the first group of the second column. That is, 280 divided by 280, minus 1 is zero for the first entry in the second group of the second column. The second entry is 9,352 ÷ 280 − 18.666667, etc. The last two entries are the coefficients of an equation in the unknown c. The coefficients stand in the same relation to the unknowns as in the original equations.

Thus, $14.733333c = 1.15357$, and solving, $c = 0.0782966$. Returning to the first group in the second column, these are the coefficients of the equation $a + 18.666667c = 845$. Substituting the now known value of c and solving, $a = 843.538$. These values should be checked by substituting in the original equations.

In a similar manner the second pair of equations are solved to give $b = -2.87$ and $d = 0.172$. You may want to carry out this calculation yourself. The complete equation may now be written

$$y''' = 843.54 - 2.87x + 0.078x^2 + 0.172x^3 \qquad \text{(8-11)}$$

If making a number of least squares fits of a cubic equation, computational labor may be saved by judicious selection of the number of data points. You can precompute a portion of the solution for any given number of data points and use this part of the solution for all problems of this given number of points. Further, for some numbers of data points the relations are such that the intermediate quotients are small whole numbers, thus reducing the additional work. This can be important if doing the computation by hand. As an example, the Gauss reduction format for the number of data points, $N = 13$, for the cubic equation is given below:

13	1	
182	14	
Σy	$\Sigma y/13$	$\Sigma y/13 - 14c = a$
182	0	
4,550	11	
$\Sigma x^2 y$	$\Sigma x^2 y/182 - \Sigma y/13$	$[\Sigma x^2 y/182 - \Sigma y/13] \div 11 = c$
182	1	
4,550	25	
Σxy	$\Sigma xy/182$	$\Sigma xy/182 - 25d = b$

$$\begin{array}{ll} 4550 & 0 \\ 134{,}342 & 4.525714 \\ \Sigma x^3 y & \Sigma x^3 y/4{,}550 - \Sigma xy/182 \quad [\,\Sigma x^3 y/4{,}550 - \Sigma xy/182\,] \div 4.525714 = d \end{array}$$

The solution may be further simplified giving the coefficients as follows:

$$c = \Sigma x^2 y / 2{,}002 - \Sigma y / 143 \qquad\qquad d = \Sigma x^3 y / 20{,}592 - \Sigma xy / 823.67994$$

$$a = \Sigma y / 13 - 14c \qquad\qquad\qquad\quad b = \Sigma xy / 182 - 25d$$

for $N = 13$, a very useful number of data points for market data. You may set up partial solutions for other data spans which you desire to use frequently.

DETRENDING DATA

Let us further explore the use of curve fitting to extract the individual components. The third-degree Equation (8-11) represents a combination of components consisting principally of an uptrending line and a cyclic component. If the y' values of the straight-line Equation (8-7) are subtracted from the 10-day smoothed data points, we will have a set of data which is said to be *detrended*. These values are tabulated in column (4) of Table 8-2 (see page 100). Solving as before, the equation is, when using detrended data

$$y_1{}''' = -1.46 - 5.73x + 0.078x^2 + 0.172x^3 \qquad\qquad \textbf{(8-12)}$$

This curve is plotted in the lower part of Figure 8-1. If Equation (8-7) for the straight line is subtracted from the third-degree Equation (8-11), the resulting equation is identical with Equation (8-12), as would be expected.

CORRESPONDING TRIGONOMETRIC CURVE

The plot of the third-degree Equation (8-12) has the appearance of a sine wave over its central portion. If Equation (8-12) is differentiated, and the derivative set equal to zero, we have

$$dy'''/dx = -5.73 + 0.156x + 0.516x^2 = 0$$

Table 8-2

Data and computations used to make a least squares fit of the cubic equation to detrended data.

(1)	(2)	(3)	(4)	(5)	(6)	(7)	(8)
x	y	y'	$y-y'=y_i$	xy_i	$x^2 y_i$	$x^3 y_i$	y_i'''
−7	823	825	−2	14	−98	686	−16.5
−6	818	828	−10	60	−360	2,160	−1.4
−5	821	831	−10	50	−250	1,250	7.6
−4	837	834	3	−12	48	−192	11.7
−3	857	836	21	−63	189	−567	11.8
−2	854	839	15	−30	60	−120	8.9
−1	854	842	12	−12	12	−12	4.2
0	860	845	15	0	0	0	−1.5
1	845	848	−3	−3	−3	−3	−6.9
2	824	851	−27	−54	−108	−216	−11.2
3	821	854	−33	−99	−297	−891	−13.3
4	843	856	−13	−52	−208	−832	−12.1
5	861	859	2	10	50	250	−6.7
6	876	862	14	84	504	3,024	4.1
7	881	865	16	112	784	5,488	21.2
Σ0			0	5	323	10,025	

The two values of x which make this equation true give the location of the reversal points of the cubic curve. Using the formula for solving this quadratic for the two values of x (see "Algebraic Equations" in Chapter 16),

$$x = \frac{-b \pm \sqrt{b^2 - 4ac}}{2a}$$

$$= \frac{-0.156 \pm \sqrt{(0.156)^2 - 4(0.516)\,(-5.73)}}{2(0.516)}$$

$$= -0.1511627 \pm 3.3357908 = -3.4869535, +3.1846281$$

and $x = -3.5$ and $+3.2$, or -17 and 16 days since the interval of x is 5 days. The difference between these two values of x equals 33 days which may be considered one-half period of a sine wave. Further, the amplitude of such a sine wave can be considered as half the difference in y values at these points or 12.8 Dow points. If we assume the corresponding sine wave goes through the point $y = 0$ at a value of x midway between the reversal points (that is at $x = -0.15$), we have the three quantities necessary to write down the desired sine wave—period (which gives the frequency), amplitude and phase. The equation is

$$y_s''' = -12.8 \sin \frac{360}{2(3.5+3.2)} (x+0.15) = -12.8 \sin 26.87 (x+0.15)$$

We see y_s''' is zero when $x = -0.15$ which establishes the phase together with the negative sign which is chosen because the curve in the graph is seen to be moving negatively as x increases from zero. The equation is plotted on Figure 8-1 as x's, and shows good agreement over the center portion between reversal points. The phase as established here is approximate. More will be said later on this point.

ERRORS IN PERIOD AND AMPLITUDE

In Figure 8-1 it is seen that the sine wave falls *outside* the cubic curve beyond the reversal points. This effect is worth exploring further. Let us fit a third-degree equation to a portion of a pure sine wave. The results are shown in Figure 8-2 for several different portions of the sine wave. The unit value of x is taken as $15°$. One period is therefore 24 x units.

In example (a) the data span is one sine wave period and is plotted as the solid line. The value of x is taken as zero at the midpoint where the sine is zero. The resulting equation is

$$y''' = -0.2197x+0.00160x^3 \tag{8-13}$$

Neither the constant term nor the x^2 term appears because of the symmetry of the situation. That is, $\Sigma y = 0$ and $\Sigma x^2 y = 0$. Although the calculated values y''' follow closely the sine curve over this one cycle (they are plotted as o's), there is a slight deviation. If the derivative of Equation (8-13) is set equal to zero and solved for the values of x, these give the location of the reversal points and they are ± 6.77 instead of the values ± 6.0 of the pure sine equation. Thus, if a corresponding sine wave equation were to be set up whose period is taken as twice the difference between the reversal points of Equation (8-13), the period would be too long. In fact, one should reduce the implied period by a factor $6.0/6.77$ or 0.89 (89%). Likewise one may determine the value of y''' at these reversal

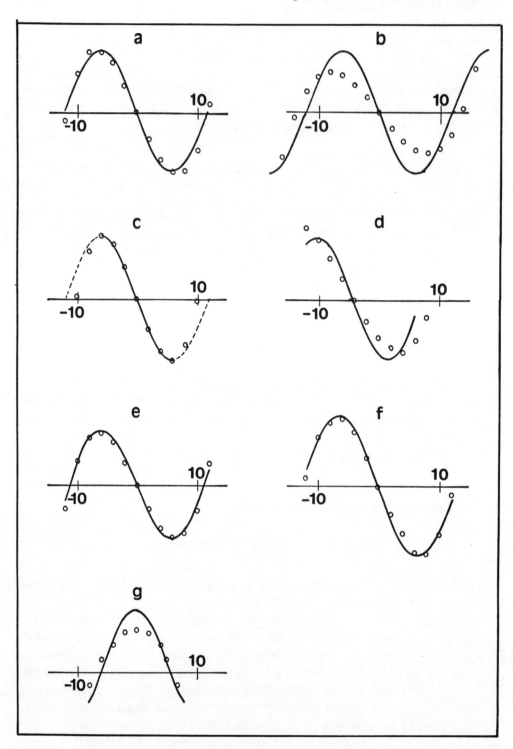

Figure 8-2. Cubic equations (plotted as circles) fitted to various portions of a sine wave.

points to imply the amplitude of the corresponding sine wave. In this case, the cubic equation falls slightly under the pure sine wave and the implied amplitude should be multiplied by 1.01 to give the amplitude of the pure sine wave.

In example (b) the data span is equal to one-and-a-half periods and again is symmetrical with x = 0 being where the sine equals zero. The cubic fit gives the equation

$$y''' = -0.124x + 0.000658x^3 \qquad \text{(8-14)}$$

The resulting fit (plotted as o's) is not as good, as may be seen by inspection. In fact the implied period needs to be corrected by a factor 0.76. Although this fit is the best from the least squares criterion, it does not closely follow the sine curve. This illustrates the desirability of using data spans of about one period or less if good agreement over the central portion is to be achieved.

Example (c) shows the fit for a data span of only half a period. The agreement over the data span is perfect for practical purposes but diverges for a complete sine wave as may be seen in the plot where the sine wave is extended as a dotted line. The cubic equation for this fit is

$$y''' = -0.258x + 0.00256x^3$$

The implied period is slightly short in this case, needing to be multiplied by 1.035 to give the sine wave period. The amplitude correction factor is 1.003, being practically perfect.

In example (d), the data span is unsymmetrical with respect to x = 0. The length of the span is 24 x units, or one period, with x = 0 spaced four units (60°) from the point where the sine equals zero. The cubic equation is found to be $y''' = -0.632 - 0.1098x + 0.0128x^2 + 0.0008x^3$. All terms are present since the data is not symmetrical about x = 0 as in the previous examples. This represents the usual result when applied to practical situations. A reasonably good fit to the data span is again achieved, though the period based on reversal points is too long, requiring a correction factor of 0.7. The amplitude correction factor is 0.98. This illustrates the desirability of trying to center the data span to be symmetrical about a point midway between the reversal points.

In all the above examples the data is a simple sine wave. In practice, the data are more complex. In general, we might expect any sine wave to be combined with a trend. This trend may be either a straight line or a section of some longer sine wave which changes its curvature slowly and can be approximated by a straight line. It is therefore worth exploring the effect of adding a trend. The trend, or linear equation

$$y' = a + bx \qquad \text{(8-15)}$$

may merely be added to any of the equations we have derived for the sine wave data. The second term only (the x term) adds the slope to the data. The constant merely shifts the data up and down the y axis. This constant does not influence the computed value of the period or amplitude of the corresponding sine wave. Since the reversal points are found by solving the first derivative equated to zero, we can see that the constant a has no influence because the derivative of a constant is zero. On the other hand, increasing or decreasing the coefficient of x in the cubic equation will result in a change in the values of x at the reversal points. If b in Equation (8-15) is positive, the trend is upward as x increases from left to right and if b is negative the trend is downward. If an upward trend (b positive) is added to Equation (8-13), the coefficient of x becomes less negative, that is, its magnitude is decreased and the values of x at the reversal points will be smaller in magnitude. For example, if a trend of 0.02x is added to Equation (8-13) resulting in y going from 0.02(-12) to 0.02(12) over one period or a change of 0.48, the equation becomes

$$y''' = -0.1997x + 0.00160x^3$$

Solving $dy'''/dx = 0$ we find $x = \pm6.45$ in comparison with ±6.77 without the trend. We see the reversal points are pushed toward each other by an uptrend in this example. If instead, we add a downtrend (b negative), the magnitude of the coefficient of x in Equation (8-13) is increased resulting in the reversal points being pushed away from each other. If the sine wave of Equation (8-13) is reversed, that is, if in example (a) of Figure 8-2, the sine wave curve first moves downward (180° phase shift), the cubic equation would be the same except the signs would be reversed, that is $y''' = 0.2197x - 0.0016x^3$. In this case adding an upward trend would push the reversal points outward and the downtrend would push them toward each other. A little thought results in a general rule that the higher reversal point always moves toward the higher trend value and the lower reversal point moves toward the lower trend value. These trend effects are illustrated in Figure 8-2e for an uptrend and Figure 8-2f for a downtrend where a trend of $\pm0.02x$ is added to the sine wave curve of Figure 8-2a.

Figure 8-2g illustrates fitting the cubic equation to a span of data centered about a reversal point, such as a high or low market region. The equation is $y''' = 0.69 - 0.0138x^2$. The terms in x and x^3 do not appear because this symmetrical span where y is a maximum at $x = 0$ causes $\Sigma xy = 0$ and $\Sigma x^3y = 0$. The cubic in fact reduces to a quadratic and shows only one reversal point. We therefore can not establish an indicated period for this solution in general. If we knew that the data had no constant term other than the average of the sine wave component, then the period could be established as twice the difference between the values of x where $y = 0$. In this example, this can be done and we find the values of x

are ±7.07 giving a period of 28.3. The amplitude would be the value of y for x = 0, or the constant term. In stock market data where we would want to use a second-degree equation to fit the data we will not have detrended data and we would not be able to set up a corresponding sine wave. This illustrates again the desirability of selecting the data span to include a portion characteristic of the shape of the cubic equation.

In the cubic equation

$$y=a+bx+cx^2+dx3 \tag{8-16}$$

we saw in Chapter 5 that an *S Shaped* curve is produced by the terms in the first and third powers of x. These two terms taken alone represent a curve symmetrical about the origin. The constant a shifts the curve up or down the y-axis. If the symmetrical curve is shifted along the x-axis, both the a and the cx^2 terms appear. We have seen in Figure 8-1 that the central portion of the cubic equation closely follows a sine wave shape. The series expansion of a sine function, where the angle x is expressed in radians, is

$$\sin x=x-x^3/3!+x^5/5! -x^7/7! + \ldots$$

and using only the first two terms (a symmetrical cubic equation) give a fair approximation, for example,

Angle x	sin x	x - x³/3!
15°	0.2588	0.2588
30	0.5000	0.4997
60	0.8660	0.8558
90	1.0000	0.9248

For purposes of finding the indicated period of a sine wave which corresponds to the midportion of the cubic equation, we can drop the constant a and the cx^2 terms and find the reversal points of the reduced equation

$$y=bx+dx^3 \tag{8-17}$$

These points are equally spaced from the point of symmetry of Equation (8-16). The indicated period (I.P.) then is four times the value of x which makes the derivative of Equation (8-17) zero. That is, $dy/dx = b + 3dx^2 = 0$, and

$$x_m =\pm\sqrt{- b/3d} \tag{8-18}$$

$$\text{I.P.} = 4\sqrt{-b/3d} \qquad\qquad (8\text{-}19)$$

The period thus determined is independent of the location of the data span relative to the symmetry of the curve. Also the value of the period so determined is less in error than if determined from the reversal points of Equation (8-16). Furthermore, the calculation is somewhat less involved. We therefore will adopt Equation (8-19) as the form to use in finding the indicated period to be used in setting up the sine wave representation.

We have said the amplitude of the corresponding sine wave is indicated by finding half the difference between the values of y in Equation (8-16) at the reversal points, that is, the difference between the maximum and minimum in the central region. We previously located these points by solving for x in the derivative of Equation (8-16) set equal to zero. Since we have chosen to find the period by Equation (8-19), we have the values of x_m given by Equation (8-18) measured from the point of symmetry. We need to find this point as it will determine where $y = 0$ in the corresponding sine wave, or in other words will determine the phase of the sine equation.

The *point of inflection* of the cubic equation is the point where the curvature changes from concave downward to concave upward or vice versa. This point is easily found by solving for x in the second derivative of y''' equated to zero. This becomes $d^2y'''/dx^2 = 2c + 6dx = 0$ or $x_i = -c/3d$ and is usually near the point of symmetry, but when the span is quite unsymmetrical the point of inflection may differ significantly from the point of symmetry. Again, a good reason for selecting the data span to be symmetrical. The phase of the sine wave equation will be taken so that the sine equals zero at the value of x equal to x_i, the point of inflection.

Returning to the determination of amplitude, we will evaluate the cubic equation (y''') at the two points established by the relation $x_i \pm x_m$. These two values of x will be designated x_1 and x_2 and the corresponding values of y as y_1 and y_2. The sine amplitude is then half the difference between y_1 and y_2. The sign of the amplitude, positive or negative, is established by inspection of the data curve to make the sine wave move in the same direction as the data.

As an example of these procedures, take the equation for Figure 8-2d

$$y''' = -0.632 - 0.1098x + 0.0128x^2 + 0.00080x^3$$

$$x_m = \pm\sqrt{-b/3d} = \pm\sqrt{0.1098/3(0.0008)} = \pm 6.76$$

$$\text{I.P.} = 4(6.76) = 27.0 \qquad \text{or} \qquad \omega = 13.3$$

$$x_i = -c/3d = -0.0128/3(0.0008) = -5.33$$

$$x_1 = -12.09 \qquad\qquad x_2 = 1.43$$

$$y_1 = 1.153 \qquad\qquad y_2 = -0.76 \qquad\qquad A = 0.956$$

Putting this all together, the corresponding sine wave equation is $y_s''' = 0.956 \sin 13.3(x + 5.3)$. The sine equation which we started with for the data is $y = 1.0 \sin 15(x + 4)$. We have an error in amplitude of y of 4.4%, in frequency of 11% and in phase of 20° or 5% of a period.

A study of Figure 8-2 shows that these errors will vary as different data spans, relative to the length of the period, are used. In practical applications, situations similar to Figure 8-2a are encountered. However, when choosing the data span it may be somewhat longer or shorter than one period in length. By fitting the cubic equation to a pure sine wave using various lengths of data span, Chart I of Appendix C was developed which gives the factor that multiplied by the indicated period gives the period of the true sine wave. This curve applies within the range of span lengths shown and without regard to the symmetry of the span to the sine wave when the data being fitted *is a pure sine wave*. In a similar manner, the curves of Chart II, Appendix C, are produced, showing the errors in indicated amplitude. Here, however, the error is not independent of the symmetry. These curves show that the error is minimized if the data span is symmetrical about a point midway between the reversal points of the cubic curve, and the span length is about one period in length. Results should be improved by giving attention to these factors whenever feasible.

THE EFFECT OF TREND

If a linear trend is added to the data, the coefficient of the first power of x in the cubic equation is changed. That is, if a trend given by the straight line equation $y_1 = b_1 x$ is added to the cubic equation $y = a + bx + cx^2 + dx^3$, the resulting cubic equation is

$$Y = y + y_1 = a(b + b_1)x + cx^2 + dx^3$$

This change produces an error in the indicated period (I.P.) given by Equation (8-19). For example, a trend which increases the value of y over one cycle of the sine wave by 25% of the amplitude of that wave will produce an error of about 12% in I. P. This follows from Equation (8-19) where we see that I.P. varies with the square root of b. We also see that I.P. is decreased when the trend decreases the magnitude of b and I.P. is increased when the magnitude of b is increased. When feasible, it is desirable to eliminate the trend to give an improved value of I.P.

In analyzing data whose available span is comparable to the period of the prominent cycle, one can not get a reliable trend directly. A procedure which works well is to make the cubic fit to the basic data (y), set up a corresponding sine wave and subtract the y_s''' values from the y values to leave a *detrended remainder* consisting principally of the long-term trend on which is superimposed the higher frequency components. A second degree equation may be fitted to these data to obtain the trend (y'') which follows the combined curve of all longer cycles. The short cycles which remain in the y - y_s''' data tend to average out in y'' so produce little if any error. Thus, one may make a correction of the cubic equation y''' by subtracting the bx term of the y'' equation from the corresponding term of the y''' equation. Having done this, the indicated period is recomputed and a correction for span length is obtained from Appendix C to give a corrected value of the period to be used in setting up the final sine wave equation which best represents the dominant cycle of the data span being studied.

Note that for purposes of obtaining a trend correction using either a first- or second-degree trend curve you only need to find the bx term which is given for either case by the normal equation $\Sigma\, xy = b\, \Sigma\, x^2$. Since Σx^2 can be obtained from the table of Appendix B, the computational effort is reduced to finding Σxy.

EFFECT OF HIGHER-FREQUENCY COMPONENTS

Figure 8-3 illustrates the effect of higher-frequency components. In market price movements, the frequencies are often related by a ratio of about two or three to one. Also they are often phased so that the different frequencies reach a maximum near the same time giving rise to strong peaks and deep minima. This figure shows, as dotted and dashed lines, two sine wave frequencies with their sum as a solid line. A cubic fit is made to the sum curve using a span of one period of the lowest frequency and the result is shown by circles (o o o). Note that the cubic tends to agree rather well with the longest period sine component. The higher frequencies tend to be averaged out. Such movements are always found in the actual market data but have little effect on the representation of the dominant cycle.

This also illustrates the necessity of *not* using a data span much greater than the period of the cycle desired to be fitted. If the data span is too long, the resulting equation tends to revert to one of lower degree.

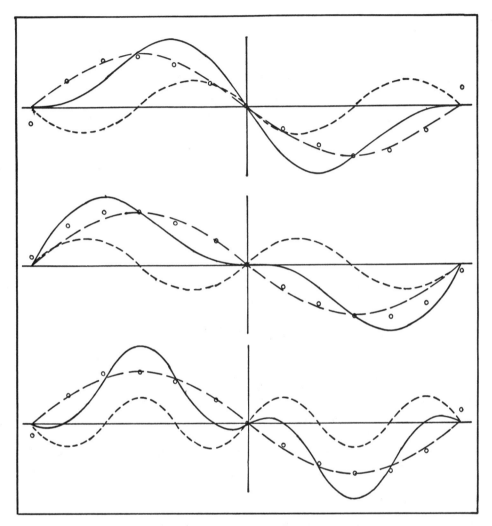

Figure 8-3. The cubic equation (plotted as circles) fitted to a curve which is the sum of two sine waves (solid line) tends to average out the short period wave and follow the long, more prominent period.

SINE-COSINE CURVE FITTING

Since stock market prices often follow a sine wave movement, it is useful to be able to fit a sine wave to the data. It is not only possible to make a mathematical best fit of such a curve but one can fit any combination of a number of sine waves of different periods, phases and amplitudes to a single series of data. One can either assume the frequencies inferred from other analysis, and then determine the amplitude and phase of each so that the combination best fits the data, or one can make a best frequency determination of frequencies, then proceed to obtain the amplitudes and phases. There is a generalized least squares method which is described in References 3 and 7, and other numerical analysis books. However, for the purposes of simple stock market use more than two frequencies are not necessary and it is simpler to describe each case separately depending on the number of frequencies used.

FITTING A SINGLE FREQUENCY

A single frequency wave of any phase and amplitude may be represented by a function of time t written

$$f(t) = A \cos \omega t + B \sin \omega t \qquad \text{(8-20)}$$

The first step is to determine the frequency ω, which involves finding α in the equation[2]

$$\cos \omega - \tfrac{1}{2} \alpha = 0 \qquad \text{(8-21)}$$

then solving for ω.

First prepare a table of values of $f(t)$ vs. time t for equally-spaced values of t covering the span of time over which the fit is to be made. Let $t = 0$ at the start of the data to be fitted, then select the units of t to give the desired number of points at which the curve is to be fitted. If the data is smoothed by a moving average or otherwise, the number of points N need not be large—say about 10 to 20 for spans of about one period. The time t will be in days, weeks, months or years, depending upon the nature of the data plot. Let the value of $f(t)$ for $t = 0$ be $f_0(t)$, for $t = 1$ be $f_1(t)$, etc. Now write down the set of equations

$$\alpha f_1 = f_0 + f_2$$

$$\alpha f_2 = f_1 + f_3$$

$$\cdot \quad \cdot \quad \cdot$$

$$\cdot \quad \cdot \quad \cdot \qquad \text{(8-22)}$$

$$\cdot \quad \cdot \quad \cdot$$

$$\alpha f_{N-2} = f_{N-3} + f_{N-1}$$

When $N = 10$, the last equation is $\alpha f_8 = f_7 + f_9$.

---

[2] The symbol α is the Greek letter Alpha.

Let us fit a curve to the 10-day moving average of the mean of the DJI Average daily high and low for the region from August 1973 to December 1973, and shown plotted as a dotted line on Figure 8-4. First, in order to detrend the data, we will make a straight-line fit. Table 8-3 tabulates the data needed in columns (1) and (2) for 10-day intervals between x = −5 to +5. Solving the normal equations results in the least squares fit being the equation y_{LT} = 900 − 5.6x. This equation is solved for the values of x (column 3 in Table 8-3) and is shown on Figure 8-4 as a solid line. The data is now detrended by subtracting the *long-term trend* from the moving average (column 2 minus column 3) giving f(t) (column 5). In Table 8-3 the coefficients of Equation (8-22) in α are listed with the first equation opposite t = 1. Column (8) gives the numerical values of the coefficients listed in column (6), and column (9) gives the numerical values of the sum given in column (7). For convenience, column (8) is denoted as *a* and column (9) is denoted by *b*. (See pages 112 and 113.)

The least squares solution of Equation (8-22) is accomplished by finding the coefficients in the equation

$$\alpha \Sigma a^2 = \Sigma ab \qquad\qquad \textbf{(8-23)}$$

where Σa^2 is the sum of the squares of each value listed in column (8) and Σ ab is the sum of the products of the values found in columns (8) and (9) for each value of t. The unit of t is taken as 10-days. The frequency will then be in terms of degrees per 10-days. Proceeding with the solution of Equation (8-23) gives Σa^2 = 19,766 and Σ ab = 26,072, or 19,766 α = 26,072 and α = 1.3190. Thus Equation (8-21) gives cos ω = ½(1.3190) or 0.6595 and the frequency ω = 48.7°, corresponding to the period 360/48.7 = 7.4 (in 10-day units) or 74 days.

The next step is to determine the amplitude and phase which involves finding A and B in Equation (8-20) where ω has been determined to be 48.7° per 10-days. Columns (10), (11) and (12) of Table 8-3 are completed · and the normal equations

$$A \Sigma \cos^2 \omega t + B\Sigma \cos \omega t \sin \omega t = \Sigma f(t) \cos \omega t \qquad \textbf{(8-24)}$$

$$A \Sigma \sin \omega t \cos \omega t + B \Sigma \sin^2 \omega t = \Sigma f(t) \sin \omega t \qquad \textbf{(8-25)}$$

solved for A and B. We find,

$\Sigma \cos^2 \omega t \quad\bullet\quad = 5.469776 \qquad\qquad \Sigma \sin \omega t \cos \omega t = 0.0399152$

$\Sigma \cos \omega t \sin \omega t = 0.0399152 \qquad \Sigma \sin^2 \omega t \qquad = 5.529907$

$\Sigma f(t) \cos \omega t \quad = 57.5577 \qquad\qquad \Sigma f(t) \sin \omega t \quad = -322.3253$

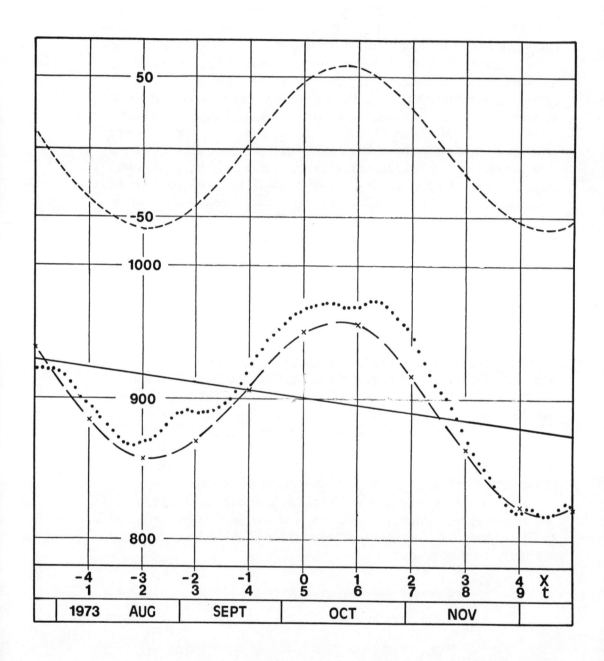

Figure 8-4. A one-frequency trigonometric fit (upper curve) to the detrended 10-day moving average of the DJI Average.

Table 8-3

Data and computations required to detrend the DJI 10-day moving average and make a one-frequency trigonometric fit over a 100-day span in the fall of 1973.

(1) x	(2) y	(3) y_{LT}	(4) t	(5) f(t)	(6)	(7)	(8) a	(9) b	(10) ωt	(11) $\cos \omega t$	(12) $\sin \omega t$	(13) $f(t)_c$
-5	923	928	0	-5					0.0	1.0000	0.0	10
-4	898	922	1	-24	f_1	f_0+f_2	-24	-52	48.7	.6600	.7513	-37
-3	869	916	2	-47	f_2	f_1+f_3	-47	-44	97.4	-.1288	.9917	-59
-2	891	911	3	-20	f_3	f_2+f_4	-20	-33	146.1	-.8300	.5577	-41
-1	919	905	4	14	f_4	f_3+f_5	14	42	194.8	-.9668	-.2554	2
0	962	900	5	62	f_5	f_4+f_6	62	86	243.5	-.4462	-.8949	48
1	967	895	6	72	f_6	f_5+f_7	72	123	292.2	.3778	-.9259	58
2	950	889	7	61	f_7	f_6+f_8	61	66	340.9	.9449	-.3272	28
3	878	884	8	-6	f_8	f_7+f_9	-6	1	29.6	.8695	.4939	-20
4	818	878	9	-60	f_9	f_8+f_{10}	-60	-55	78.3	.2028	.9792	-55
5	825	874	10	-49					127.0	-.6018	.7986	-53

which when substituted in Equations (8-24) and (8-25) results in two simultaneous equations which may be solved for A and B (the Gauss reduction may be used), giving A = 10.948787 and B = -58.366679. Then,

$$f(t)_c = 10.9 \cos 48.7°t - 58.4 \sin 48.7°t$$

Expressing this as a sine function (see "Periodic-Wave Equations" in Chapter 5), C = $\sqrt{A^2+B^2}$ = 59.4, tan ϕ = A/B = -0.1876 and ϕ = 169.4°

$$\text{Then } f(t) = 59.4 \sin (48.7t + 169.4) = 59.4 \sin 48.7(t + 3.5) \quad \text{(8-26)}$$

Equation (8-26) is plotted in the upper portion of Figure 8-4 and represents the cyclic component which gives the best one-frequency fit to the 10-day moving average of the DJIA, when this average is detrended by a first-degree equation. If this cyclic component is added to the detrending curve, the dashed curve is obtained which is seen to give a good fit to the moving average data. Remember that this is only a curve-fitting technique and does not necessarily mean that the components obtained occur in the original data. Making different basic assumptions may give different results.

When making a trigonometric fit, the data span should be great enough to include a sizable portion of one cycle. If you try to fit a portion of a sine wave between the reversal points, you may get a poor representation of the frequency. In the extreme condition, if the data is a straight line, α is 2.0 and cos ω = 1. This is zero frequency or infinite period. If cos ω is nearly one, a different data span should be tried.

Although a best frequency fit can be made to a data span extending over several cycles, the results will be an average value which may not best represent the data over any one cycle. Because the cycles of stock market data generally vary in period and amplitude from one to the next, better results for projection to predict the future trend of prices is achieved if the data span is about one cycle or somewhat less.

FITTING TWO FREQUENCIES

Two frequencies of any amplitude, phase and frequency may be represented by

$$A_1 \cos \omega_1 t + B_1 \sin \omega_1 t + A_2 \cos \omega_2 t + B_2 \sin \omega_2 t = f(t) \quad \text{(8-27)}$$

The frequencies ω_1 and ω_2 are determined from the two roots of x in the equation $2x^2 - \alpha_1 x - (1 + \alpha_2/2) = 0$, where $x = \cos\omega$, that is,

$$x = \frac{\alpha_1 \pm \sqrt{\alpha_1^2 + 8(1 + \alpha_2/2)}}{4} \quad (8\text{-}28)$$

To find the values of α_1 and α_2 by the least squares method we proceed in a manner similar to the single frequency case. The set of equations

$$\alpha_1(f_1+f_3)+\alpha_2 f_2 = f_0+f_4$$

$$\alpha_1(f_2+f_4)+\alpha_2 f_3 = f_1+f_5$$

$$\cdot \quad \cdot \quad \cdot$$
$$\cdot \quad \cdot \quad \cdot \quad (8\text{-}29)$$
$$\cdot \quad \cdot \quad \cdot$$

$$\alpha_1(f_{N-4}+f_{N-2})+ \alpha_2 f_{N-3}=f_{N-5}+f_{N-1}$$

are evaluated.

Let us make a two-frequency fit to the 13-week moving average of the DJI Average shown in Figure 8-5 for the 27-month period from January 1972. The data is detrended by fitting a straight line to this span of data. The data for this fit is given in Table 8-4, columns (1), (2) and (3). From these data the normal equations provide

$$\Sigma y = 11,986 = 13a \qquad \text{and} \qquad a = 922$$

$$\Sigma xy = b\,\Sigma x^2 \quad \text{or} \quad -1,052 = 182b \quad \text{and} \quad b = -5.78$$

which results in the equation $y'_{LT} = 922 - 5.8x$. This straight line, taken as the long-term trend (y'_{LT}), is plotted as a solid line on Figure 8-5. Subtracting the long-term trend from the 13-week moving average gives $f(t)$ (column 6).

The coefficients of the α's in Equation (8-29) are tabulated in Table 8-4 and summed to give the simultaneous equations

$$\alpha_1 \Sigma a^2 + \alpha_2 \Sigma ab = \Sigma ac \quad \text{or} \quad 30,217\alpha_1 + 15,594\alpha_2 = 20,214$$

$$\alpha_1 \Sigma ab + \alpha_2 \Sigma b^2 = \Sigma bc \quad \text{or} \quad 15,594\alpha_1 + 11,829\alpha_2 = 4,880$$

which when solved give $\alpha_1 = 1.4266314$ and $\alpha_2 = -1.4681624$. Substituting these values in Equation (8-28) we obtain the two roots

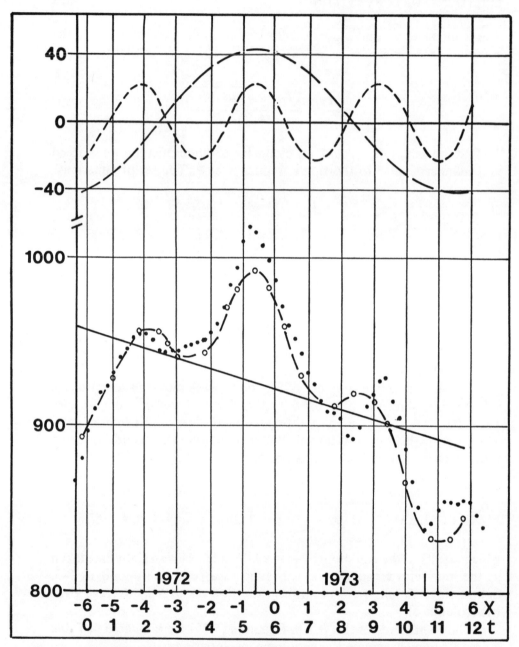

Figure 8-5. A two-frequency trigonometric fit is made to the detrended 13-week moving average of the DJIA (dotted curve) over a two-year section of data. The extracted cycles are shown above and are added to the solid detrending line below to show the overall fit to the moving average.

Table 8-4

Data and calculations required for determining the frequencies in a two-frequency trigonometric fit to detrended data for the DJI 10-day moving average of Figure 8-5.

(1)	(2)	(3)	(4)	(5)	(6)	(7)	(8)	(9)	(10)	(11)	(12)
x	y	xy	y_{LT}	t	f(t)				a	b	c
−6	872	−5232	957	0	−85						
−5	930	−4650	951	1	−21						
−4	953	−3812	945	2	8	f_1+f_3	f_2	f_0+f_4	−17	8	−62
−3	943	−2829	939	3	4	f_2+f_4	f_3	f_1+f_5	31	4	60
−2	957	−1914	934	4	23	f_3+f_5	f_4	f_2+f_6	85	23	71
−1	1009	−1009	928	5	81	f_4+f_6	f_5	f_3+f_7	86	81	19
0	985	0	922	6	63	f_5+f_7	f_6	f_4+f_8	96	63	13
1	931	931	916	7	15	f_6+f_8	f_7	f_5+f_9	53	15	94
2	900	1800	910	8	−10	f_7+f_9	f_8	f_6+f_{10}	28	−10	49
3	918	2754	905	9	13	f_8+f_{10}	f_9	f_7+f_{11}	−24	13	−29
4	885	3540	899	10	−14	f_9+f_{11}	f_{10}	f_8+f_{12}	−31	−14	−43
5	849	4245	893	11	−44						
6	854	5124	887	12	−33						

$$\cos \omega_1 = 0.8667 \quad \text{and} \quad \omega_1 = 30° \quad \text{or} \quad T_1 = 120 \text{ weeks}$$

$$\cos \omega_2 = -0.1534 \quad \text{and} \quad \omega_2 = 99° \quad \text{or} \quad T_2 = 36 \text{ weeks}$$

The amplitudes of the sine and cosine waves for the two frequencies are found in a manner similar to that for one frequency by solving the normal equations

$$A_1 \Sigma \cos^2 \omega_1 t + B_1 \Sigma \cos \omega_1 t \sin \omega_1 t + A_2 \Sigma \cos \omega_1 t \cos \omega_2 t$$
$$+ B_2 \Sigma \cos \omega_1 t \sin \omega_2 t = \Sigma f(t) \cos \omega_1 t$$

$$A_1 \Sigma \sin \omega_1 t \cos \omega_1 t + B_1 \Sigma \sin^2 \omega_1 t + A_2 \Sigma \sin \omega_1 t \cos \omega_2 t$$
$$+ B_2 \Sigma \sin \omega_1 t \sin \omega_2 t = \Sigma f(t) \sin \omega_1 t$$

$$A_1 \Sigma \cos \omega_2 t \cos \omega_1 t + B_1 \Sigma \cos \omega_2 t \sin \omega_1 t + A_2 \Sigma \cos^2 \omega_2 t$$
$$+ B_2 \Sigma \cos \omega_2 t \sin \omega_2 t = \Sigma f(t) \cos \omega_2 t$$

$$A_1 \Sigma \sin \omega_2 t \cos \omega_1 t + B_1 \Sigma \sin \omega_2 t \sin \omega_1 t + A_2 \Sigma \sin \omega_2 t \cos \omega_2 t$$
$$+ B_2 \Sigma \sin^2 \omega_2 t = \Sigma f(t) \sin \omega_2 t$$

Using the Gauss reduction method of solving these simultaneous equations from data calculated using Table 8-5, the amplitudes are: $A_1 = -42.51$, $B_1 = 12.55$, $A_2 = -23.65$ and $B_2 = 1.15$. Changing to the sine wave form, $C_1 = -44.3$, $C_2 = -23.7$, $\phi_1 = 106.5°$ and $\phi_2 = 92.8°$ giving the two sine wave equations

$$f_1(t) = -44.3 \sin 30 \, (t+3.6) \qquad\qquad (8\text{-}30)$$

$$f_2(t) = -23.7 \sin 99 \, (t+1) \qquad\qquad (8\text{-}31)$$

Equations (8-30) and (8-31) are plotted in the upper portion of Figure 8-5. When they are added to the long-term trend, the dashed curved line is obtained representing the fit of these three components to the moving average data. This analysis illustrates the formation of a head and shoulders pattern.

Table 8-5

Data and calculations for finding the amplitudes of the cosine and sine terms of a two-frequency trigonometric fit for frequencies determined using data of Table 8-4.

(1)	(2)	(3)	(4)	(5)	(6)	(7)	(8)	(9)	(10)
t	$f(t)$	$\omega_1 t$	$\cos \omega_1 t$	$\sin \omega_1 t$	$\omega_2 t$	$\cos \omega_2 t$	$\sin \omega_2 t$	$f_1(t)_c$	$f_2(t)_c$
0	−85	0	1.000	0.000	0	1.0000	0.0000	−42	−23
1	−21	30	.866	.500	99	−.1564	.9877	−30	7
2	8	60	.500	.866	198	−.9511	−.3090	−9	21
3	4	90	0.000	1.000	297	.4540	−.8910	14	−14
4	23	120	−.500	.866	36	.8090	.5878	33	−17
5	81	150	−.866	.500	135	−.7071	.7071	43	19
6	63	180	−1.000	0.000	234	−.5878	−.8090	42	11
7	15	210	−.866	−.500	333	.8910	−.4540	30	−23
8	−10	240	−.500	−.866	72	.3090	.9511	9	−4
9	13	270	0.000	−1.000	171	−.9877	.1564	−14	24
10	−14	300	.500	−.866	270	0.0000	−1.0000	−32	4
11	−44	330	.866	−.500	9	.9877	.1564	−43	−23
12	−33	360	1.000	0.000	108	.3090	.9511	−42	11

SIMPLIFYING THE CALCULATION

When fitting a single frequency, if one chooses a data span equal to any multiple of a half period and divides the span into a number of data intervals so that 90° is divided evenly by ω, a symmetrical arrangement is established. The sine and cosine functions only need to be looked up for the first quadrant. The remaining values repeat in absolute value and it is only necessary to attach the correct sign. This saves considerable look-up time. Further, since for each product of the cosine and sine of ωt in the first quadrant there is one in the second quadrant equal in magnitude and opposite in sign, the coefficients involving these products equal zero. In addition, where the number of data points, N, is even the coefficients involving the squared terms each equal $\frac{1}{2}N$. If an odd number of data points is used, the extra point being the end of the period, or the beginning of a second period, then, the sum of the cosine squared term is $\frac{1}{2}(N-1)+1$ and sine squared term is $\frac{1}{2}(N-1)$. (See Table 8-5 where the frequency $\omega_1 = 30°/10$-weeks provides an illustration of this arrangement.)

One has freedom in setting up the data interval. In our data we usually have points on a moving average plotted weekly or daily but only desire to sample every tenth point. We could as well sample every ninth or eleventh point, or we could choose any other convenient interval including fractional values, interpolating between points as necessary. Also we are not limited to a specific data span, so it may be chosen as a half period or some multiple of a half period. Having set up the problem in this manner, Equations (8-24) and (8-25) simplify to

$$A \cdot \tfrac{1}{2}N = \Sigma f(t)\cos \omega t \quad\text{ or }\quad A = (2/N)\,\Sigma f(t)\cos \omega t \quad \text{(8-32)}$$

$$B \cdot \tfrac{1}{2}N = \Sigma f(t)\sin \omega t \quad\text{ or }\quad B = (2/N)\,\Sigma f(t)\sin \omega t \quad \text{(8-33)}$$

when N equals an even number of data points.

If making a multiple-frequency fit, one can sometimes choose the data interval so that more than the one frequency is symmetrical. This is particularly true for market data because the cyclic components frequently are related by periods having ratios of 2:1 or 3:1.

When several frequencies are indicated, it is often acceptable to fit one frequency at a time starting with the lowest (longest period), removing this component, then fitting the next lowest frequency, etc. The sampling interval may be individually chosen for each frequency to take advantage of a symmetrical arrangement.

Tables are given in Appendix G for products of the trigonometric functions used in curve fitting which will save computation time. When fitting a single frequency, a good approximation may be had by adjusting the data interval to make the frequency fall between 30 and 59 degrees per data interval and rounding to an integral number so as to use the precomputed sums given in Table V.

THE GENERAL SOLUTION

One may proceed to fit three or more frequencies following similar procedures as described for the one and two frequency cases. When the frequencies must be established by least squares methods, this is carried out, as before, as a separate calculation. The general equations for m frequencies, using what is known as Prony's method are

$$(f_1+f_{2m-1})\alpha_1+(f_2+f_{2m-2})\alpha_2 + \ldots +(f_{m-1}+f_{m+1})\alpha_{m-1}$$

$$+f_m\alpha_m = f_0+f_{2m}$$

$$(f_2+f_{2m})\alpha_1+(f_3+f_{2m-1})\alpha_2 + \ldots + (f_m+f_{m+2})\alpha_{m-1}$$

$$+f_{m+1}\alpha_m=f_1+f_{2m+1} \qquad \text{(8-34)}$$

. . . .

$$(f_{N-2m}+f_{N-2})\alpha_1+(f_{N-2m+1}+f_{N-3})\alpha_2+ \ldots +(f_{N-m-2}+f_{N-m})$$

$$\alpha_{m-1}+f_{N-m-1}\alpha_m=f_{N-2m-1}+f_{N-1}$$

A table is prepared similar to Table 8-4 for values of f(t), that is, the data points vs. values of t from 0 to N covering the span of data. As before, it is convenient to designate the coefficients of α_1 under a column a, for α_2 under b, etc., the last column being the right-hand term. A second set of equations is set up by summing the terms a^2, ab, ac etc., then ba, b^2, bc etc. which results in m equations containing m + 1 terms that are the coefficients of the α's and the right-hand term where the α's are in the same position as in the first set. This second set of equations is solved simultaneously for the α's. These α's are now substituted in

$$T_m-\alpha_1T_{m-1}- \ldots -\alpha_{m-1}T_1 - \tfrac{1}{2}\alpha_m = 0 \qquad \text{(8-35)}$$

where the values of the T's are given by the Chebyshev polynomials

$$T_o(x) = 1.0 \qquad\qquad T_3(x) = 4x^3 - 3x$$

$$T_1(x) = x \qquad\qquad \cdots\cdots\cdots\cdots\cdots \qquad \text{(8-36)}$$

$$T_2(x) = 2x^2 - 1 \qquad\qquad T_{R+1}(x) = 2xT_R(x) - T_{R-1}(x)$$

where $x = \cos \omega$. Solving Equation (8-35) for the values of x gives the cosines of the frequencies which are best to fit the data span used in deriving them. When the data span used covers several periods of the higher frequencies, this best fit may not in fact produce as good a fit as if the frequencies were redetermined for shorter data spans, because of the period varying from cycle to cycle.

For three frequencies, Equation (8-35) becomes the cubic equation

$$x^3 - \frac{\alpha_1}{2}x^2 - \frac{\alpha_2 + 3}{4}x + \frac{2\alpha_1 - \alpha_3}{8} = 0 \qquad (8\text{-}37)$$

whose solution may be obtained by the procedure given in "Algebraic Equations" in Chapter 16. Given the frequencies $\omega_1, \omega_2, \ldots, \omega_m$, the amplitudes $A_1, B_1, A_2, B_2, \ldots, A_m, B_m$ must be determined in

$$A_1 \cos \omega_1 t + B_1 \sin \omega_1 t + A_2 \cos \omega_2 t + B_2 \sin \omega_2 t + \ldots$$
$$+ A_m \cos \omega_m t + B_m \sin \omega_m t = f(t) \quad (8\text{-}38)$$

This equation must be true for each value $t_0, t_1, \ldots, t_N$, giving rise to $N+1$ equations. The least squares solution is obtained in the same manner as for the two frequency case. That is, a second set of equations is set up as follows: The first equation is found by multiplying the coefficient of A_1, that is $\cos \omega_1 t$, by the coefficients of $A_1, B_1, A_2, B_2, \ldots$ and the right hand side for each value of t and summing corresponding terms. This gives

$$A_1 \sum_{t=0}^{N} \cos^2 \omega_1 t + B_1 \sum_{t=0}^{N} \cos \omega_1 t \sin \omega_1 t + A_2 \sum_{t=0}^{N} \cos \omega_1 t \cos \omega_2 t +$$
$$\ldots + B_m \sum_{t=0}^{N} \cos \omega_1 t \sin \omega_m t = \sum_{t=0}^{N} \cos \omega_1 t \cdot f(t)$$

for the first equation. The second equation is similarly found by multiplying all the coefficients of the A's, B's and the right-hand member by the coefficient of B_1, that is $\sin \omega_1 t$, and summing corresponding terms. This is continued until $\sin \omega_m t$ is used as the multiplier, thus giving $2m$ equations which are solved simultaneously for the A's and B's. As an example for three frequencies, the coefficients of the A's and B's may be set up for solution by the Gauss reduction method as shown in Table 8-6.

The first term in Equation (8-39) is the coefficient of A_1, the second is the coefficient of B_1 etc. Likewise for Equation (8-40), etc. Following the Gauss reduction, the value of B_3 is first found when Equation (8-44) has been reduced to two terms, the A_3 will be found from Equation (8-43) by substituting the value of B_3 in the reduced three-term equation, etc. When all values of the A's and B's are found, substitute them in the original Equation (8-44) as a check on accuracy.

Having found the A's and B's, Equation (8-38) may be expressed as a sum of sine wave equations by the transformation described on   Page 67, resulting in the equation of the form

$$C_1 \sin \omega_1 (t+\phi_1) + C_2 \sin \omega_2 (t+\phi_2) + C_3 \sin \omega_3 (t+\phi_3)$$

Table 8-6

The coefficients in the set of simultaneous equations to be solved for the amplitudes in a three-frequency trigonometric fit arranged for the Gauss reduction method of solution.

$$
\begin{aligned}
\Sigma \cos^2 \omega_1 t &= \\
\Sigma \cos \omega_1 t \ \sin \omega_1 t &= \\
\Sigma \cos \omega_1 t \ \cos \omega_2 t &= \\
\Sigma \cos \omega_1 t \ \sin \omega_2 t &= \\
\Sigma \cos \omega_1 t \ \cos \omega_3 t &= \\
\Sigma \cos \omega_1 t \ \sin \omega_3 t &= \\
\Sigma \cos \omega_1 t \cdot f(t) &=
\end{aligned}
\qquad (8\text{-}39)
$$

$$
\begin{aligned}
\Sigma \sin \omega_1 t \ \cos \omega_1 t &= \\
\Sigma \sin^2 \omega_1 t &= \\
\Sigma \sin \omega_1 t \ \cos \omega_2 t &= \\
\Sigma \sin \omega_1 t \ \sin \omega_2 t &= \\
\Sigma \sin \omega_1 t \ \cos \omega_3 t &= \\
\Sigma \sin \omega_1 t \ \sin \omega_3 t &= \\
\Sigma \sin \omega_1 t \cdot f(t) &=
\end{aligned}
\qquad (8\text{-}40)
$$

$$
\begin{aligned}
\Sigma \cos \omega_2 t \ \cos \omega_1 t &= \\
\Sigma \cos \omega_2 t \ \sin \omega_1 t &= \\
\Sigma \cos^2 \omega_2 t &= \\
\Sigma \cos \omega_2 t \ \sin \omega_2 t &= \\
\Sigma \cos \omega_2 t \ \cos \omega_3 t &= \\
\Sigma \cos \omega_2 t \ \sin \omega_3 t &= \\
\Sigma \cos \omega_2 t \cdot f(t) &=
\end{aligned}
\qquad (8\text{-}41)
$$

$$
\begin{aligned}
\Sigma \sin \omega_2 t \ \cos \omega_1 t &= \\
\Sigma \sin \omega_2 t \ \sin \omega_1 t &=
\end{aligned}
$$

$$\Sigma \sin \omega_2 t \cos \omega_2 t =$$
$$\Sigma \sin^2 \omega_2 t \qquad =$$
$$\Sigma \sin \omega_2 t \cos \omega_3 t = \qquad\qquad (8\text{-}42)$$
$$\Sigma \sin \omega_2 t \sin \omega_3 t =$$
$$\Sigma \sin \omega_2 t \cdot f(t) \quad =$$

$$\Sigma \cos \omega_3 t \cos \omega_1 t =$$
$$\Sigma \cos \omega_3 t \sin \omega_1 t =$$
$$\Sigma \cos \omega_3 t \cos \omega_2 t =$$
$$\Sigma \cos \omega_3 t \sin \omega_2 t = \qquad\qquad (8\text{-}43)$$
$$\Sigma \cos^2 \omega_3 t \qquad =$$
$$\Sigma \cos \omega_3 t \sin \omega_3 t =$$
$$\Sigma \cos \omega_3 t \cdot f(t) \quad =$$

$$\Sigma \sin \omega_3 t \cos \omega_1 t =$$
$$\Sigma \sin \omega_3 t \sin \omega_1 t =$$
$$\Sigma \sin \omega_3 t \cos \omega_2 t =$$
$$\Sigma \sin \omega_3 t \sin \omega_2 t = \qquad\qquad (8\text{-}44)$$
$$\Sigma \sin \omega_3 t \cos \omega_3 t =$$
$$\Sigma \sin^2 \omega_3 t \qquad =$$
$$\Sigma \sin \omega_3 t \cdot f(t) \quad =$$

A NOTE ON NUMBER OF DATA POINTS

When making a trigonometric least squares fit remember there are three unknowns for each frequency—the frequency, amplitude and phase. You must have at least as many equations as unknowns for the simultaneous solution. To determine the frequency, two more data points are required than equations for a one-frequency fit, four more for two frequencies, etc.

Up to a point, the greater the number of data points used, the better the resulting fit. Some judgement should be used considering the variation in the data and the amount of calculation required.

A NOTE ON NOMENCLATURE

We will follow a notation in the remainder of this book, where curve fitting is being carried out, like the scheme used in this chapter. The data points will be designated by the letter y, as well as the dependent variable in general equations involving powers of x used in these procedures. A triple prime will be applied to y ($y^{i\prime\prime}$) when the equation is a calculated fit of a cubic equation. Likewise, a second-degree equation will be $y^{\prime\prime}$, etc. The sine wave equation derived from $y^{\prime\prime\prime}$ will be represented by $y_{\rm s}^{\prime\prime\prime}$, and the corrected value by $y_{\rm sc}^{\prime\prime\prime}$.

The basic time reference will be day number, or week number, as may be appropriate. The day number will *count* market days only. The zero will be arbitrarily located, and relocated as desired to avoid excessively large values. Calendar dates will be noted merely to orient the analysis to calendar time. Days noted on this axis will be Mondays. When using weekly charts, Friday's data will be used as the date for point plotting and calendar dates will be marked as the first Friday of each month. In making the least squares fit, centered spans will be used with intervals designated in terms of x, where x = 0 at the span center. The data points to be used in the analysis will be at integral values of x. The value of x may be any convenient number of days (or weeks). Time of points are determined by relating the value of x to the day (or week) number. Remember the calculations will be expressed in the units of the interval of x. To get days (or weeks) one must multiply by the number of days (or weeks) in one interval of x.

Data points which represent detrended data will be designated as f(t) (read f of t). A curve designated as f(t) will designate a trigonometric curve fit. Subscripts of f will be used to designate the various components when more than one is extracted. Likewise, subscripts will denote the corresponding values of frequency (ω) and period (T). The independent variable for trigonometric curve fitting is designated as t where t = 0 at the beginning of the data span. The intervals, in units of t, are chosen, as with x, to designate the data points used in the calculation.

Summary

Mathematical curves may be fitted to stock market charts which closely represent the time variations found in the data. A projection of these curves indicates the likely trend of future data. Least squares curve fitting of cubic and lesser degree and of trigonometric form in one or two frequencies are useful for stock market analysis. Methods and approximations are described which simplify and reduce the calculations.

9

Cycles and Their Determination

A SIMPLE APPROACH TO CYCLE ANALYSIS

Cycle analysis is somewhat of an art. There are various ways to proceed and devices to aid one in extracting cyclic information contained in various data. More generally the area is known as Time Series Analysis. Such studies are of interest in economics, business and various scientific endeavors. These series contain a number of components which may occur separately or in combination.

DATA STRUCTURE

First of all there may be a long-term drift. This is called the *secular trend* or merely the *long-term trend*. Stock price averages exhibit an upward drift when viewed over many years. While in general one need not know the cause of any particular component, it is obvious that the continuous inflation could produce an upward drift upon which other influences are superimposed to give wide as well as small swings.

Many series show a *seasonal variation*. This may not be obvious in market averages, but some stock prices exhibit marked seasonal variations, which stem from the nature of their business. These may not be as pronounced today as in the past due to companies diversifying to smooth out their business peaks and valleys.

Of most importance to the market analyst is the cyclic component, or components, which range from over long periods of time related to alternations in the business cycle, general prosperity and depression (or reces-

125

sion) which may last for several years, to the shorter but prominent movements which repeat their patterns with regularity.

Finally, there is the irregular component which contributes movements that are of short duration and relatively small in magnitude and add roughness to the whole picture. They are frequently associated with day-by-day news. With respect to this, commentators on the stock market often associate price movements with news items when the relationship is merely that the news serves as a trigger to set in motion a cyclic pattern already poised to make its move. The news may cause the price to jump, even ahead of time, but when smoothed out you can see that it should have happened anyway. Also note how often the comment is that the market did not react to the news; this merely means the market was not ready for a movement in the direction expected from the news.

DETRENDING DATA

In making a cycle analysis, it is frequently useful to remove the secular or long-term trend. This can sometimes be done by eye; just draw a straight or curved line through the plotted data. However, there are ways of mathematically fitting the curve to the data that give a unique answer to a given situation as was described in the previous chapter. Another approach is to draw the "Hurst envelopes," the pair of curved lines which enclose the plotted data in a band of equal vertical width, then draw a line through the midpoints defined by this band. Finally, one may use a long-span moving average but the delay (one-half span) may be too great to be useful for the particular analysis you have in mind.

If this long-term trend is determined either by eyeball smoothing, Hurst envelope, or some mathematical procedure, the points on this line may be subtracted from the corresponding points of the data and the resulting differences treated as detrended data.

CYCLE IDENTIFICATION

The simplest approach to finding cycles is to mark successive low points in the plotted data. A low may be defined as any point lower than the points to either side in time. This strictly followed will identify the shortest cycles in the raw data. Longer and more prominent cycles can be similarly located by marking the lows which are lower than the lows to either side (see Figure 6-1 as an example). These frequently contain about three of the shorter cycles. At times the proper low will be higher than one to the side if it occurs on the upswing of a still longer cycle. This situation is apparent from the general trend of the data and the general location in time of the expected low in comparison to the series of lows being marked.

Enclosing the data in "Hurst envelopes" is useful for extending the marking of cycles by finding the low points. Points touching the lower boundary curve are usually bottom cycle points. High points may also be used in the same manner but usually the lows are more pronounced than the highs. When more sophisticated methods of extracting cycles are used, one may find that the cycle lows do not exactly correspond to the data lows. This is to be expected. Refer back to Figure 3-3 which shows how the peaks of pure sine waves may be displaced when added.

LONG DATA SPANS

There has been a lot of cycle analysis of economic data, and even stock averages and stock group averages, covering spans of many years. These studies, for the most part, search for cyclic components expressed in terms of a periodic wave whose period represents the average of many periods. Techniques have been developed to aid in identifying the cycle and the best fit obtained over the span of many cycles. At any time there may be a marked difference in phase between the periodic wave and the actual data. For the market technician, this is not helpful when trying to predict the price trend. Also these long-term studies frequently use moving average smoothing of long spans and other analysis methods that do not allow carrying the result up to current day data.

For the purpose of making market predictions, these long-term analyses are not of too much use. More useful results are obtained by restricting the data span to either that corresponding to about one period of the cycle being extracted, or a few periods at most, if the data suggests several periods of similar amplitude and durations are present. In some procedures, amplitudes are determined, which vary from period to period, and these should be extracted to indicate the amplitude trend.

The chapters on moving averages and on curve fitting discuss the use of mathematical procedures for cycle analysis. The treatment of time series data in general may be found in various statistical and numerical analysis books such as References 5 and 7.

ANALYZING A MARKET AVERAGE

Examination of the chart of any stock market average covering many years discloses a prominent cyclic movement whose lows occur on an average of about 4½ years. Any market study should include this cycle. Longer cycles which may be present can be grouped together into a long-term trend component, but this major cycle represents the bull and bear markets as we have known them for many years. Shorter cycles are always present, some of which are quite significant and others only of primary interest to the short-term trader. If you have access to a large computer and the necessary background in mathematics and programming you can make as sophisticated an analysis as you may want. The methods described here, however, are intended for the use of anyone interested in studying for himself the cyclic behavior of the market without undue computational effort.

It has been found convenient to start the analysis with the identification of this nominal 4½-year cycle which we will call the *major cycle*. Prices never go negative, of course, and in fact seldom go to zero. The cyclic motion occurs around some average level, or some trend value. It is not easy to immediately identify this trend from a limited span of data. We have seen that a moving average can be used to smooth the data and in fact to reduce the amplitude of components having periods of about the length of the data span and shorter. If used to smooth the 4½-year cycle, the span should be at least one period long. The delay of over two years makes this method useless for one interested in what the market is now doing and is likely to do in the future. Curve fitting can be applied to the data right up to present time but if used to smooth out or average the data over a 4½-year cycle, must be applied to spans considerably longer than the major cycle, or something like nine years or more. This takes a lot of data and may not yield the best of results for the latest time period. An approach which has worked well is to make a least squares fit of the cubic equation to a section of price data of about one period in time of the major cycle. This procedure does not require detrended data and produces a result which includes any constant bias and trend inherent in the data, but still shows up a cyclic component in the region around and between the reversal points of the normal cubic equation. The data should first be smoothed to eliminate short-term fluctuations and a short-span moving average is satisfactory for this purpose. When working with the major 4½-year cycle, a three-month (or 13-week) span is a good choice. The delay of 6½ weeks is of little consequence for this time scale.

We have described in Chapter 8 how to establish a sine wave based on the cubic curve, which closely follows the central portion of the cubic, and can be used to represent the cyclic component over the data span, and even projected into the future to indicate how the prices are likely to move. Also, methods were described which make corrections to period and amplitude to provide an even better sine wave representation. In selecting the span of data to be analyzed it is desirable to try to cover a region which resembles the central portion of the cubic. That is, where the data makes two reversals such as a high followed by a low, or vice versa. These reversals must be clearly associated with the period of interest, not some secondary movement.

Having found a representation of the major cycle component, its y values may be subtracted algebraically from the original data to leave the long-term trend on which are superimposed the shorter cycles. We can now find the appropriate long-term trend by a least squares fit to the remainder data. Several periods of the shorter cycles will be present and so will average out. Also, any remnants of the major cycle will be present only as a fraction of its amplitude and will be smoothed to some extent resulting in little, if any, effect on the trend. Normally you would make a second-degree curve fit for the trend because the trend is most likely a small section of some longer cycle thus having some curvature. Upon occasion this section may revert to a straight line. This trend curve may be extended into the future but some care must be exercised as to how far. If in fact it is a part of some longer cycle or cycles, there will be a reversal sometime. If a second-degree equation resulted, remember it must continue its curvature, concave up or down as the case may be, and the extension may be forced into ever increasing errors as time goes on. I'm referring to time intervals of a year or more for this situation. Therefore, it is wise to update the analysis if this curve becomes suspect.

Having now a representation for the trend and the major cycle, the original data may be detrended by subtracting algebraically these two components. The detrended data will contain the shorter cycles which will oscillate above and below the zero value, and when plotted will normally show up one or two intermediate cyclic movements. This data is susceptible to trigonometric least squares fitting, described in Chapter 8, Page 109 and following. If only one intermediate frequency is evident, then a single frequency fit may be carried out. You may observe two or more cycles of this frequency and the period may appear to differ between the cycles; also the amplitude may be changing. Since we are interested in what the prices are going to do in the future, the most recent data is what we are interested in. We may, therefore, shorten the data span to that covering about one period, or even somewhat less. This reduces the labor and gives a more up-to-date result. When this cycle is found, its value may be subtracted from the data for further detrending. There will probably be another cycle of shorter period showing up and one can proceed in like manner as long as it is fruitful. If at any time two frequencies seem to be more or less equally prominent, a two-frequency trigonometric fit should be carried out. You may at times merely find the two frequencies, then choose the one which seems more pronounced and continue with a determination of amplitude and phase for this one frequency, detrending further and proceed with the next frequency.

The original data in most cases would start with weekly values. At some point, as the periods become shorter, it is desirable to shift to daily data. At the same time, a shorter-span moving average should be selected, such as 30-days. This reduces the delay, so the results are more current. Also, the data amplitudes are not as suppressed as in the longer span when our interest shifts to the higher frequencies.

Eventually a point will be reached where it is not productive to continue this process. In fact, the components generally desired are the long-term trend, the major cycle, the intermediate cycle and one or two shorter cycles which are of such duration as to be termed trading cycles. Still shorter cycles may be identified merely by marking the low values on a market average high-low plot, determining their average period and projecting these lows into the future one at a time. Their occurrence relative to the longer cycles should be observed. The short low-amplitude cycles will be most prominent when occurring near the flat regions, tops or bottoms, of the longer-term cycles.

10

Practical Formulas for Estimating Option Prices and Ranges

A contract which entitles the holder to buy a number of shares (typically 100) of a stock at a designated price within a stated time is known as a *call option*. That is, it is an option to call the stock from the option seller. Conversely a *put* entitles the holder to sell 100 shares of a designated stock at a designated price within a stated time. That is, it is an option to put your stock to the option seller for him to buy at the previously agreed price.

The purchase and sale of stock options, such as puts and calls, have been available in the over-the-counter market for many years, but their popularity increased immensely with the advent of the Chicago Board Options Exchange (CBOE) and the start of trading in call options in April 1973.[1] This was followed by the AMEX in January 1975 using a similar arrangement. Their success encouraged other exchanges to add options. What was new was that these exchanges provided a secondary market in standardized call options of a selected number of NYSE listed common stocks.

There are combinations of puts and calls and various strategies for hedging which are discussed in Reference 6, various advisory services and financial publications, from time to time. If interested, the reader is advised to study some of this reference material.

---

[1]The prospectus of the Options Clearing Corp., available from your broker, contains an excellent introduction to the options market.

EXCHANGE-TRADED OPTIONS

Our interest here is one of predicting the price of an option contract at some future time in terms of the expected price of the underlying common stock. The basic evaluation will be in terms of the expected performance of the common stock. We want to transfer this evaluation to an estimated value of the option. A participant in the option market may approach it from two aspects. The one considered most conservative is the option writer. For example, if you own 100 shares of a stock covered by the CBOE, you may sell (write) a call on it on this exchange. A choice of three expiration times is usually available. Calls expire at the end of specified months and trading in the expiring call stops on these exchanges at a specified time before the last of the month. As one call date is passed, a new call, expiring nine months later, is introduced. There is frequently a choice of the price at which the stock may be called, known as the *striking price*, or exercise price. The longer the time to expiration, the higher the price of the call. If you follow this program, your considerations include how to produce the maximum return on a yearly basis. When calls expire, you are free to write another call on the same stock. If the call is exercised, your stock is called (sold), but you will of course have the proceeds to enter the market again in the same or different stock. If the market price of the stock falls below the striking price, it certainly will not be called and you retain the stock, but you may suffer a paper loss. If the stock price is above the striking price, the call is most likely to be exercised.

The second approach is to trade in the options directly. You may purchase a call on the Option Exchange in the expectation that it will go up in price and you can sell it at a profit. There are other reasons for purchase of a call but the trading aspect will suffice to bring out the price considerations. The leverage is very great so profits can be large, but also losses can be total as the option becomes worthless at expiration if not exercisable.

A word of caution is in order if you become interested in the various hedge strategies. Calculate all costs involved and be sure you can make a profit worth the risk. You must include the commission costs which tend to be neglected, because of their low dollar amount, but may be a large percentage of your differential gain. Frequently, recommendations are presented on the basis of using margin; be sure to include all margin costs. When trading low-priced options, commission costs can often be reduced by dealing in two or more of the same options, since in most cases there is a minimum commission charge. Find out what the current commission rates are and make the computation.

Also think through the tax situation. Remember that under present tax laws gains and losses on short sales are treated as ordinary income, but gains and losses on the long side are treated as capital gains or losses which may be either short or long term. This different treatment can be an advantage or a disadvantage depending upon the circumstances. You will find most hedges presented on the basis of possible profits assuming a direct offset of loss on one side against a gain on the other side. You can fall into a trap here if the situation involves gain on the short side and loss on the long side. You have to include the entire short side gain as ordinary income which is fully taxed. The loss on the long side is treated as a capital loss and can only be used to offset ordinary income to a maximum of $1,000 each year, though it can be carried over to succeeding years. Further, should it be long term it takes a $2,000 loss to produce the $1,000 offset. Depending on your tax bracket, you could end up actually losing money. On the other hand, if the transaction involved a loss on the short side against a capital gain on the long side, they would balance out, but if the gain were long term, then it would be taxed at a lower rate and the tax treatment would be to your advantage since the short-side loss would reduce taxable income at one hundred percent. Also, tax laws change, so check it out.

OPTION PRICE

The active option markets establish the option price in terms of the underlying stock price, the striking price, the length of time the option has to run until expiration, and certain assessments the public places on these vehicles relative to market conditions and stock characteristics. If one wants to trade in options, it is important to understand how the price of an option is likely to vary in the future.

Confining our discussions to exchange-traded calls, first of all the call price varies with the price of the underlying stock. When the stock price is above the striking price, the call will be worth at least as much as the spread between the striking price and the stock price. Actually the call usually will be worth somewhat more by an amount corresponding to the value placed on the privilege to buy the stock at a predetermined price prior to the expiration date. Table 10-1 lists those calls on the CBOE as of August 1, 1974 where the common stock was selling near a striking price. The *adjusted call price* is the quoted call price minus the difference between the stock price and the striking price. That is, it is the portion of the call quoted price attributed to the privilege of holding the option. This is expressed as a percent of stock price in the last column. The price of April calls, having about seven months to go to expiration, are seen to range from about 10 percent to as much as 25 percent of the stock price with an average of about 16 percent.

As the expiration date approaches, the value of the call decreases. Referring to Table 10-1 again, the January calls having about four months to go are quoted at a lower value and average about 12 percent of the stock price. Further, the October calls which are one month from expiration are lower yet.

During the last few weeks of the life of the call, if the stock price rises well above the striking price, the call price becomes very close to the difference between the stock price and the striking price. See Table 10-2 listing a number of July calls as of June 24, 1974, having 24 days to go. The quoted call price varies by only a fraction of a point from the differences between the stock price and the call striking price, as shown by the last column. This Table also shows April calls having 14 days to go.

When the stock price is closer to the striking price, the call has a value beyond that due to the difference between the stock price and the striking price as illustrated in Table 10-3. The stocks are arranged in decending order of striking price and are as of June 24, 1974.

When the call has longer to run, its value is greater. See Table 10-4 which lists January calls as of October 5, 1973, thus having about four months to expiration, and April calls having about seven months to go showing even greater values. These tables illustrate how the call value varies with its time to expiration.

If the stock price falls considerably below the striking price, the value of the call decreases but of course can not fall below zero. It may continue to trade at some low fractional value. Such calls are not necessarily cheap just because they are low in price. They may not rise appreciably until the stock price begins to approach the striking price.

When two striking prices for the same expiration date are available, the call quoted prices will differ by something less than the difference in the striking prices. This is illustrated in Table 10-5 for April calls having about seven months to expiration. For this situation the calls differ in price by about two-thirds of the spread between the striking prices. The call spread increases somewhat as the expiration date approaches and reaches 100 percent at expiration.

Table 10-1

Certain CBOE calls as of August 1, 1974 in which the stock was selling near the call striking price. The last column represents the portion of the price of the option in excess of that attributed to the difference between the price of the underlying stock and the option striking price expressed as a percent of the stock price. That is, it is the part of the option price attributed to the privilege of being able to call the stock.

Stock	Call	Stock Price	Call Price	$\dfrac{\text{Adj. Call Price}}{\text{Stock Price}}$ %
Beth St	Apr 30	29 ⅞	3 ¾	13.0
Citicorp	Apr 30	30 ⅛	5 ¾	18.7
Ford	Apr 45	44 ½	3 ¾	9.6
Gt Wes Fin	Apr 10	10 ⅛	2 ⅝	24.7
IBM	Apr 200	201 ¾	27	12.5
Loews	Apr 15	15 ⅛	2 ½	15.7
Monsan	Apr 60	60 ¼	8 ½	13.7
N W Air	Apr 20	19 ⅞	3 ¾	19.5
				Average 15.9
Beth St	Jan 30	29 ⅞	2 ⅞	10.0
Citicorp	Jan 30	30 ⅛	4 ½	14.5
Ford	Jan 45	44 ½	3	7.9
Gt Wes Fin	Jan 10	10 ⅛	2	18.5
IBM	Jan 200	201 ¾	22 ¾	10.4
Loews	Jan 15	15 ⅛	1 $^{15}/_{16}$	12.0
M M M	Jan 65	65 ½	6	8.4
Monsan	Jan 60	60 ¼	6 ¾	10.8
N W Air	Jan 20	19 ⅞	3	15.7
				Average 12.0
Beth St	Oct 30	29 ⅞	2	7.1
Ford	Oct 45	44 ½	2 ¼	6.2
Gt Wes Fin	Oct 10	10 ⅛	1 ⅝	14.8
IBM	Oct 200	201 ¾	15 ⅞	7.0
Loews	Oct 15	15 ⅛	1 ¼	7.4
M M M	Oct 65	65 ½	4	5.3
Monsan	Oct 60	60 ¼	4 ⅝	7.3
N W Air	Oct 20	19 ⅞	2	10.7
				Average 8.2

Table 10-2

When the calls are close to expiration and the stock is selling well above the striking price, the call price is very nearly the difference between the stock price and the striking price. The July calls are as of June 24, 1974, and have 24 days to expiration. The April calls are as of April 5, 1974, and have 14 days to expiration.

Stock	Call	Stock Price	Call Price	Stock Price less Striking Price	Difference
Ford	July 45	52 ⅛	7 ⅛	7 ⅛	0
Kresge	July 30	36 ¼	6 ⅝	6 ¼	+ ⅜
Monsan	July 50	65	15 ⅛	15	+ ⅛
N.W. Air	July 20	24 ½	4 ⅞	4 ½	+ ⅜
Upjohn	July 65	79 ½	14 ¾	14 ½	+ ¼
Atl Rich	Apr 80	91 ¼	11 ½	11 ¼	+ ¼
Beth St	Apr 25	32 ⅞	7 ⅜	7 ⅞	− ½
Ford	Apr 40	49 ⅛	9	9 ⅛	− ⅛
Gt Wes Fin	Apr 15	18 ½	3 ¼	3 ½	− ¼
Weyerhs	Apr 30	41	11 ½	11	+ ½

Table 10-3

When the stock price is near the striking price, the call has an appreciable value as shown by the values in the last column. These prices are as of June 24, 1974, with about one month to expiration.

Stock	Call	Stock Price	Call Price	Stock Price less Striking Price	Adjusted Call Value
Atl Rich	July 90	89 ½	2 ¾	− ½	3 ¼
Merck	July 80	82	4	2	2
M M M	July 75	73 ⅝	1 ⅞	−1 ⅜	3 ¼
Kerr MG	July 65	66 ¾	4 ¼	1 ¾	2 ½
Weyerhs	July 40	38 ⅝	1 ¼	−1 ⅜	2 ⅝
Kresge	July 35	36 ¼	2 ½	1 ¼	1 ¼
Beth St	July 30	29 ¼	¹³⁄₁₆	− ¾	1 ⁹⁄₁₆
N W Air	July 25	24 ½	1 ³⁄₁₆	− ½	1 ¹¹⁄₁₆
Int Har	July 25	24 ¾	⅞	− ¼	1 ⅛
ITT	July 20	19 ⅝	¹³⁄₁₆	− ⅜	1 ³⁄₁₆
Bruns	July 15	14 ¼	½	− ¾	1 ¼

Table 10-4

When the calls have a long time to expiration, they have a time value much larger than when they are close to expiration. These prices are as of October 5, 1973.

Stock	Call		Stock Price	Call Price	Stock Price less Striking Price	Adjusted Call Value
Atl Rich	Jan	90	93 ⅜	8 ⅞	3 ⅜	5 ½
Exxon	Jan	90	96 ½	9 ½	6 ½	3
Exxon	Jan	100	96 ½	4 ½	−3 ½	8
Gt Wes Fin	Jan	20	21 ⅞	7	1 ⅞	5 ⅛
Kresge	Jan	40	41	5	1	4
McDlds	Jan	70	68 ⅞	12 ⅛	−1 ⅛	13 ¼
N W Air	Jan	25	26 ⅛	4 ⅛	1 ⅛	3
Pennzoil	Jan	25	25 ¾	6 ¼	¾	5 ½
Sperry R	Jan	55	53 ⅝	4 ½	−1 ⅜	5 ⅞
Tex Instr	Jan	120	129 ⅝	18	9 ⅝	8 ⅜
Atl Rich	Apr	90	93 ⅜	11 ½	3 ⅜	8 ⅛
Exxon	Apr	90	96 ½	12 ¾	6 ½	6 ¼
Exxon	Apr	100	96 ½	6 ¾	−3 ½	10 ¼
Gt Wes Fin	Apr	20	21 ⅞	8 ⅞	1 ⅞	7
N W Air	Apr	25	26 ⅛	8 ⅜	1 ⅛	7 ¼
Pennzoil	Apr	25	25 ¾	7	¾	6 ¼
Sperry R	Apr	55	53 ⅝	6	−1 ⅜	7 ⅜
Weyerhs	Apr	70	74 ¾	10 ¾	4 ¾	6

Table 10-5

The difference between the prices of two calls on the same stock at two striking prices is only about two-thirds the difference between striking prices when the time to expiration is several months. Prices are as of October 5, 1973.

Stock	Call		Stock Price	Call Price	Difference	Dif. (S_2-S_1)
Atl Rich	Apr	80	93 ⅜	19 ⅜		
	Apr	90		11 ½	7 ⅞	.79
Beth St	Apr	25	33 ¼	9 ¼		
	Apr	30		5 ⅝	3 ⅝	.73
Bruns	Apr	20	28	9 ¼		
	Apr	25		6 ¼	3	.60
Exxon	Apr	90	96 ½	12 ¾		
	Apr	100		6 ¾	6	.60

Table 10-5 (Continued)

Stock	Call		Stock Price	Call Price	Difference	Dif. (S_2-S_1)
Gt Wes Fin	Apr	15	21 ⅞	8 ⅞		
	Apr	20		5 ⅛	3 ¾	.75
N W Air	Apr	20	26 ⅛	8 ⅜		
	Apr	25		5 ⅜	3	.60
Pennzoil	Apr	20	25 ¾	7		
	Apr	25		4 ⅛	2 ⅞	.58
Sperry R	Apr	45	53 ⅝	12 ½		
	Apr	55		6	6 ½	.65
Weyerhs	Apr	60	74 ¾	16 ¾		
	Apr	70		10 ¾	6	.60

Average .655

A FORMULA FOR OPTION PRICE

If the prices of calls are examined for stock prices at the striking price, it has been found that the call price varies approximately with the square root of the number of market days to expiration. Taking this and other observations, which have been illustrated, into consideration, an expression has been found which gives a good value for the calls traded on an exchange as follows:

$$C=PV(\sqrt{D}-3/\sqrt{D}+2)+ (P-S) (1.5+1/\sqrt{D})\div2.5 \qquad (10\text{-}1)$$

where C is the computed value of the call; P is the price of the underlying stock; V is a constant factor established for each stock and averages about 0.01; D is the number of market days to expiration; and S is the striking price. This expression works well for calls where the stock price (P) and striking price (S) are not widely different. When P = S, the second term becomes zero. When the stock price varies from the striking price, the call price changes by approximately two-thirds the change in stock price. The first term contributes some to the price change but the second term predominates. This observation is important in estimating how much of a change to expect in the call price for an expected price change of the underlying stock.

When D = 1, the last day the option is traded, the first term is zero and the call price becomes just equal to the difference between the stock price and striking price when P is greater than S. In fact there is very little contribution from the first term during the last few weeks of the call life.

When the stock price drops well below the striking price, the call will trade at some very small value. Don't be misled into expecting much of a price rise if the stock increases in price until the negative second term ceases to be overpowering.

The computation using the empirical formula can be simplified by preparation of a table given in Appendix D where the expression is written

$$C = P{\cdot}V{\cdot}A + (P-S)B \qquad (10\text{-}2)$$

where $A = \sqrt{D} - 3/\sqrt{D} + 2$ and $B = (1.5 + 1/\sqrt{D}) \div 2.5$. The value of V should be determined for each stock. The value may be written as

$$V = \frac{C+B\,(S-P)}{P{\cdot}A}$$

and an average found using several price values. Select points using the striking price nearest above and below the stock price and use the full range of stock price swings. Select times where options have over one month to expiration. Avoid using points where the second term of Equation (10-1) is quite negative, that is, where the stock price is well below the striking price.

Equation (10-1) gives good values for *in the money calls*, that is, when the stock price is above the striking price, and for stock prices at or somewhat below the striking price when the option has several weeks or longer to expiration. For *out of the money calls*, that is, when the stock price is less than the striking price, Equation (10-3) gives good results for both long and short times to expiration:

$$C = \frac{\tfrac{1}{2}\,P{\cdot}V{\cdot}A^2 \log D}{\tfrac{1}{2}\,A \log D + (S-P)/P{\cdot}V} = \frac{P{\cdot}V{\cdot}A{\cdot}E}{E + (S-P)/P{\cdot}V} \qquad (10\text{-}3)$$

where the symbols have the same meaning as in Equation (10-1). The same value of V is used as determined above. Appendix D gives values of $E = \tfrac{1}{2}A \log D$.

The value of D, the number of market days to expiration, may merely be counted but a quick and practical way is to use the calendar day numbers found on most desk calendars. Subtract the present date number from the date number of the day the option expires and multiply by 0.7.

The values of calls computed using the above formulas are average values, or nominal values. At times the options will trade above or below the computed value, indicating they are overpriced or underpriced. You may use this information to advantage in selecting the particular option for purchase or sale and for setting up hedges. When several options are available, you may find one overpriced while another is underpriced. They may revert to nominal values or even reverse positions but this of course can not be depended upon.

You may find an average value of V over a long period of time including different types of markets and consider this the long-term nominal value. Comparisons of computed values and current values of the options give you an insight into the current option climate. Since options have a short life, buying and selling decisions are better made using values determined over a recent period of time. A good method is to use the average of the high and low values for the week of the options and of the underlying stock for substitution in the equation to determine V. Use options where the stock price and striking price are not widely different and where the option has over a month before expiration. The values for several different options on one stock are averaged and if desired the values for several weeks may be combined.

You may use the equations to investigate how different options behave. For example, if buying a call with the expectation of selling later at a profit, you can investigate which call stands to be the most profitable. You will find purchasing a call that is a few points out of the money (stock price a few points below the striking price) should yield a larger percentage gain, for a given increase in the stock price, than in the money calls. In fact, if you are fortunate enough to pick a stock which goes "straight up," it may be profitable to sell when the call becomes in the money and purchase the option having the next higher striking price, even though you will be paying extra commissions. A good "roll-over" point is near midway between striking prices. Conversely, if writing (selling) options, you should choose in the money calls.

EXAMPLES OF PRICE RELATIONS

Figure 10-1 shows the high-low-close price of the common stock of Atlantic Richfield. In addition, the January 100 and April 100 calls closing price on the CBOE are plotted. The value of V was determined by taking the average of four calculations ranging from 45 to 60 days before expiration for the January 100 call. During this time the common moved downward from about 110 to 100. Using the average value thus found of 0.0084, the values of the January and April calls were computed by Equation (10-2), using the closing price of the stock, at 10-day intervals. These values are shown on Figure 10-1 by circles. The agreement with the actual

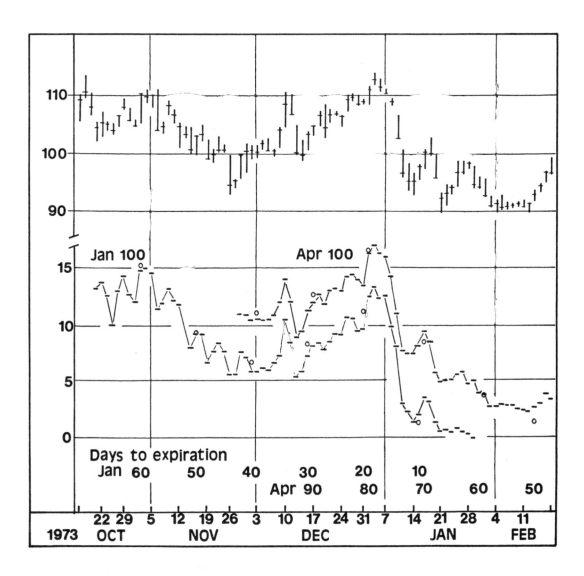

Figure 10-1. This chart of Atlantic Richfield illustrates how the prices of calls move. The closing prices of the January and April calls with striking price of 100 are plotted. The circles are call prices computed by use of the empirical Equation (10-2). Note the spread between the calls having the same characteristics except for time to expiration. Also note how the price of the calls decreases as the expiration date approaches.

call price is quite satisfactory. Note the computed point for February 13 which is low but also note the stock is selling nearly 10 points below the call striking price which is getting beyond the range suggested for good agreement. Using Equation (10-3) gives good agreement.

Figure 10-1 also illustrates other points previously discussed. Note how the value of the January 100 call trends downward as its expiration date approaches and vanishes on the last trading day since the stock price is under the striking price. Even though the common rose early in January 1974 to a value higher than the previous high of November 1973, the call did not even equal its previous high. This illustrates the time factor that must be taken into consideration in evaluating the future price of the option.

The high leverage of calls is well illustrated. The common fell from about 110 (closing price) to 95 during November, or 13%, but the January 100 call fell from 15 to 6, or 60%. Again in December the stock moved up from 100 to 113, or 13%, but the January 100 call increased from 5 ½ to 13, or 135%. At the same time the April 100 call moved up from 9 to 17, or 89%. Although the shorter-term calls undergo the greater percent swings, as just illustrated, if the prices fail to move in the expected direction, the call can expire before gains have been achieved.

Figure 10-2 is a chart of Brunswick with October and January calls. The value of V was determined from data over a three-week period in July and August 1973 using the October 20 call. The circles show computed values of the various calls. Note the low computed values of the October 15 call at 30 and 20 days before expiration. The quoted values are equal to the difference between the stock price and the striking price as expected when the time to go becomes short and the spread is large (over 10 points on a 15-point striking price). The computed values are satisfactory for the longer times to expiration for both the October and January calls and for the October 20 call where the price is closer to the striking price. This and the previous figure illustrate what can be expected from Equation (10-2).

When computing V it is better to throw out any *wild points*. When using closing price data there is no way of knowing when the closing price of the call occurred relative to the closing price of the stock. While only four data points were used in the examples and were taken over a short data span, you may want to use more points over a greater range.

Figure 10-3 is the chart of Sears showing the price of the common and the April call for a striking price of 60. The price of the common stock rounded a bottom in December 1974 at a price of about 45 and continued a determined upward path thereafter. The call was selling at about one-and-a-half to two and continued at about this level while the common gained 10 points or about 20%. It wasn't until late January 1975 that the

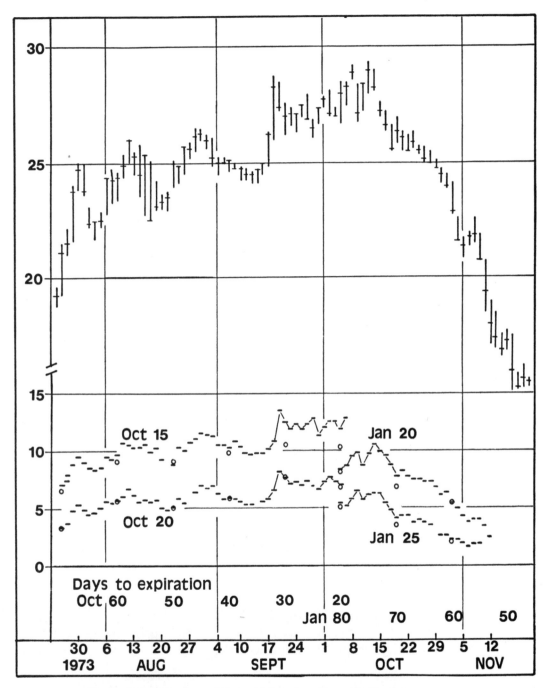

Figure 10-2. This chart of Brunswick and various calls illustrates the agreement of the prices given by Equation (10-2) with the actual call prices. The value of V, the only quantity characteristic of the stock, was determined from a short span of data near the beginning of the plot of the October 20 call, and used for all calls and for times up to three months later.

143

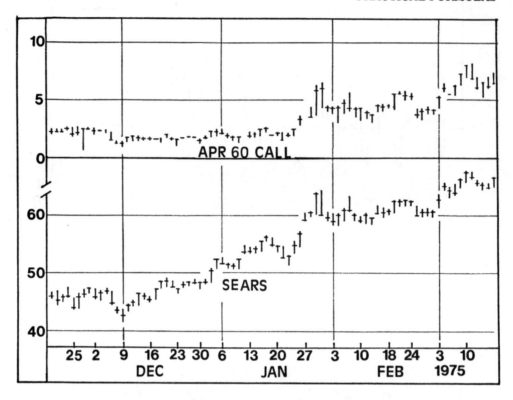

Figure 10-3. The price of Sears call did not move appreciably, even though the common stock was in a good uptrend, until the stock approached the striking price.

call came to life and began to respond to the uptrend of the common, as Sears rose to near the striking price of 60. This illustrates how a call will sell for some appreciable value even though the striking price is far above the price of the common, and how the call does not move appreciably while the stock price catches up. For trading purposes, this call would not have been a good buy in December or early January even though it might appear cheap. Your funds would have been tied up without being productive. As the stock price moves closer to the striking price, the call begins to respond and good profits are attainable.

COMPUTING DAILY RANGE

Most daily newspapers quote only the closing price for the exchange-traded options. When trading in options it is useful to know how much the option swings during the day. Equation (10-2) can provide a good estimate of the daily price range of the call in terms of the daily price range of the common stock. Let the subscript one denote the values in Equation (10-2) for one price relationship and the subscript two denote the values for a second price. Then, we can write

$$C_1 = P_1 \cdot V \cdot A + (P_1 - S)B \qquad (10\text{-}4)$$

$$C_2 = P_2 \cdot V \cdot A + (P_2 - S)B \qquad (10\text{-}5)$$

If Equation (10-5) is subtracted from Equation (10-4), then

$$C_1 - C_2 = (P_1 - P_2)V \cdot A + (P_1 - P_2)B \qquad (10\text{-}6)$$

Let $C_1 - C_2 = \Delta C$ and $P_1 - P_2 = \Delta P$, then[2]

$$\Delta C = (V \cdot A + B)\Delta P \qquad (10\text{-}7)$$

which involves only the constant V characteristic of the stock and constants A and B associated with the time the option has to go before expiring. The expression is independent of the price of the stock and the striking price of the call. Use of Equation (10-7) should be limited to conditions where the stock price and striking price are not widely different as discussed in the previous sections.

Summary

Exchange-traded call options are valued in terms of the price of the underlying stock, the time to expiration, the striking price, and a relative constant factor for each stock which can be determined from past data. Empirical formulas have been found to provide good estimates for assumed conditions. An option has a value that may be attributed to the privilege to purchase the stock at an agreed to price which combined with the spread between stock price and striking price gives the price at which the option trades. The time value part decreases as the expiration date approaches. When writing calls with the intent to cover (buy back) before it expires, this trend works with you, but if purchasing a call with the intent of selling at a higher price, time is against you as the decrease in time value cuts your profit spread.

---

[2]The symbol Δ is the Greek letter Delta.

When an option has several months to expiration, its price change is approximately two-thirds the price change of the underlying stock when the stock is selling near the striking price. When the stock is selling far below the striking price, the option will trade at some small value which remains nearly constant until the stock price catches up. Such an option is not cheap merely because its price is low.

11

Measuring the Market

HOW'S THE MARKET DOING?

Most people expect as an answer some response in terms of the Dow Jones Industral Average. It is the oldest market average, the most widely followed, most available in newspapers and radio and is computed nearly continuously. There are many who claim it does not measure the market, and other market averages have been developed which claim to do a better job. The various averages are derived in different ways. Their individual characteristics serve their own purposes. We are interested in selecting measures which serve our particular purpose.

THE DOW JONES INDUSTRIAL AVERAGE

The DJI Average is made up of 30 blue chip stocks traded on the NYS Exchange. Even though only 30 stocks are represented, they account for about 30% of the dollar asset value of all the companies listed on the NYSE. It is formed by adding together the prices of the 30 stocks and dividing by a number which has been adjusted over the years for stock splits etc. Thus, the higher-priced stocks affect the average more than a lower-priced stock. It is said to be *price-weighted*, which is held up as a fault as well as the stocks not being representative of the market as a whole.

This average has an advantage from the point of view that it is so readily available, and even the prices are published for hourly intervals daily in *The Wall Street Journal* and weekly in *Barron's*, and further the daily high and low values are provided. These features make it desirable to follow this average on a daily basis for short-term analysis. The left-hand side of Figure 11-1 compares several averages on a short-term basis and it may be observed that about the same fluctuations occur in all the averages. This figure shows the daily closing price which is the only value generally available for most of the averages. Using the high and low range plot of the DJIA, the very short-term variations are brought out even to a greater extent. This plot is carried in *The Wall Street Journal* and may be used to analyze the price movement showing cycles of a few days to a few weeks. However, I prefer to maintain my own plot for the reasons that price and date values can be more easily read if plotted on graph paper and I also join the pages of such a graph together to provide a longer time span than shown in the *Journal*.

THE STANDARD & POOR'S COMPOSITE AVERAGE

This average comprises 500 issues making it more representative than the DJIA. It also is *price-weighted* and furthermore is *size-weighted* by multiplying each stock price by the number of its shares outstanding.

THE NEW YORK STOCK EXCHANGE COMMON STOCK INDEX

This average uses all common stock issues listed on the exchange and is also *size-* and *price-weighted*.

UNWEIGHTED AVERAGES

With the aid of the electronic computer, averages are being computed in which equal weight is given to all stocks. Such averages as Value Line and Indicator Digest are commonly referred to. These are not as readily available as one might desire when doing your own thing. However, one of these or a similar average is frequently published by advisory services or shown in other financial publications. Of course you can subscribe for one of the services regularly supplying the desired data, usually on a week-ly basis, which may serve your purpose for long-term analysis. There is, however, an alternative in the Advance-Decline Line as a measure of the long-term market conditions.

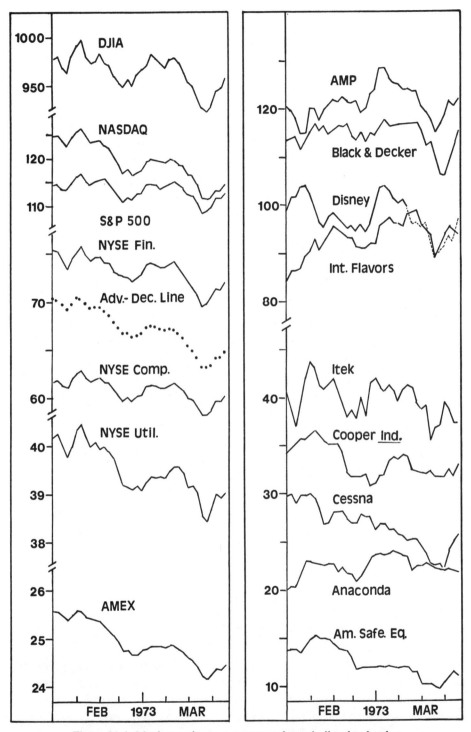

Figure 11-1. Market and group averages show similar day-by-day movements. Stocks generally show similar movements but have their own variations.

ADVANCE-DECLINE LINE

The *Advance-Decline Line* for the NYS Exchange is formed by cumulating the difference between the number of stocks advancing and the number declining on that exchange each day. The procedure is very simple. Just start with any arbitrary number such as 10,000 and each day add the number of stocks advancing and subtract the number of stocks declining. There are variations such as using weekly data, rather then daily data, and taking moving averages, ratios, etc., but the basic procedure is adequate and simple.

Much is written about divergence between advance-decline lines and stock averages and the ability to predict tops and bottoms of the market. It is true that usually the A-D line starts trending downward before the DJI Average reaches its peak at the end of a bull market in the DJIA. You are not primarily concerned, or shouldn't be, with when the DJI Average tops out but rather when your stocks top out, and your stocks have their own individual ideas. It is useful, however, to know what the majority of stocks are doing, or in other words what the state of the market is. The A-D line tells this. It is a broad measure and is independent of price and size. It also is independent of inflation factors. It has the characteristics of the unweighted market averages and is practical to compute from readily available data. A-D lines can of course be computed for the AMEX and the NASDAQ OTC markets but data is a little less available. The NYSE line is adequate for the average investor. The A-D line for the NYSE is shown as a dotted curve in Figure 11-1. It has the same variation as the averages on this short-term basis.

The A-D line should be considered merely as a measure of the state of the stock market. Its comparison with the DJI Average should be thought of as how one special group (the 30 blue chips) is behaving relative to the market. Don't get things turned around.

INDIVIDUAL STOCK MOVEMENTS

The right-hand side of Figure 11-1 shows plots of the closing prices of a variety of individual stocks for comparison with the averages. They all tend to show similar movements to the averages but exhibit certain individual characteristics. They may do better than the market (Anaconda), worse than the market (Cessna Aircraft), agree very closely with the market (Cooper Industries) and show sharper swings (Itek). Nevertheless, on a day-by-day basis the stocks in general move with the market.

Therefore, when market movements of a few days can be anticipated, it would be profitable to assume your stocks of interest will move likewise.

LONG-TERM BASIS

We have seen that almost any market average could be used for short-term movements, but we selected the DJI Average because of its greater availability and publication of daily high and low prices. This average may not serve as well for the longer trend. We want to know what the market as a whole is doing and when the DJIA is compared with an unweighted average, the long-term trends may differ considerably.

We have noted that the Advance-Decline Line has desirable characteristics for measuring the market. Because it is based only on the number of stocks advancing and declining there is no price or size weighting, that is, a high-priced stock has the same effect as a low-priced stock and the number of shares outstanding has no influence. Also dollar inflation does not enter into the result. While every stock listed may contribute its bit, use of the NYSE restricts the kinds of stocks to eliminate the more speculative and less well known. Therefore, the NYSE Advance-Decline Line is a good long-term measure of the market.

Measuring the market in this manner must be done by observation of trends, not absolute values which have no significance. The advances and declines do not permit prediction of the dollar value of some price average but only long-term trends. After all, there is no real need to know what price the DJIA is going to reach, even though there seems to always be an interest in predicting on this basis. What one really wants to know is what price one's stocks of interest are going to reach—up or down. This can be determined only by an analysis of the stock performance together with appropriate market *trends*. If one feels the necessity to predict the price of an average, then treat that average as an individual stock.

Summary

For the short term, any market average or general group average, will serve to show the short-term fluctuations. Likewise, the A-D Line shows the same characteristics. However, the better availability of the DJI Average together with publication of daily high and low makes it preferable for disclosing the short-term market movements. A daily high-low-close plot of the DJI Average is recommended. It may be observed that the day-by-day price movements of individual stocks will follow your market average. The short-term cycle prediction from the average (usually running from 5 to 9 days) may be expected to show up in the individual stocks and should be used for timing of transactions.

On a long-term basis, the *market averages* readily available are price and/or size weighted and in some cases represent a group average rather than a market average, including the DJIA. One desires an unweighted average but these are not as readily available as may be desired. A good alternative is the Advance-Decline Line of the NYS Exchange which has the characteristic of an unweighted average, also eliminates the dollar inflation factor and is easy to compute from data readily available on a daily basis. The A-D Line should be interpreted as *the market* and the *limited market averages* thought of as representing a group, including the long standing DJIA. Divergences, etc., between these representations should be considered as indicating how the group is responding relative to the market, rather than considering the group as the market.

12

Applying the Mathematical and Analytical Techniques (or Tools) You've Learned

In this chapter we will carry out an analysis of the DJI Average as an illustration of the procedures which have been described and as an example of the results which may be obtained. In order to fully bring out the range of results, a number of sections of data will be treated where one working in present time might be interested in only the more recent data.

The analysis is restricted to the single index (DJIA) to provide a common price reference for the various methods. It should be remembered that the DJIA may not be the best measure of the market for the long term. An unweighted average or advance-decline line is preferred for that purpose; so we will in the long term be investigating the movement of a market group—the 30 industrial blue chips. The short-term treatments work equally well with any of the measures and for the very short term the more frequent reporting of the DJIA makes it preferred.

THE SOURCE OF DATA

If one were merely updating the analysis, then past data should be on file. Regardless of what data one may use at a given time it is useful to retain the tabulations for future use.

In starting out without the benefit of a data file, there are various sources available which give much stock market data for past years. The

153

most complete is the *ISL Daily Stock Price Index* published by Investment Statistics Laboratory. The data is available from 1962. It consists of quarterly volumes, one for the NYSE, one for the AMEX and one for OTC stocks. It gives the daily data for all stocks listed on the Exchanges and for a large number of OTC stocks. Contained in these volumes are tabulations of the more common stock market statistics on a daily basis. These publications are usually available in the larger public libraries.

The DJI Average is reported daily in *The Wall Street Journal* and weekly, by the day and hour, in *Barron's*, other averages and statistics are also found in these publications. Back copies of these are frequently available in Public Libraries.

Lacking any of the above, one can purchase large wall charts of the market averages which go back many years. These usually provide a plot of the high-low-close price by the week. Values can be read off these charts for long-term analysis. See the advertisements in *Barron's* if you are interested in purchasing such a chart.

THE LONG-TERM TREND

When we speak of the long-term trend we are most likely referring to a cyclic movement whose period is several years in duration. When this cycle is long enough, even a straight line may satisfactorily represent the trend for the time span of the data desired to study. For the purpose of price prediction, we are usually interested in what is expected to happen in the matter of a few weeks to several months, or a year or two at the most. As has previously been pointed out, prediction is more accurate for the shorter times. As one looks farther into the future, the prediction can only be in broad general terms.

Studies have been made of very long spans of data to obtain the cyclic components which persist throughout the years. For example, a cycle of 9.225 years has been observed in both the DJI Average and Standard and Poor's Combined Stock Index[1]. Also a cycle ranging from 38 to 52 months has been observed[2] which has been quite reliable for long spans of time, but whose period has possibly shifted at times. These studies look for a cycle whose average period remains constant for many cycles, but at any one time the real data may move ahead or behind the ideal cycle. That is, the observed period is the average of many values.

---

[1] Shirk, Gertrude, "Current Status: The 9-year Cycle in Stock Prices", *Cycles*, vol. XXIV, No. 3 March 1973, 75-76.
[2] Shirk, Gertrude, "A Cycle Puzzlement", *Cycles*, vol. XXV, No. 6, June 1974, 130-134.

Our interest is in obtaining the best representation at the present time which will produce the most accurate near-term projection. We therefore confine our analysis to the most recent periods and even the last half period in some cases. Thus, the period and its timing (phase) may differ considerably from that given by the long-term average of many cycles.

Figure 12-1 is a plot of the average of the monthly high and low of the DJI Average taken from a large wall chart. This is easily done with the aid of a pair of dividers. Find the center of the high and low for the month by trial and error, then read this one value from the chart. Arrows indicate major lows which are obvious by inspection and are seen to be spaced by about four years. This is an indication of a prominent cycle. Also note a rather sizable low between each of these major lows indicating the presence of some shorter cycle.

THE 1970 LOW

We will apply the various methods of analysis to the DJI Average for the period including the 1966 major cyclic low and leading up to the 1970 low. This period covers about one period of the recurring four-year prominent cycle. Figure 12-2 is a plot of the DJI Average weekly high-low covering this period. Also shown, as dotted lines, the 3-month and 9-month moving averages of the mean of the weeks high and low. The smoothing of the price variation by these averages brings out the long cycle of perhaps about four years duration, and a shorter cycle also having a low in 1966, and a following low around early 1968. The amplitudes of both these cycles appear significant. Other shorter cycles are evident in the moving average as well as in the price data.

By observation we see the apparent long cycle closely resembles a third-degree polynomial curve. The data moves downward during 1966, reverses direction and generally swings upward until 1969, reverses again and trends downward. We will use the techniques of Chapter 8 and the procedure outlined in "Analyzing a Market Average" in Chapter 9. This procedure is relatively easy, the calculation is within reason, no detrending of the data is required, and a sine wave may be set up corresponding to the polynomial curve to give a representation of the desired long-term component of about four years, which has been a major recurring cycle over many years.

Proceeding with the calculation, we prepare Table 12-1 related to the plot of Figure 12-2 which gives in column 2 the data required to make a third-degree polynomial curve fit to 21 points taken at 10-week intervals of the 3-month centered moving average, over the 200-weeks span starting

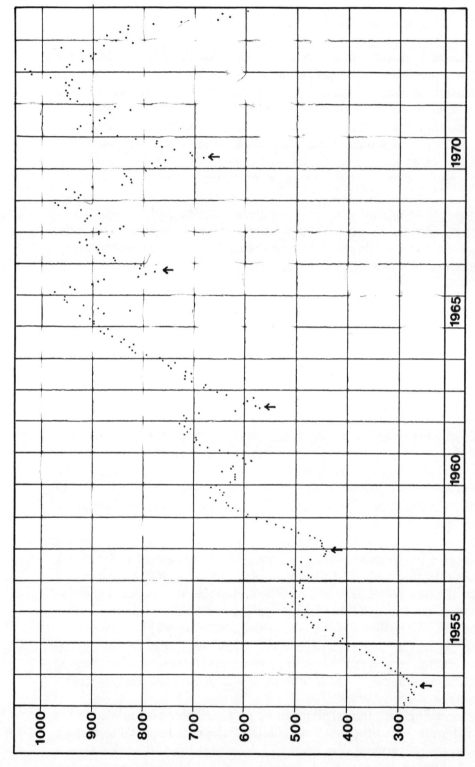

Figure 12-1. Mean of the monthly high and low of the DJI Average taken from a large wall chart.

156

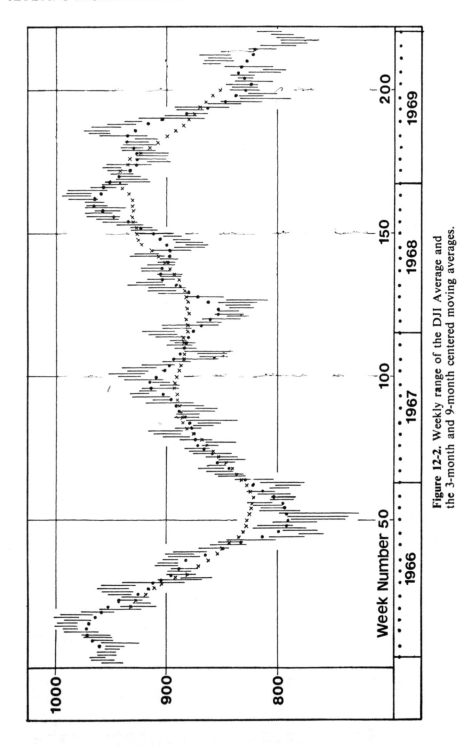

Figure 12-2. Weekly range of the DJI Average and the 3-month and 9-month centered moving averages.

Table 12-1

Data and calculations for least squares curve fitting to the DJI Average leading up to the 1970 low.

(1) Week No.	(2) 3-mo. Avg. y	(3) x	(4) y_s'''	(5) $f_1(t)$	(6) y''	(7) y_{sc}'''	(8) $f_2(t)$	(9) t	(10) a	(11) b	(12) ωt	(13) $\cos \omega t$	(14) $\sin \omega t$	(15) y_1	(16) Sum
0	968				929	56	−17	0			0	1.0000	.0000	−16	969
10	970	−10	14	956	925	38	7	1	7	0	53	.6018	.7986	8	971
20	953	−9	−2	955	920	16	17	2	17	6	106	−.2756	.9613	25	961
30	905	−8	−17	922	915	−9	−1	3	−1	−13	159	−.9336	.3584	22	928
40	848	−7	−31	879	911	−33	−30	4	−30	−66	212	−.8480	−.5299	2	880
50	790	−6	−41	831	907	−52	−65	5	−65	−55	265	−.0872	−.9962	−21	834
60	814	−5	−47	861	903	−64	−25	6	−25	−43	318	.7431	−.6691	−26	813
70	853	−4	−47	900	899	−68	22	7	22	19	11	.9816	.1908	−11	820
80	876	−3	−43	919	895	−63	44	8	44	71	64	.4384	.8988	13	845
90	891	−2	−32	923	891	−49	49	9	49	95	117	−.4540	.8910	27	869
100	910	−1	−19	929	888	−29	51	10	51	53	170	−.9848	.1736	19	878
110	883	0	−3	886	884	−5	4	11	4	10	223	−.7314	−.6820	−4	875
120	860	1	13	847	881	20	−41	12	−41	−36	276	.1045	−.9945	−23	878
130	880	2	27	853	878	42	−40	13	−40	−76	329	.8572	−.5150	−25	895
140	898	3	39	859	875	58	−35	14	−35	−68	22	.9272	.3746	6	927
150	912	4	46	866	873	67	−28	15	−28	7	75	.2588	.9659	17	957
160	965	5	47	918	870	67	28	16	28	−10	128	−.6157	.7880	27	964
170	943	6	44	899	867	58	18	17	18	52	181	−.9998	−.0175	15	940
180	930	7	36	894	865	41	24	18	24	39	234	−.5878	−.8090	9	897
190	903	8	23	880	863	19	21	19	21	−3	287	.2924	−.9563	−26	856
200	828	9	8	820	861	−6	−27	20	−27	19	340	.9397	−.3420	−22	833
210	827	10	−6	833	859	−30	−2	21			33	.8387	.5446	−1	828

at December 31, 1965 (week No. 10). From Appendix B, for $N = 21$, we find

$$\Sigma x^2 = 770 \qquad \Sigma x^4 = 50{,}666 \qquad \Sigma x^6 = 3{,}956{,}810$$

and we calculate the sums

$$\Sigma y = 18{,}639 \qquad \Sigma xy = -94 \qquad \Sigma x^2 y = 686{,}718 \qquad \Sigma x^3 y = -150{,}868$$

Setting up the coefficients for the Gauss reduction solution of the normal equations, we obtain the coefficients in $y_c''' = a + bx + cx^2 + dx^3$

$\Sigma Na =$	21	1	
$\Sigma x^2 =$	770	36.667	
$\Sigma y =$	18,639	887.571	$a = 882.20$
$\Sigma x^2 =$	770	0.0	
$\Sigma x^4 =$	50,666	29.1333	
$\Sigma x^2 y =$	686,718	4.271	$c = 0.147$
		- - - - - - - -	
$\Sigma x^2 =$	770	1	
$\Sigma x^4 =$	50,666	65.8	
$\Sigma xy =$	-94	-0.122	$b = 15.160$
$\Sigma x^4 =$	50,666	0.0	
$\Sigma x^6 =$	3,956,810	12.296	
$\Sigma x^3 y =$	-150,868	2.856	$d = -0.232$

and
$$y''' = 882.2 + 15.2x + 0.147x^2 - 0.232x^3 \tag{12-3}$$

The indicated period of the corresponding sine wave is $4\sqrt{-b/3d}$ or $4\sqrt{-15.2/3(-0.232)} = 18.69$ (in ten week units) or 187 weeks. The point of inflection of y''' is $x_i = -c/3d = 0.147/3(0.232) = 0.21$, which may be rounded to 0.2. This corresponds to week number 112. The reversal points are taken to be one-quarter period to either side of x_i, or at $x_m = -4.45$ and $+4.88$. Equation (12-3) is evaluated at these points and the indicated amplitude for the corresponding sine wave is taken as half the difference of the two values thus determined. Evaluating Equation (12-3) at point $x_m = -4.45$ is most easily accomplished by writing in the form (see Page 225, "Evaluating a Polynomial" in Chapter 16).

$$y_m = [\{(-0.232)\,(-4.45) + (0.147)\}\,(-4.45) + 15.2]\,(-4.45) + 882.2 = 837.9$$

In like manner, the value when x = 4.88 is 932.9. With a minicomputer, the value of x is stored in memory and recalled for multiplication each time. The indicated amplitude is taken as 47.5. We now have all the information required to write down the corresponding sine wave equation. The frequency is found to be $\omega = 360°/$I.P., or $360°/18.69 = 19.3°/10$ weeks. At the midpoint, taken as x_i, the sine must be zero which determines the phase. The complete equation is then

$$y_s''' = 47.5 \sin 19.3\,(x - 0.2) \tag{12-4}$$

We will use Equation (12-4) as a tentative representation of the dominant cycle in this time span and examine the data for trend by the procedures described in "The Effect of Trend" in Chapter 8. The values of y_s''' are tabulated in column 4 of Table 12-1 and the *detrended data* $y - y_s''' = f_1(t)$ is tabulated in column 5. A second degree fit to these data gives the equation

$$y'' = 884.4 - 3.27x + 0.075x^2 \tag{12-5}$$

This equation indicates a rather strong downward trend, the term $-3.27x$ producing a drop of 65 points from $x = -10$ to $+10$, or 68% of the peak-to-peak amplitude of the y_s''' wave. Correcting Equation (12-3) for this trend, the coefficient of x becomes $15.2 + 3.3 = 18.5$ and recomputing the indicated period gives a value of 20.6 or 206 weeks.

We saw in "Errors in Period and Amplitude" in Chapter 8 that the period derived from the cubic equation is usually too long. Using Appendix C to correct the period results in one of about 174 weeks. The phase is not changed by these corrections and thus x_i remains at x = 0.2. The new cubic equation needs to be evaluated at $x_1 = -4.15$ and $x_2 = 4.55$ for a new determination of amplitude. This results in $y_1 = 824.7$ and $y_2 = 947.4$ giving A = 61.4. The ratio of data span to corrected period is 1.15 and the span is well centered. Obtaining a correction for amplitude from Appendix C gives the amplitude as 68.46. The corrected sine wave equation is now, (rounding values)

$$y_{sc}''' = 68 \sin 21\,(x - 0.2) \tag{12-6}$$

This cycle has a low at week number 69 and a high at 155. Projecting into the future, the next low will occur when sin 21 (x − 0.2) is minus one, or when the angle 21 (x − 0.2) is 270°. Solving for x, its value is 13.06 corresponding to week number 241, or about 21 weeks beyond January 1970, that is, late May.

Since Equation (12-6) differs from Equation (12-4), one could use this *improved* equation to detrend the basic data, then determine a new long-term trend and a new correction, etc. We will, however, proceed with the analysis.

The original data y will now be detrended by subtracting the long-term trend y'' and the major cycle just found, y_{sc}'''. The resulting values are designated $f_2(t)$ and are tabulated in column 8 of Table 12-1. We note that these data exhibit a cyclic movement covering something over two cycles. We will make a single frequency trigonometric fit to these data starting at week number zero and designating this time as $t = 0$. See "Fitting a Single Frequency" in Chapter 8 for the procedures. The calculations are tabulated in columns 9 through 15 of Table 12-1. The frequency is determined first. We have

$$\Sigma a^2 = 21{,}675 \qquad \alpha = 1.1902 \qquad \omega = 53.48°/10 \text{ weeks}$$

$$\Sigma ab = 25{,}793 \qquad \cos \omega = 0.5951 \qquad T = 6.73 \text{ or } 67 \text{ weeks}$$

Rounding the frequency to 53°/10 weeks, the amplitudes A and B are found. The sums required and the solution using the Gauss reduction are

$\Sigma \cos^2\omega = 11.523793$	1.0	
$\Sigma \cos \omega t \sin \omega t = 0.3402717$	0.0295277	
$\Sigma \cos \omega t \cdot f_2(t) = -187.0431$	−16.231036	$A = -15.583193$
$\Sigma \sin \omega t \cos \omega t = 0.3402717$	0.0	
$\Sigma \sin^2 \omega t = 10.475938$	30.757452	
$\Sigma \sin \omega t \cdot f_2(t) = 224.10055$	674.82401	$B = 21.940179$

Writing in sine form, (see "Periodic-Wave Equations" in Chapter 5) we have $C = \sqrt{A^2+B^2} = -26.9$ (C has the sign of A), $\tan \phi = A/B = -0.71026$ giving $\phi = 144.6°$ resulting in

$$y_1 = -26.9 \sin 53 (t+2.73) \qquad (12\text{-}7)$$

Evaluation of this equation is tabulated in column 15 of Table 12-1. Column 16 gives the sum of y'', y_{sc}''' and y_1 and this sum is plotted on Figure 12-3 as Y together with the 3-month moving average for comparison, and to illustrate the agreement. The individual components are also plotted in this figure.

It is important to remember that these components do not necessarily occur in the basic data but are merely a *best fit* to the data under various assumptions. Had different spans of data been used the results could have been somewhat different. The y_1 curve, whose period is 68 weeks, was fitted to a span of data of 210 weeks or three periods. The period probably varies over this span, and to get the best fit over the entire span with a fixed period, the amplitude will be different from the best amplitude for each period. If we split up the 210-week span into three sections and make separate fits, a better overall representation may be obtained. You may want to experiment with this as an exercise. All the basic data are contained in Table 12-1. Remember there are shorter-term components, some in the data used, and others smoothed out by the moving average. To get a more accurate estimate, one should examine the near-term data on an expanded scale. For example, use a daily plot of the past year with shorter moving average smoothing, such as a 30-day span.

HOW IT CAME OUT

The analysis made to this point can be used to make general predictions for the next few months. Although these long-term components will be modified as time goes on, they do not change rapidly so we can predict the general time and price on average. The farther into the future, the greater the likely error. Near-term movements may appear at considerable variance due to shorter components not considered, but these will correct themselves bringing prices back to the general long-term movement. Keeping these variations in mind, let us compare the projection of the major components we have found with what actually happened.

We noted that the next projected low of the 3.3 year cycle, y_{sc}''', is at week number 241. The 68-week cycle y_1, has its next projected low about week number 262. We may be particularly interested in the next major low. Except for shorter cycles not included in the analysis, this should occur in the region of the broad bottom of the 3.3 year cycle when the next shorter, 68-week cycle makes its bottom. If its period continues, this will be somewhat before week number 262 as the 3.3 year bottom will have been passed before the bottom of the shorter cycle. There is a tendency for

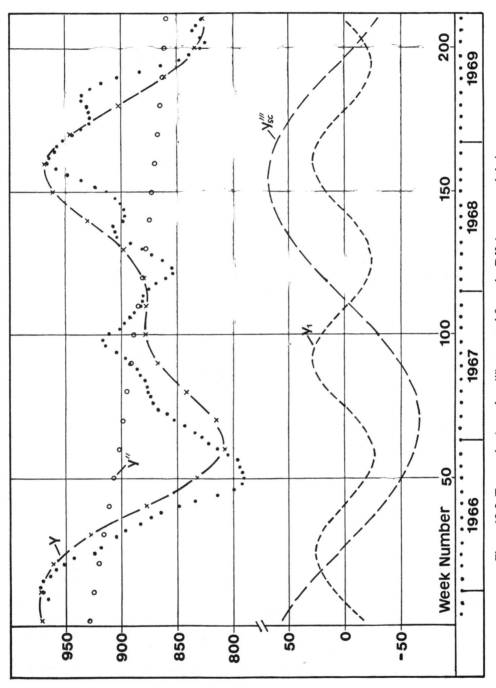

Figure 12-3. Two cycles (y_1 and y_{SC}''') extracted from the DJI Average and their sum added to the extracted long-term trend (y'') to give (Y) which may be compared with the 3-month moving average (dotted curve).

cycles to move into phase at major tops and bottoms. We should be alert for the low occurring between week numbers 240 and 262. The long-term trend y'' will fall to between 856 and 853. The major cycle y_{sc}''' will drop the price about 68 points and the y_1 cycle can drop the average another 27 points. These values represent a smoothed average which is thus projected to be as low as $853 - 68 - 27 = 758$.

The 9-month moving average made its low of 744 at week 241, or the week ending June 5, 1970. It was within 5 points of its low over the period between week numbers 234 and 249. The 3-month moving average made its low of 703 at week number 242. The DJI Average made its low of the year at 627.5 on May 26 at week number 239. This absolute value includes all the shorter cycles which we have ignored.

THE 1972-3 HIGH

The time is early November 1971, the market has fallen since spring after a good rise over a period of a year. Was a market high made and a major decline started, or do we have another chance? We will make a cycle analysis and see what it implies. Figure 12-4 shows, as a dotted line, the 3-month centered moving average of the DJI Average. It is similar to Figure 12-2 except inverted, or opposite in phase.

If we compare the rise from the 1966 low to the 1968 high in Figure 12-2 with the rise starting from the 1970 low, the present price movement could be a secondary reaction like that of the last half of 1967. On the other hand, it may be that the top has been made and the market will continue downward. We will proceed as in "The 1970 Low" in this chapter and first make a cubic equation fit to the 3-month moving average between weeks 130 and 310. Next we will find a corresponding sine wave representation, remove this cyclic component from the data, and fit a second-degree polynomial to the remaining data to give a long-term trend y''. From this trend we will take the coefficient of the first power of x and subtract it from the corresponding coefficient of the cubic equation to correct it for trend. A new indicated period is computed from the modified cubic equation and this value is then corrected for span length by Appendix C to give the corrected period which will be used to determine the frequency in the final sine wave equation representing the long cycle. The values of the modified cubic equation are determined at points a quarter period either side of the point of inflection of this cubic equation and half the difference is used as a tentative value of the sine wave amplitude which is then corrected by Appendix C. The final sine wave

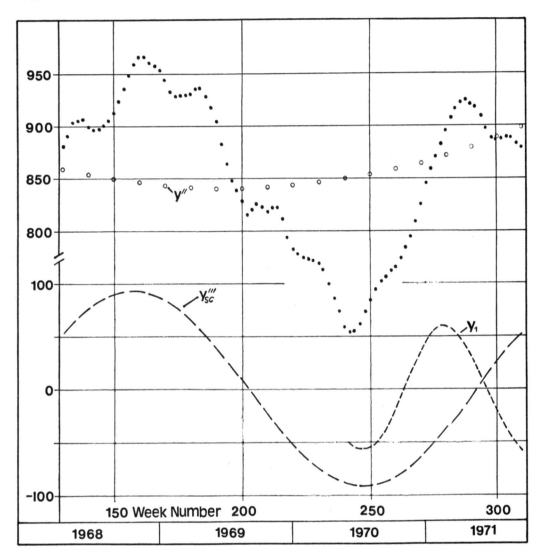

Figure 12-4. The 3-month moving average of the DJI Average (dotted curve) and the extracted long-term trend (y''), together with the extracted major cycle (y''') and intermediate cycle (y_1).

equation y_{sc}''' is now written down with its phase so that it is zero at the point of inflection of the cubic equation. The next step is to find the next longest cycle. We detrend the original moving average data by subtracting the long-term trend y'' and long cycle y_{sc}'''. Usually these data show a single prominent shorter cycle which is determined by a one-frequency trigonometric fit.

The sums required for the cubic equation fit are found from Table 12-2 and Appendix B. They are:

$$\Sigma y = 16{,}246 \qquad\qquad \Sigma x^2 = 570$$

$$\Sigma xy = -2{,}535 \qquad\qquad \Sigma x^4 = 30{,}666$$

$$\Sigma x^2 y = 507{,}089 \qquad\qquad \Sigma x^6 = 1{,}956{,}810$$

$$\Sigma x^3 y = -50{,}889$$

The cubic equation is $y''' = 811.5 - 19.43x + 1.453x^2 + 0.278x^3$. We obtain

Indicated period = 19.307 (in 10-week units)

Point of inflection, $x_i = -1.7422$

$$x_1 = -6.569 \qquad\qquad x_2 = 3.08453$$

$$y_1 = 923.0 \qquad\qquad y_2 = 773.6 \qquad\qquad A = 74.72$$

The tentative sine wave equation is $y_S''' = -74.7 \sin 18.65\,(x + 1.74)$. Removing the values of y_S''' from the original data, y, and making the long term fit we obtain for the trend

$$y'' = 842.7 + 2.112x + 0.438x^2 \tag{12-8}$$

The cubic y''' is adjusted for trend by subtracting $2.112x$ to give

$$y_C''' = 811.5 - 21.54x + 1.453x^2 + 0.278x^3 \tag{12-9}$$

The indicated period from this equation is 20.3 in 10-week units. The ratio of span length to indicated period is $180/203 = 0.89$. Using Appendix C to correct for span, the corrected period becomes 180 weeks. Equation (12-9) is evaluated to obtain new values of the indicated amplitude where $x_1 = -6.2$, and $x_2 = 2.8$ giving $y_1 = 935$ and $y_2 = 769$. Using Appendix C, a corrected amplitude of 93 is established. The corrected equation is

$$y_{SC}''' = -93 \sin 20\,(x + 1.74) \tag{12-10}$$

The original data y is detrended by subtracting the long-term trend y'' and the long-period cyclic component y_{SC}''' to give $f_1(t)$. The evaluation of these quantities is tabulated in Tables 12-2 and 12-3. A trigonometric fit is made to these data over the span between weeks 240 to 310. The calculations are tabulated in Table 12-3 in the portion above the heavy broken

Table 12-2

Data and computations for making least squares fits to the DJI Average for the period leading up to the 1972-3 high.

Week No.	x	3-mo. y	y_s'''	f(t) $y-y_s'''$	y''	y_{sc}'''
130	−9	880	52	828	859	53
140	−8	898	66	832	854	76
150	−7	912	74	838	849	90
160	−6	965	73	892	846	93
170	−5	943	65	878	843	84
180	−4	930	50	880	841	66
190	−3	903	30	873	840	40
200	−2	828	6	822	840	8
210	−1	827	−18	845	841	−24
220	0	781	−40	821	843	−53
230	1	768	−58	826	845	−76
240	2	709	−70	779	849	−90
250	3	733	−74	807	853	−93
260	4	765	−74	839	858	−84
270	5	825	−60	885	864	−66
280	6	895	−43	938	871	−40
290	7	920	−22	942	879	−8
300	8	886	2	884	888	28
310	9	878	26	852	897	53

Table 12-3

Computations used in making a trigonometric fit of the intermediate cycle approaching the 1972-3 high for the span between weeks 240 and 310. The data below the broken line is used to update the frequency of this cycle.

Week No.	y	y''	y_{sc}'''	t	$f_1(t)$	a	b	ωt	$\cos \omega t$	$\sin \omega t$	y_1
240	709	849	−90	0	−50			0.0	1.0000	.0000	−49
250	733	853	−93	1	−27	−27	−59	54.8	.5764	.8171	−56
260	765	858	−84	2	−9	−9	0	109.6	−.3355	.9421	−16
270	825	864	−66	3	27	27	55	164.4	−.9632	.2689	37
280	895	871	−40	4	64	64	76	219.2	−.7749	−.6320	59
290	920	879	−8	5	49	49	34	274.0	.0698	−.9976	31
300	886	888	28	6	−30	−30	−23	328.8	.8554	−.5180	−24
310	878	897	53	7	−72	−72	−152	23.6	.9164	.4003	−58
320	862	908	76		−122	−122	−158				
330	923	919	90		−86	−86	−193				
340	953	931	93		−71						

line. This covers about one period of a cycle which appears to be building up at this time. This results in the equation, where t = 0 at week 240,

$$y_1 = -59.5 \sin 54.8 \, (t+1) \qquad \text{(12-11)}$$

The maximum of Equation (12 - 10) will occur when the angle $20(x + 1.74) = 270°$ or at x = 11.8 corresponding to week number 338. The maximum of Equation (12-11) occurs when angle $54.8(t + 1) = 630°$ or at t = 10.5 corresponding to week number 345. These two cycles are peaking some six or more months in the future. It is clear that the market has not reached its high. The present decline is due to a cycle of about 66-weeks duration. This cycle with the 3.5-year major cycle should carry the average to a new high in 1972. A better estimate of when can be made after a few more months of data become available. The intermediate cycle is at its low so prices should rise very soon with both cycles pushing upward.

At this point it is interesting to compare the results of this analysis with that previously carried out for the 1970 low. The long-term trend is seen to be downward from 1966 to 1969 where it turns upward.

The two trends are offset by about 20 points where they overlap. There is an indication that this trend is in reality a cycle of long duration. Greater data spans will be required to obtain its value. One may make a new fit to the overall span, giving a better value. You may want to do this from the data provided in the Tables. I suggest using a longer interval for the samples, 20 or 30 weeks, to reduce the computations. The major cycle had a period of 174 weeks in the first analysis and 180 weeks in this last analysis—nearly the same. The amplitude increased by 36%. This could be a trend to watch to see if it continues to build up. A peak amplitude occurred at week 155 for the first and 158 for the second, showing a good phase agreement. In other words, this major cycle continued through this six-year period with little variation except possibly an increasing amplitude.

The next shorter cycle had a period of 68 weeks during 1967-69 and 66 weeks during 1970-71. The maxima occurred at week 270 for the first and 279 for the second. This agreement is good, particularly considering the number of cycles involved. It indicates that there was a cycle of about one-and-a-third years running through this entire time span.

TIME FOR UPDATING

By early June, 1972, 30 weeks later than our last analysis, the secondary reaction due to the 66-week cycle was complete and the Dow had risen a hundred points to new highs. If the major cycles continue, as predicted, this could be the top. The Dow dropped 30 points the past week. It is time to update the analysis. We have 30 weeks of new data up to week number 340 in the 3-month moving average, which hasn't started turning down yet. We would not expect much change in the long-term trend or the major long cycle, but the next shorter cycle has advanced about half a period. We simply extend Equations (12-8) and (12-10) and detrend the moving average by subtracting these two components. A one-frequency trigonometric fit is made to this detrended data between weeks 240 and 340 where t = 0 at week 240. The resulting equation is

$$y_2 = -80 \sin 38.3 (t+3.3) \qquad \textbf{(12-12)}$$

We see an increase in amplitude and period over that of Equation (12-11). The next predicted high will be where the angle 38.3(t + 3.3) = 630° or at t = 13.15 corresponding to week number 372 or early December 1972. This implies the market may have a way to go before a final downturn. The long cycle previously found is in its flat top portion at the present time and should be about 32 weeks or one-third the way down by December. This corresponds to a 15% drop in amplitude or about 13 points. This will not show up to any extent against the strong upward swing of the 94-week updated cycle, Equation (12-12).

Prior to this updating we should have been watching the intermediate cycle. It was last analyzed when the moving average data reached week number 310 and we were using 10-week intervals for data points. It is very easy to check the period at each 10-week interval. Refer to Table 12-3 which contains the tabulation for the trigonometric curve fit previously made in the numbers above the heavy broken line. Also in this table are three additional lines of numbers which provide the extension of the moving average y, the long-term trend y'' and the major cycle y_{sc}'''. These values and the numbers in columns a and b are filled in one interval at a time as the data becomes available. The two sums required to recompute the frequency are simply found by adding on the proper quantity to the sum previously found. The results are:

As of Week No.	Σa^2	Σab	cos ω	ω deg./10-wks.	T weeks
310	8 936	10 298	0.5762	54.8	67
320	14 120	21 242	0.7522	41.2	87
330	29 004	40 518	0.6985	45.7	79
340	36 400	57 116	0.7846	38.3	94

This shows that the length of the period was increasing as early as the first check. It is not necessary to find the amplitude and phase each time. This increasing period indicates the turning point is going to be farther into the future so we can wait until we are closer to that time and when the data has advanced enough to make it worthwhile.

Figure 12-5 shows in the lower portion the extended plot of the major cycle given by Equation (12-10), and the updated intermediate cycle given by Equation (12-12). In the upper portion the extended long-range trend, Equation (12-8), is shown. The two sine waves, shown below, are added to this trend to produce a projected DJI Average shown as a dashed line. The dotted line is the actual 3-month moving average. This average did peak at about the same time as the projection, though at a somewhat lower level. The rather strong upward trend of Equation (12-8) is suspect in this region. It can only bend in one direction and the x square term becomes overpowering as x is extended to the larger values. For better price agreement, this equation should be updated if such information is important. You may want to run an update analysis from the data provided in Tables 12-2 and 12-3 to see how well the price values are predicted.

THE 1974-5 LOW

We plot, as before, the 3-month moving average of the DJI Average in Figure 12-6 as a dotted line. The span of data from 1969 through 1974, including the 1970 low and the 1972-3 high, appears to cover about one period of our recurring 4-year cycle. We will fit a cubic equation to this span of data between week numbers 190 and 470. The data values are given in Table 12-4. The sums for 15 data points taken at 20-week intervals are

$$\Sigma y = 12{,}866 \qquad \Sigma x^2 = 280$$

$$\Sigma xy = -262 \qquad \Sigma x^4 = 9{,}352$$

$$\Sigma x^2 y = 226{,}782 \qquad \Sigma x^6 = 369{,}640$$

$$\Sigma x^3 y = -68{,}236$$

which results in the solution

$$y''' = 918.3 + 33.75x - 3.244x^2 - 1.03844x^3 \qquad \text{(12-13)}$$

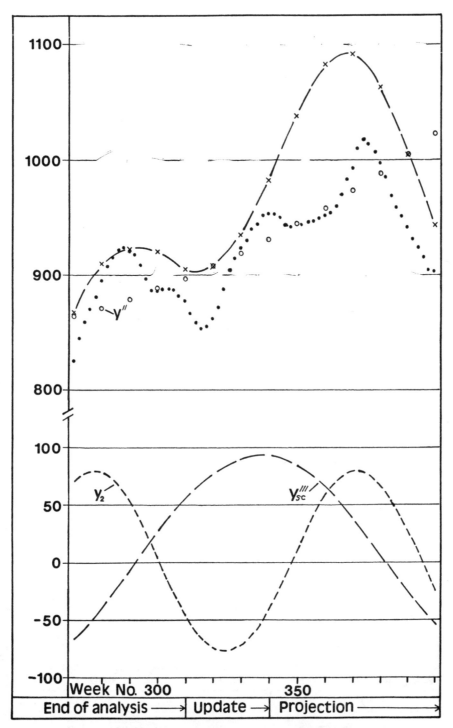

Figure 12-5. Extracted components are projected and combined to predict the future trend of the DJI Average (dashed line) compared with the 3-month moving average (dotted line).

171

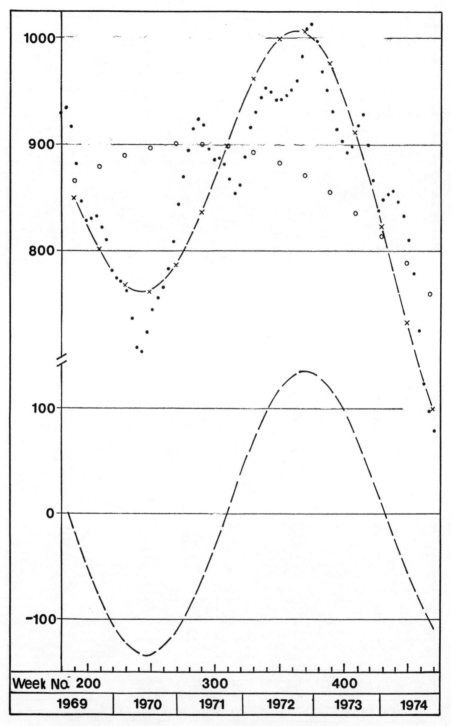

Figure 12-6. The 3-month moving average of the DJI Average, the long-term trend, the major cycle and the sum of the extracted components.

172

Table 12-4

Computations for the analysis of the DJI Average in the period 1969 to 1974.

Week No.	x	y	y_s'''	$y-y_s'''$	y''	y_{sc}'''	$y''+y_{sc}'''$
190	−7	904	−25	929	866	−16	850
210	−6	827	−59	886	880	−79	801
230	−5	768	−81	849	890	−123	767
250	−4	733	−84	817	897	−136	761
270	−3	825	−68	893	901	−114	787
290	−2	920	−38	958	901	−64	837
310	−1	878	0	878	899	0	899
330	0	923	40	883	893	69	962
350	1	943	70	873	883	117	1000
370	2	993	84	909	871	136	1007
390	3	941	80	861	855	121	976
410	4	911	58	853	836	75	911
430	5	841	22	819	814	10	824
450	6	821	−18	839	789	−57	732
470	7	638	−54	692	760	−110	650

The inflection point is $x_i = -c/3d = -1.04$. The reversal points are displaced from this point by $\sqrt{-b/3d} = 3.29$. These locations are then $x_1 = -4.33$ (minimum) and $x_2 = 2.25$ (maximum). The y values at these reversal points are $y_1 = 795.6$ and $y_2 = 966$ giving the indicated amplitude as 85.2. The indicated period is $4 \cdot 3.29 = 13.17$ (in 20-week units) and the frequency is $27.3°/20$ weeks. The corresponding sine wave equation is then

$$y_s''' = 85 \sin 27.34 \, (x+1.04) \qquad (12\text{-}14)$$

Detrending the moving average with Equation (12-14) and making a second degree fit to the remainder gives the long-term trend

$$y'' = 892.6 - 7.664x - 1.623x^2 \qquad (12\text{-}15)$$

Correcting Equation (12-13) for trend by subtracting the term $-7.664x$ gives a corrected cubic equation from which we compute the period and amplitude and make corrections from Appendix C to give the final sine wave representation

$$y_{sc}''' = 136 \sin 29.1 (x+1.04) \qquad \text{(12-16)}$$

This equation has a period of 247 weeks or 4.75 years. Its low is at week 495 (Spring of 1975) and the next high will be mid 1977.

The moving average is now detrended by subtracting the long-term trend Equation (12-15) and the major cycle Equation (12-16). These two equations, and their sum, are plotted in Figure 12-6. The difference between the sum and the 13-week moving average shows the shorter cycles which remain. From week number 430 to the end of the plot there appear about three-quarters of an intermediate cycle. This is determined by a trigonometric fit. Its equation

$$y_I = 87 \sin 46.55 (t+0.22) \qquad \text{(12-17)}$$

where t = 0 at week 430 and is in 10-week intervals. This equation had a maximum at week 447 (mid May, 1974) and a minimum is due at week 485, or early February, 1975.

At this point, our analysis shows a downward sloping long-term trend, a major cycle approaching its low at week number 495, Spring of 1975, and an intermediate cycle approaching its low at week number 485. In other words, we are near a major market reversal.

The next high of the intermediate cycle is due at week number 525, or around the Fall of 1975. This should be a good secondary recovery but the market should again fall off. The major cycle moving upward and the long-term trend moving downward will more or less neutralize each other so the movement will be largely due to the intermediate cycle together with short-term components. The extreme range could, however, amount to 200 Dow points.

Comparing this analysis with the previous ones, we note that the amplitude of the major cycle has increased again. It went from 68 to 93 to 136. The period increased again, even to a greater extent than before. The 4.75-year period is more in keeping with the average over the years. The first low in the 1974 analysis was at week number 247 compared with 241 found for the previous time span.

THE LONG-TERM REPRESENTATION

We now have nine years of data on a weekly basis used in the three time spans which have been treated individually. Also we have extracted the major cyclic component from the 3-month moving average. Figure 12-7 shows the plot of this major cycle for the three time periods. We will assume a composite curve made up as follows: Curve 1 is used to week number 120, then curve 2 to week number 190 and, thereafter, curve 3. This composite curve is subtracted from the 3-month moving average at 20-week intervals and a second-degree fit is made to the resulting data. In this 9-year span, any remnants of the major cycle will be smoothed out. This then will give us a better long-term trend. The resulting equation for x = 0 at week 250 using 20-week intervals is

$$y'' = 885.5 - 3.22x - 0.356x^2 \qquad \text{(12-18)}$$

THE SHORTER CYCLES

Having obtained a better estimate of the long-term trend, the projection into the future will now use these values. This long-term component and the major cyclic component are now combined and the 30-day moving average detrended to give data for a revised determination of the recent intermediate trend. Using the shorter-span moving average introduces less delay in the data than the 3-month average and it is not significantly different in this region. The data are tabulated in Table 12-5. The one-frequency trigonometric fit to f(t) for weeks 430 to 475 where t = 0 at week 430 is

$$y_2 = -69 \sin 35.7 \, (t + 4.6) \qquad \text{(12-19)}$$

We used five-week data intervals for the units of t. The period thus is 50 weeks compared to 77 weeks previously obtained, Equation (12-17). This intermediate cycle is added to all longer period components and plotted on Figure 12-8, as a dashed line, together with the DJI Average daily high-low range, the 10-day moving average and the 60-day moving average. We note the sum of all components found thus far (dashed line) follows closely the 60-day moving average. This average passes 95% of the

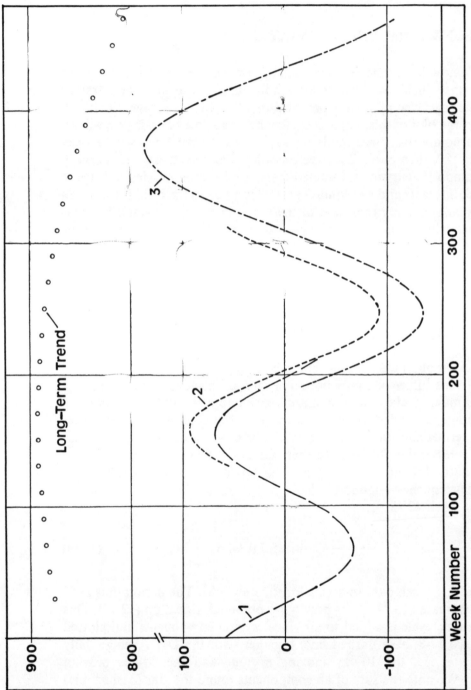

Figure 12-7. The major cycle of the DJI Average as extracted for three time periods shows good phase agreement and an increasing amplitude with time. The long-term trend resulted from fitting the data after detrending by a composite of the three sections of the major cycle.

Table 12-5

Computations used in projecting the longer cycles and making a fit to data of a daily chart.

Week No.	Day No.	y''	y$_{sc}$'''	Sum Long Comp.	30-day Avg.	t	f(t)	a	b	ωt	cos ωt	sin ωt	y₂
430	141	828	9	837	851	0	14			0.0	1.0000	.0000	−19
435	165	825	− 8	817	847	1	30	30	81	35.7	.8121	.5835	24
440	190	823	− 25	798	865	2	67	67	94	71.4	.3190	.9478	57
445	214	820	− 42	778	842	3	64	64	131	107.1	−.2940	.9558	69
450	238	818	− 58	760	824	4	64	64	108	142.8	−.7965	.6046	55
455	263	815	− 73	742	786	5	44	44	60	178.5	−.9997	.0262	20
460	288	812	− 87	725	721	6	− 4	− 4	− 25	214.2	−.8271	−.5621	−22
465	311	809	− 99	710	641	7	−69	−69	− 48	249.9	−.3437	−.9391	−56
470	336	807	−110	697	653	8	−44	−44	−137	285.6	.2689	−.9632	−69
475	360	804	−120	684	616	9	−68			321.3	.7804	−.6252	−56

50-week cycle and all longer cycles, but smooths out most of the shorter components present (see Chapter 7). If allowance were made for the 5% loss of amplitude, the two curves would be even closer together.

We can see that there is a significant short cycle exhibited by the 10-day moving average moving about the projected dashed line. This can be analyzed using daily data. The 10-day average is detrended by the dashed line and a one-frequency trigonometric fit results in the equation

$$y_3 = -38.6 \sin 24.3 (t+7.1) \tag{12-20}$$

when fitted to the span of days 320 to 375 using five-day intervals for t and where $t = 0$ at day 320. The values of $f(t)$ may be read graphically from Figure 12-8. The sum of all components is plotted as a solid line on Figure 12-8. This short cycle of 74 days constitutes a trading cycle whose low was at day number 377 and will reach its next high at day 414 or near the middle of February 1975. A mild reaction should then follow at a level of about 750, but the market will then be moving up strong under the influence of the 50-week intermediate cycle and should soon resume its upward trend.

Besides this short cycle, we see in Figure 12-8 that there are minor fluctuations of the daily prices whose periods are even shorter. These can be picked out by noting the low values of the daily range. A low is defined as a day which reaches a lower price than reached on the previous or following day. On this basis, lows occured as follows:

Day Number	318	321	324	330	332	337	342	345	349	355	357	363
Difference		3	3	6	2	5	5	3	4	6	2	6

indicating a very short cycle of about three days. If we also mark the lows that are lower than the lows to either side, we have

Approximate Day No.	307	321	336	355	366
Difference		14	15	19	11

indicating a cycle whose period averages about 15 days. These short cycles can add or subtract 20 to 30 points on the average.

CYCLE SUMMARY

We have derived numerous equations representing the components found in the DJI Average for various spans of time. Those that apply to

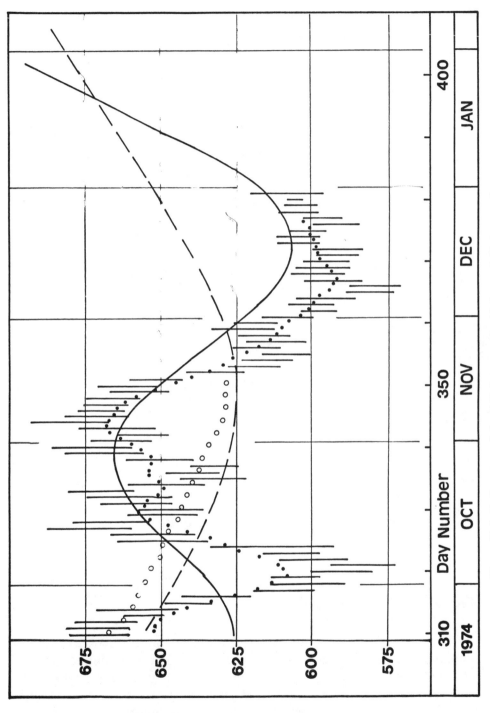

Figure 12-8. Daily range of the DJI Average, the 10-day and 60-day moving averages, and the sum of all extracted components (solid line) projected into the future.

the most recent data will be restated on a common basis. In each case we made the independent variable x equal zero at the center of the least squares data span in order to eliminate the odd powers of x in the calculation. We chose the data interval as some convenient value. Likewise, the independent variable t always equaled zero at the beginning of the data span for trigonometric curve fitting. We will change the equations so that the independent variable is expressed as week number, N_w, or day number N_d. For example, the long-term trend, Equation (12-18), $y'' = 885.5 - 3.22x - 0.356x^2$ is for $x = 0$ at week 250 and units of x represent 20 weeks. This becomes

$$y'' = 885.5 - 3.22\frac{1}{20}(N_w - 250) - 0.356\frac{1}{20^2}(N_w - 250)^2$$

That is, when $N_w = 250$ the quantity in parentheses becomes zero and when $N_w = 270$, the quantity in parentheses equals 20 or one interval of x. This equation, and others modified in the same manner, are then:

Equation Number	Equations	Designation
12-18	$y'' = 885.5 - 0.161(N_w - 250) - 0.0009(N_w - 250)^2$	L. T. Trend
12-16	$y_{sc}''' = 136 \sin 1.455(N_w - 309)$	Major Cycle
12-19	$y_2 = -69 \sin 7.14(N_w - 407)$	Intermediate Cycle
12-20	$y_3 = -38.6 \sin 4.86(N_d - 285)$	Trading Cycle

where week number zero is the week ending Friday October 22, 1965 or week number 500 is the week ending Friday May 23, 1975. Day number zero is June 28, 1973 and day number 500 is June 20, 1975.

FREQUENCY SCANNING

In "Time for Updating" in this chapter, the intermediate cycle was updated by adding a data interval to the trigonometric solution for determining frequency. This is a very simple calculation to carry out. One may want to follow a cycle on a more or less continuous basis. When the cycle is defined by a single-frequency trigonometric solution, changes in frequency may be picked up as they occur. The calculation may be carried out in a manner similar to a moving average—that is, a moving frequency. One first sets up a complete solution for an appropriate data span of N data points separated by uniform time intervals. The best frequency is determined by solving the equation cos ω = $\frac{1}{2}\alpha$, where α is given by $\alpha \Sigma a^2 = \Sigma ab$ (see "Fitting a Single Frequency" in Chapter 8). One maintains a running total of Σa^2 and of Σab, that is, as time increases by one-data interval, the new value of a^2 is added and the oldest value of a^2 is subtracted from Σa^2, likewise for Σab, and the new frequency is computed. This gives a running frequency for this component. As may be desired, the solution can be completed for amplitude and phase but unless the frequency changes, the amplitude and phase may be expected to remain about constant.

This technique of frequency scanning is useful for any detrended data, where the longer period components have been computed or extended through the region being scanned. One may want to track the trading cycle at 5-day intervals and the intermediate cycle at 10-week intervals.

Summary

Curve-fitting techniques may be used to obtain a cyclic representation of the price movement of a stock market average, group average, or even an individual stock. The cyclic components thus found are not necessarily in the basic data but only represent the best fit of a set of assumed mathematical curves to the past price movement.

Although average values of period and amplitude may be found for long spans of data, better overall representation is achieved by using short sections of data, of the order of one cycle, and letting the period, amplitude and phase vary from section to section. These sections may be combined to give a total cyclic representation. When done in this manner the changes from section to section are gradual and the individual cycles may be extended into the future and combined to predict the price. The results are satisfactory for times measured in fractions of the cycle period. That is, for long cycles of several years the projection can be expected to hold for a year or two with the agreement possibly deteriorating for the longer times. For best results the analysis should be updated when sufficient new data is accumulated to be significant. The short cycles need to be updated frequently in time, such as every half cycle. When the analysis has been completed for extended periods of time one can often observe a pattern in change of amplitude and period. This pattern should be taken into consideration in making estimates of future prices both as to value and time of occurrence of maxima and minima. Also remember that price movements may include significant very short cycles measured in days, which you may have averaged out in your curve-fitting analysis. These short time movements can best be estimated from observation of high-low charts of price movements.

For many years stock market averages have moved in cycles of bull and bear markets having a period of about four years, plus or minus several months. Any analysis should be built around this major cycle. Market data includes some positive price value as well as cycles of longer periods. Such components are of interest primarily only to provide a base value upon which the major and minor cyclic motions are superimposed. It is satisfactory to combine these components into a single polynomial curve of second degree. For short periods of time, as months, it may appear essentially as a straight line and may be extended on this basis. When projected for several years, care must be taken to avoid a large distortion showing up as a major curvature resulting from the fact that the second-degree equation can bend in only one direction, whereas the data may in fact go through a point of inflection.

In this chapter we have demonstrated an analysis technique using curve fitting to about nine years of the DJI Average. We first obtained individual representations of the major cycle around two bear bottoms and the high between. We then subtracted this cycle and found the long-term representation. Using detrended data, shorter cycles were determined for specific spans of data and the sum of all extracted components was used to predict the price movement into the future. The three major sections analyzed showed a major bear-bull-bear movement in which the major cycle increased in period and amplitude with time. It is typical for the amplitude and period to increase and decrease together. Figure 12-7 illustrates this effect. It is well to remember that as major reversal areas are approached, if the prices seem to move beyond the predicted analysis, the cycle is likely to be longer. Likewise, if the prices tend to reverse early, the period is likely to be shorter in the future. Again the movements tend to be gradual and a trend is likely to continue. These deviations must be evaluated over an appropriate span of time so as to avoid being misled by the movements of the shorter cycles.

In practice, the minor movements should first be removed from the data with a centered moving average, then the major cyclic component removed, after which the long-term trend is found and the data detrended for further analysis of the shorter cycles as may be desired. A 13-week moving average is satisfactory to smooth weekly data for curve fitting of components with periods of a few years or longer. Always select a data span which shows by observation a movement resembling the shape of the mathematical curve selected for the representation. In particular, one or more reversal areas must be included, otherwise the best fit solution may in fact not represent the likely price movement. For example, don't try to make a sine wave fit to data around the midpoint of a sine wave curve. The result will likely be a very long or even an infinite period. Curve-fitting techniques, as well as moving average analysis, works better for regions around major reversal areas. The rapid rise or fall sections of the longer cycles tend to swamp the appearance of the short cycles making it difficult to obtain their representation even though they are present in full strength. Refer to Figures 4-3 and 4-4 which illustrate this point.

This chapter illustrated various analysis techniques but did not exhaust the computations possible to make using the nine years of weekly data of the DJIA. For example, you could detrend the 3-month moving average with the long-term trend, Equation (12-18), then obtain new major cycle fits, either using the cubic equation to establish the corresponding sine waves, or you could make a trigonometric fit to the detrended data. These fits can be made at more than the three time increments selected in this chapter and the results combined into a composite for the entire data span. After obtaining the new major cyclic component, you may subtract it from the original moving average and determine a new long-term trend. These iterations may give a better fit to past data and the carrying through of the shorter cycles over the full span of data may give you more confidence in the cyclic concept of stock price movements as well as practice in the techniques of analysis. The basic data required is found in the tables of this chapter.

13

Observations of Special Value to All Investors

TECHNICIANS AND FUNDAMENTALISTS

PRICE-VOLUME RELATIONS

Prices, either of individual stocks or of the market as a whole, require volume to make them move. The volume action is an important backup to price action analysis. There are certain well documented price-volume actions worth knowing. In a healthy bull market it is normal for volume to increase with prices and tend to dry up on reactions. In a bear market it is normal for volume to increase as prices drop and dry up as prices recover in the bear market reactions. If the volume action is opposite to this normal behavior, it is advisable to be alert for a change in trend. This may be of short duration, of interest to the trader, or it may be an indication of a major market reversal, depending on the circumstances. Moving averages may be used to remove the short-term fluctuations when you are interested in major turns in the prices.

BEAR MARKET BOTTOMS

Bear markets often end with a particular volume action which marks the turning point with considerable certainty. A *selling climax* often occurs and produces a sharp indication. It is marked by a one- or two-day price reversal that starts with heavy volume with prices falling. The days volume will be perhaps double the average of the preceding weeks. Technicians recognize this as the end of the bear market. The 1966 and 1970 bear markets ended in this manner. See Figures 13-1 and 13-2. The climactic selling occurred on August 29 and 30 of 1966 and on May 26 and 27 of 1970. Usually there is a secondary low following the climactic selling low. This is often referred to as a testing of the low and may be either lower or higher than the previous low. It is in fact nothing more than the low of a shorter cycle which shows up on the daily graphs of Figures 13-1 and 13-2. Whether it is lower or higher depends upon the phases of the various cycles present and no particular significance should be attached to the result of the testing. The climactic ending of the bear market is a result of a *panic* on the part of investors dumping their stocks only to have them be picked up by more astute bargain hunters.

Bottoms sometimes occur in an opposite manner. Volume dries up and the price drags out without much change, forming a base. As time goes on the cheap stocks are bought up and prices are forced upward and a reversal is then in process. This bottom is less sharp and more difficult to call. These are the *flat* bottoms of a long cycle without the presence of significant short cycles to *peak up* and generate the sharp reversal. Sharp reversals can occur without the climactic selling if the cycles peak up in phase.

HIGH-VOLUME STOCKS

Stocks trading with low volume seldom do much, but a stock which suddenly develops high volume is likely to be a good price mover. In fact, this is a good way to pick out stocks to watch for purchase.

UPSIDE-DOWNSIDE VOLUME

The volume of stocks trading on an *uptick*, that is at a higher price than the previous trade, and the volume trading on a *downtick* are published daily in *The Wall Street Journal* for the NYSE, the AMEX and the NASDAQ. A 10-day moving average plot of the upside volume and of the downside volume is useful in deriving short-term trading signals. As long as the downside volume predominates, the market is expected to continue downward. Likewise, as long as the upside volume predominates, the market is expected to continue upward. Convergence of these two

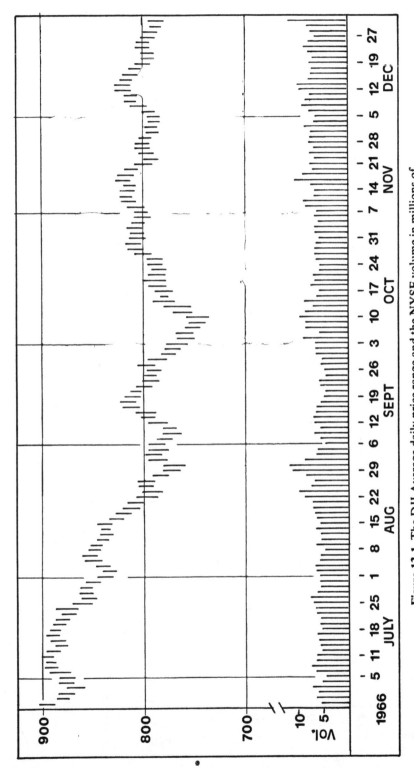

Figure 13-1. The DJI Average daily price range and the NYSE volume in millions of shares at the 1966 low.

187

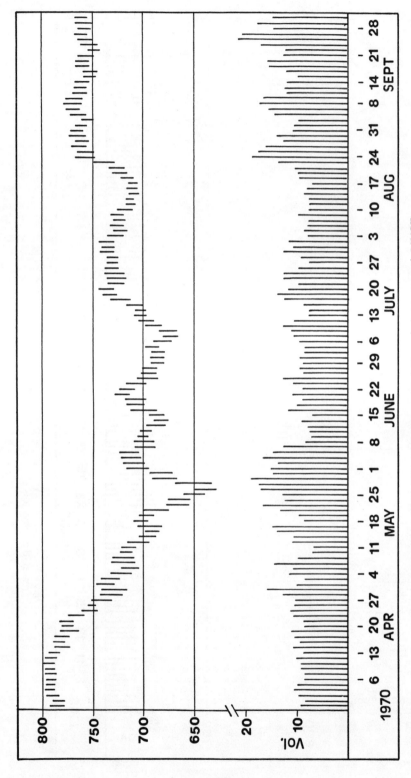

Figure 13-2. The DJI Average daily price range and NYSE volume at the 1970 low.

188

moving averages toward a crossover is an indication of a price reversal. This movement tends to show up in advance of the point of price reversal so is a leading indicator. The modified moving average (see "The Modified Moving Average" in Chapter 4) is most suitable for these indicators because of its greater sensitivity to current data and it is less responsive to the old drop-off data.

TECHNICAL VS. FUNDAMENTAL APPROACH

There are proponents of the technical approach to the stock market who take the position that everything that is known is reflected "on the tape." There are others who stand firm on the position that the performance of a stock will in the end be determined by its fundamentals. Then there are those who try to follow both approaches, or who fall in between.

The part-time do-it-yourself investor is advised to be basically a technican with a little of the fundamental thrown in. The fundamental approach is well and good but is largely beyond the capability of the lone part-time investor. One is forced to depend on others for information. The recommendations you get are as varied as the informants. Just because a stock is in a good fundamental position does not mean it will go up in price, or if it does, that it will occur soon. Your funds can be tied up earning nothing more than dividends, which may be small, for extended periods of time.

The technician approaches the market from the viewpoint of what is happening today and what will happen tomorrow. One follows the action and keeps his funds working. The information comes from the investors themselves, as a group, as reflected through the performance of the market and of individual stocks. The data is contained in your daily newspaper. The labor is within reason for a part-time investor and the techniques described in this book help to minimize the effort.

When ready for a buy action you can always have choices. Here is the place for at least a sprinkling of fundamentals. There are some very quick checks that can be made from the financial newspaper data, or statistical data obtainable from your broker or publications in your local library. What is the company's earnings trend? Try to pick one with growth and which is not erratic. If you are interested in the dividends, are they well covered by earnings? The price-earnings ratio is frequently quoted but this can not be taken literally. About the best you can do is to note whether it is out of line with comparable companies and ask yourself why. A relatively low price-earnings ratio may mean the price is depressed because the company is viewed as being in trouble, or it may mean its price hasn't caught up with the others—quite different viewpoints. There are other statistical data easily available either from your broker or public library which you can analyze and which you may consider useful.

It is also worthwhile to think about the business of the company. Is it in a live or dying industry? Are there economic factors that may create problems for this industry, or for the geographical area where the company does its business. Your broker can give you help on these factors.

When owning a stock you have only two choices, hold or sell. Normally the signal to sell would show up on the technical side before you would discover a deteriorating fundamental condition. If you practice a policy of reviewing your holdings and selling when the stock would not be a buy, fundamentals would enter into the decision. If you follow the technical approach, the sell decision should take care of itself.

BUY BACK ON WEAKNESS

How often do you hear the advice, "Buy back on weakness" or, "Take your profits on the next rally"? Is this good advice? What does it mean? Have you just as often wondered how much of a rally to wait for or how far the stock should fall before buying? Yes, this can be good advice if coupled with cyclic analysis, for this will give you the buy and sell levels. Perhaps the one giving advice has some feeling for the cyclic movement of prices. You can use such advice to bring interesting stocks to your attention. Make your cyclic study and act only if it clearly supports the recommendations.

TAXES AND LONG-TERM GAINS

Everyone knows the tax advantage of long-term gains (holding period of over six months) rather than paying on the total of short-term gains. This knowledge often leads to poor investment decisions on the sell side. If you have a paper profit and the stock should be sold, this is the thing to do. The tax problem may not be all that bad. Remember if you sell you have this money to invest and you may be able to make additional profits on another short-term holding which makes up for any tax difference or even have more after tax gain than holding out for long-term gains.

14

Short-Term Indicators

QUICK REACTION AIDS FOR THE TRADER

We have observed that all market averages tend to move together over the short term. However, we prefer a plot of the daily high and low of the DJI Average for disclosing the short cycles by inspection, primarily because it is more available. Marking the days having a low which is lower than the previous and following days' lows usually discloses a cycle ranging from about five to nine days. In a similar manner, marking the successive low areas which are lower than the adjacent areas usually discloses a cycle of about four-to six-weeks duration.

UNWEIGHTED SHORT-TERM OSCILLATOR

We have also noted that for assessing the market in the long-term, weighted averages, which include the DJIA, often give a different result from an unweighted average but the Advance-Decline Line moves more in concert with the unweighted averages and is easily constructed from readily available data. It has been recommended as a good measure of the long-term state of the market. The number of stocks advancing and declining each day is readily available and these data may be combined in various ways to produce a short-term measure of the market which is frequently referred to as an *overbought-oversold index*. Since it only involves the number of stocks and not their prices, the measure is unweighted. One combination, which I prefer, is a modified 10-day moving average of the difference between the number of stocks advancing and the number declining on the NYS Exchange. This index will oscillate between positive and negative values of a few hundred points. When in the negative region it is called an *oversold market* and when in the positive region an *overbought market*. The larger the numerical value (positive or negative) the more overbought or oversold it is said to be. The market does not stay in an overbought or oversold state forever but will correct either of these conditions. While it may appear to linger in one condition or the other as indicated by this index remaining essentially flat at one extreme or the other, when it starts to reverse it usually does so very rapidly, and at this point one may expect a price reversal in the market within a few days.

The above description of the overbought-oversold (OB/OS) index is nothing more than the extraction of a cyclic component of the market with some additional features. One is that it provides a numerical measure of the extremity of the market movement and the other is that it provides a sensitive indicator of a reversal of condition. This latter can best be treated as a warning signal to be followed up by other analysis to pinpoint buying and selling actions.

If this moving average index is plotted centered, that is, delayed by 5 days, it would be seen to be a leading indicator time-wise, but also it is 5 days behind the market data. However, using a modified moving average (see Chapter 4) the additional weight given the latest data tends to overcome the delay somewhat. In fact, it usually follows the market closely as to minor movements, thus giving pretty much a coincident index. It is normally plotted at the date of the last data point. In some cases, a purely mechanical buy and sell signal derived from this index works well. For example, one may consider the signal is produced when the index crosses zero. For large swings this usually gives good results though it tends to be a little late for pinpoint action. In long market trends, there are likely to be numerous whipsaws as there are minor corrections which bring the index back to neutral only to reverse and move into the previous overbought or oversold region.

Again, the signal point may be derived from an indication of trend change, either by breaking a trend line of this index or by moving some specified amount in the reversal direction. Whipsaws are again a problem but better timing may be attained when the market is truly reversing. Best results are obtained when this index is used as a warning, for it frequently gives an early indication and never a totally false signal, though it can produce frequent whipsaws if acted on without other confirming support. I prefer using it as a warning as to when trend reversal of the price is indicated.

UPSIDE AND DOWNSIDE VOLUME

Upside and downside volume is a useful confirming indicator. A modified 10-day moving average of each is plotted on the same scale. When the upside volume predominates, the market is bullish and when the downside volume predominates it is bearish. One can devise signal indications based on the behavior of these two curves. One method is to use points where the curves cross though this is usually late. Better timing is achieved by acting on a change of trends which indicates that the curves are moving toward a crossover. It is usually best to wait until the curves converge to within about 1.5 million shares on the 10-day modified moving average of the NYS Exchange stocks. This point is usually near the price reversal point. Using this indicator alone can produce whipsaws.

TRADING INDEX

We have now discussed two short-term indicators, one based upon the number of stocks advancing and declining and another based upon the upside and downside volume. These basic data can be combined to form another short-term indicator. It is obvious that it is bullish for more stocks to be advancing than are declining, also that it is bullish for the upside volume to be greater than the downside volume. It is also obvious that when more stocks advance we should expect the upside volume to be greater and conversely in a downside movement. Sometimes this direct correlation does not exist and often it exists to widely different degrees. It is therefore useful to measure, in an advancing market, whether the stocks advancing are receiving their fair share of volume, or receiving more or less than their fair share. On the downside we want to know whether the declining stocks are receiving more or less than their share of volume. The *Trading Index* was devised to provide this measurement[1]. It is defined as the ratio of two ratios—the ratio of advances to declines (A/D) and the ratio of the upside to downside volume (u/d). The Trading Index (I) is then $I = (A/D) \div (u/d)$. This index uses data which is produced almost continuously for the NYSE and can be calculated at times during the day, or at various periods as desired. An index less than 1.0 is bullish and one

---

[1]Richard W. Arms Jr., *Jack be Nimble*, Barron's, August 7, 1967, p 5.

greater than 1.0 is bearish. Forming a moving average of this index has not been found useful. Computed on a daily basis, it has been found highly reliable as an indicator of the market direction for the next day or two.

THE THREE RATIOS INDEX

Using the criteria that when the three ratios, A/D, u/d and I are all bullish, the market has been higher within two days 85 percent to 90 percent of the time over a span of several years that it has been checked. Likewise, it has been lower within two days when the three ratios are all bearish. This combination will be referred to as the *Three Ratios Index*.

BUY AND SELL SIGNALS

Combining the OB/OS index, the 10-day moving average of upside and downside volumes and the Three Ratios Index just discussed has produced highly reliable trading signals. The sequence of events used has been: first to obtain an alert from the OB/OS index by an indication of direction reversal using the criteria of trend line penetration and percentage reverse movement; then an indicated convergence of the upside and downside volume moving averages; and finally pinpointing the day by requiring the three ratios to be indicating the new price direction. After the first two conditions are met, the signal is given on the first day the three ratios meet the requirement, unless the OB/OS index or the upside-downside volume indicators negate the signal. This procedure eliminates many of the possible whipsaws. A whipsaw is a price movement which is not profitable to follow. This trading signal only indicates direction and provides no information on magnitude or duration of the price movement. This later is best obtained by a study of the cyclic position of prices.

Figure 14-1 illustrates the use of these short-term indicators to generate buy and sell signals for trading purposes at a time when the market was topping out in 1973. Arrows are placed next to the DJIA curve to denote the combined indication of the Three Ratios Index. The resulting signals are good except for the possible whipsaws of September 10 and 19 when measured by the DJI Average. The turns in the OB/OS Index are indicated by dots placed on this curve.

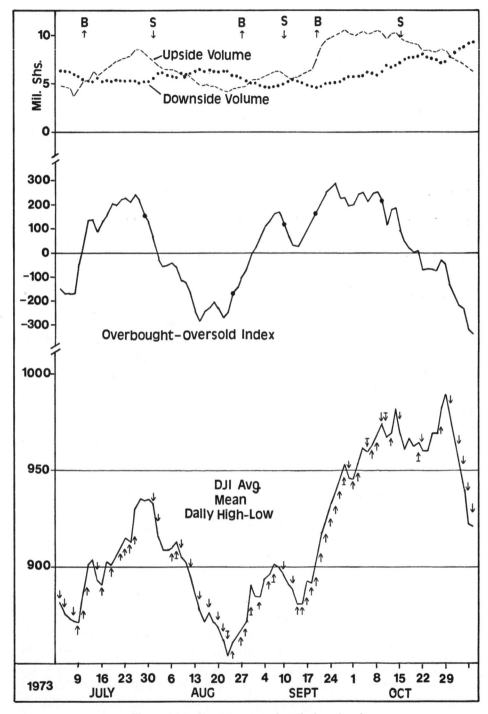

Figure 14-1. Short-term market timing signals.

195

BUYING AND SELLING A STOCK

This discussion has been in terms of "buying the Market Average" and in this sense is useful to back up decisions on individual stocks. However, the final decision must be based on the individual stock performance. It may move late, but should not be too late unless it is a contramarket mover (like golds at times). If it is delayed very much, it is wise to be cautious for the stock may be changing its performance characteristics. The stock may be early but one can often "see" the indicators developing toward a signal. Don't be afraid to commit yourself, if the stock provides a strong signal, under these conditions.

Let us now turn to the actual purchase and sale of the individual stock instead of the market averages. We will discuss the procedures from a trading viewpoint although exact timing for the best price of a stock being purchased to hold should use the same criteria.

We should have charts of a few stocks in which we are interested. For each stock there should be a weekly-entry chart showing a plot of prices for a year or more which lends itself to the drawing of Hurst envelopes bounding the price movement. This chart can be found in a chart book publication which you may find at your public library, or can be purchased by subscription most economically. A second chart using daily entries is required which I recommend plotting yourself, although daily charts, published weekly, are available. Your own daily plot will keep you updated and the process will make you more aware of what is going on.

If trading on the long side, we look for a stock in the uptrend portion of a cycle whose period is long enough to encompass several trading cycles. This may be a stock which is in a consistant uptrend, or one that has a well formed cyclic motion with a period of generally several months. Next pick a stock which has a trading cycle that moves over a price range of 10% or more. You will usually not be able to catch the extremes in price and you will have to pay commissions, so keep this in mind if you want to make a reasonable profit.

Let's look now at some stock charts which illustrate the mechanics of timing the purchase or sale, assuming we have already selected the stock for action. Following the method of trendlines described by Hurst, in Figure 14-2a, a sell signal is illustrated. The signal occurs when the uptrend line is broken on August 15. The line is drawn to connect the reaction lows. It can first be drawn after the price moved up on August 2. Continental Airlines continued in a down trend to October 3 to close at 17. The market sell signal occurred on August 16, one day later than the stock signal. This is not unusual for the market is describing the conditions of the average stock.

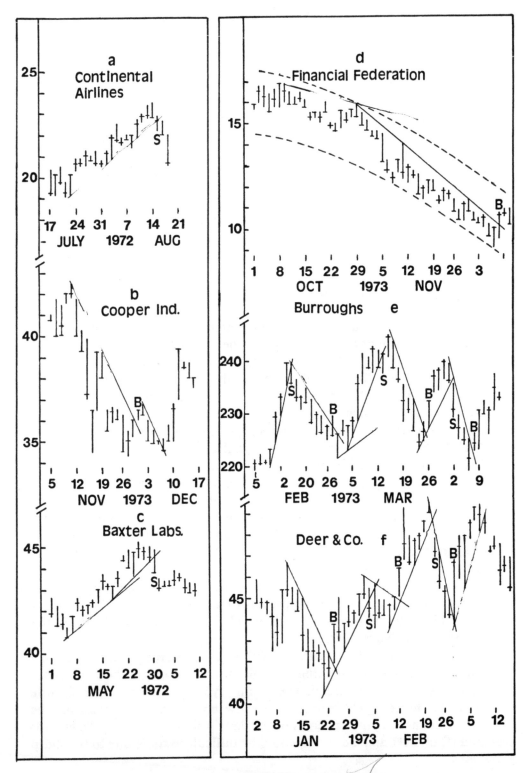

Figure 14-2. Buy and sell signals in individual stocks.

197

Cooper Industries illustrates the corresponding formation of a buy signal. The corresponding market signal wasn't given until eight days later. This stock moved to a high of 46½ on January 3, 1974 before turning down. This chart illustrates a situation often encountered. After the buy on November 28 the prices turned down to reach 34½ on December 6. Market technicians call this a pull-back. It is, of course, merely a short cycle exerting its presence. This stock made minor lows on November 6, 15 and 27, each seven days apart. We should expect another minor low in about seven days which did occur precisely on time. The prominence of this minor cycle coupled with the fact that a market buy signal had not yet occurred would justify waiting for the pull-back before buying. The second trend line drawn on this short cycle was broken on December 6, thus giving the final buy signal. A similar situation may occur at the formation of a sell signal but waiting is more serious. If you miss a good buy, there is always another stock and another chance. If you miss a sell, you lose money and worse yet it is human nature to hang on hoping to recover your losses which usually results in even greater losses. Therefore, be very cautious about ignoring a sell signal when holding stock long. At least enter a stop-loss order to protect against a turnaround.

Plot (c) for Baxter Laboratories illustrates a situation often encountered. The first trend line drawn after the low of May 17 is not as steep as the one which can be drawn connecting the lows of May 17 and 23. Always draw the steepest trend line possible. Hurst refers to this as the "valid trend line." The market sell signal occurred on May 31, one day later. There are occasions when additional trend lines may be drawn. This applies equally to formation of both sell and buy signals.

Plot (d) of Financial Federation illustrates a stock in a slower moving trading cycle than the previous illustrations. The buy signal on December 7 was one market day prior to the market signal of December 10. This stock reached a high of 15½ on February 26, 1974, continuing its consistent trading cycle. The Hurst envelope is shown as dotted lines obtained from a much longer span of price data. This cycle is in keeping with the market cycle at this time. The previous market signal was a sell on October 15. Note the three-day cycle which is especially prominent during the month of November.

In marked contrast with plot (d) is (e) of Burroughs Corp. During this time the market was going through the corresponding short cycles but in a longer-term down trend. The trading cycles are so short there is little time for shorter cycle reactions to show up. Steep trend lines may be drawn connecting the extremes of the daily price movement. Likewise for plot (f) of Deer and Co. Both would be difficult to trade due to the sharp price reversals for it would be difficult to get good executions. One would need to operate on hourly data rather than daily data. During this span of time market signals did not develop and the market was moving downward. This should be a warning even though various stocks show good cyclic motion.

While these examples may look like textbook cases if compared to a stock picked at random, the point is that clear-cut examples do occur and can be found at most any time. Stay away from the purchase of any stock which does not exhibit a clear situation. If you own a stock, then you must face up to its sale. When trading, if the purchase was made under clear-cut circumstances, conditions are unlikely to change sufficiently in the short time of a half period of the trading cycle to be confusing. If so, it is best to sell and start over with another stock.

SOME STOCK TRADES

Let's see how these signals work out when applied to trading an actual stock (see Figure 14-3). RCA was a stock which had been declining for several months and by July 1973 showed signs of bottoming out with an upturn probable. Using a break of the trend line to mark the buy and sell signals, RCA would have been a sell July 24, five days before the market sell signal at an average price the following day of 25⅜. The stock gives a buy signal August 29, two days later than the market signal with an average price the following day of 23⅜, or a two-point profit on the short side. Whether one would have been caught in the whipsaw or not is questionable. On the assumption that RCA was expected to be in a bottom region, the envelope at this time would have been extended much as shown in the figure and its upper boundary would be well above the price, so it would be reasonable under these conditions to assume this is only a minor cyclic reaction. On the other hand, if one assumes RCA is headed downward, the envelope might have been drawn to touch the top area around September 10. This attitude is at variance with the original assumption that RCA is bottoming out and one should not have been long in the stock at this point, had this been the assumption. The stock gives a sell signal on October 10, three market days beforethe market sell signal. In this case, the market indicators are in a position to be generating a sell signal in the near future, but more important RCA prices have reached a level where the upper envelope line might well pass and they have moved upward for a time comparable to one-half the previous cycle. The sale would have been at an average price of 27 on the following day for 3⅝-point gain from the August 29 buy.

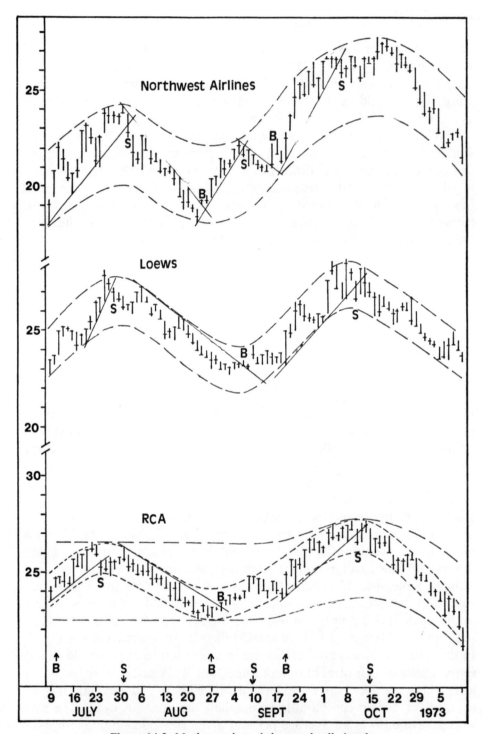

Figure 14-3. Market and stock buy and sell signals.

200

This is a good example of what one may accomplish and some of the practical situations one encounters. As a matter of record, I purchased RCA on September 4, 1973 at 23 ½ and sold it October 11 at 27 ¼. After commissions, this resulted in a profit of 120% on an equivalent annual yield basis.

The plot of Loews Corporation is another illustration. Here the stock gives a sell on July 27, two market days prior to the market sell signal, then a buy on September 6. Here the whipsaw does not appear in the stock chart. Another sell occurs on October 10, three days before the market signal. As a matter of record, I purchased Loews on September 17 at 23 ½ and sold on October 8 at 28 ½ for a profit, after commissions, of 290% on an equivalent annual yield. The October 8 sale deserves a comment since it was made prior to the sell signal and at a better price. This can often be done by noting that cycle-wise the top is due, and selling at the estimated upper channel line rather than waiting for the price to drop below the trend line. This action can be further justified by the fact that you are nailing down your gains and the money is available for further commitments. The converse is not true for purchases. Anticipating the bottom to get a better price may result in a loss as the bottom may not have been made, or the stock may linger in a base area tying up your money that could be better used elsewhere. It is best to wait for a definite buy signal and even then to delay, if the stock cyclic position is in a broad bottom with a definite short cycle (the 5-to 9-day variety) apparent. Waiting for the bottom of the next short cycle can result in improved gain with less risk.

A third stock, Northwest Airlines, is plotted which shows prices more nearly conforming to the market signals including the whipsaw signals, which in this case could have worked out to no great disadvantage. A sell signal was given on August 1, one day after the market signal. In retrospect one could have noted a prominent short cycle of about six days duration, and could have anticipated the sell signal, since the market sell signal had occurred and a 6-day cycle low was due. One might have sold for a point or more higher if alert to this prospect. The next buy was on August 23, two days prior to the market signal and followed by a sell September 6, again two days prior to the market signal. The final sell on October 5 was seven market days prior to the market signal. It may be noted that the stock did rise somewhat during this period and for a few days afterward. For the record again, my purchase was two CBOE October 20 calls on August 27 at 2 ⅛ which were sold on September 20 at 3 ⅞ for a profit, after commissions, of 1,050% on an annual basis. This sale was obviously early. However, in self defense, it was a good profit.

These actual situations illustrate that a short-term trading signal can be developed from market data other than prices and are therefore not price weighted, but they do include the total action of all stocks which change their price during the day and so are broad in nature. Many individual stocks tend to move with the market in the short term, but their individual buy and sell times will vary from the market average and should be followed, rather than acting on the market signals alone.

The stocks illustrated in Figure 14-3, RCA, Loews and Northwest Airlines, are only a few that exhibit good cyclic patterns for trading at this time. This is not to say that many stocks are completely unsuited, but enough can be found to satisfy the average trader.

Summary

Buy and sell signals for individual stocks are derived from short-term data for stocks selected to watch if buying, or for your holdings if selling long. General buying and selling times are determined from the longer-to-intermediate cyclic position. Market trading signals can be derived using an overbought-oversold index as a warning, backed up by trend reversal of upside and downside volume moving averages and finally pinpointed by the confirmation of all the three ratios—advances/declines, upside/-downside volume and trading index. Whipsaws are reduced by ignoring signals unsupported by the cyclic actions.

The market signals can often "be seen" developing ahead of their occurrence. Individual stocks may have their buy and sell signals a few days early or late compared to the market signals. It is advisable to avoid stock signals which deviate considerably from the market signals unless the stock has a consistent pattern of contramarket movement.

15

Things to Think About

MARKET INDICATORS

Many market indicators have evolved over the years and they are described in the various financial publications. They have followers who stay with them and promote their use. You can't probe into the market without encountering a number of such indicators presented by their proponents in such a way as to be very convincing. You should explore these for yourself and come to your own conclusion as to what they tell you. A common feature is a chart of the indicator plotted beside some stock market average, such as the DJI Average, showing how this indicator makes its extreme at the time the market makes its extreme. When looking at the historical record this may be very convincing. It called all the turns, or it called a large percentage of the market turns. The trouble with many of these is, when you start using them in real time, you never know when the indicator has reached its extreme until it has gotten well around the corner; by that time so has the market—you might as well have watched the price curve.

Then there are those who recognize these indicators are of the coincident type and attempt to overcome this problem by designating limits on values of the indicators which, when penetrated, tell you to expect a market turn. Again, the history may look very good but when using them in real time, you may find the indicator penetrating the limit with the

203

market continuing in the same direction. You may have committed yourself only to see losses pile up or profits forgone. Again you may decide to wait to be sure and finally realize the turn was made and you missed a good profit. Further, you often find even though the limit was penetrated, the indicator continues toward more extreme values for a long time. It seems as if the limits have changed.

Even though these indicators may tell you the market is low, or the market is high, and it is indeed true, also remember you only had to look at the prices to get this information. There may be no magic in the indicator. Look at market indicators carefully; don't be carried away by their historical performance. If they are coincident indicators, ask whether they tell you anything more than the price itself tells you. After all it is only price that matters in the end. Beware of the "early indicator." It is always right, for the market will always reverse if you wait long enough.

Work back through the development of an indicator and see if you can discover its real basis. In particular, see if it is based on anything other than something which moves with the price; if not, better use the price itself. For example, consider indicators involving yields. Dividends vary slowly when averaged. The yield variations of any group of stocks, such as the DJI Average, are principally due to price changes, at least for short to intermediate times. They tell you no more than the price itself. It is even more true of high-grade bond yields. *Barron's* reports weekly the spread between the yield on the DJI Average and Barron's High-Grade Bonds. You can make a logical argument that astute investors move into high-grade bonds when the outlook for common stocks is bad. This pushes bond prices up and yields down, but it doesn't always work this way. At the same time the selling of stocks drops prices and yields increase. The yield spread tells it all. Logical? If these people are so astute, they are astute enough to take these actions ahead of time, so here is an advance warning system. How much in advance? Try it out and see if you can tell, but be careful that your conclusions aren't influenced by already knowing the answer.

If you really want a good indicator, pick something that depends on price, plot it upside down (that is, so that it moves opposite to price) and plot it ahead in time equal to a half period of a prominent cycle thus bringing it back in phase with the price. This may be impressive, if you maintain some mystery about it, but how much simpler, and more reliable, merely to extend the cycle. Its value depends upon how well you estimate the cycle period.

CLASSES OF MARKET PARTICIPANTS

It is commonly assumed there are smart operators who make fortunes in the stock market. You always know someone who knows someone who knows someone that made it. Some market systems are built on the assumption that there are people who as a group possess the astuteness to be at least more right than wrong, particularly at market turns. Such groups are pitted against other groups who are more often wrong than right. These are commonly considered to be the public or small investors. There is always a search on to identify the two sides of the combat and devise measures which indicate how one or both groups are acting and thereby determine what the market is going to do. We will look at some special groups which can be identified and their market actions studied from published data.

NEW YORK STOCK EXCHANGE MEMBERS

Barron's publishes weekly data on the member trading on the NYSE two weeks after the close of the data week. The Stock Exchange Members form a class of traders who account for about 20 percent to 25 percent of the volume on the exchange. The data provides the total shares purchased and the total shares sold by this group. You can then determine whether they are buying or selling on balance. Also the number of shares they sold short is given along with the total shares sold short during the week. The difference represents the number of shares sold short by the public, thus providing a measure of the action of Stock Exchange Members vs. the public in selling short. Further, the short selling by the *specialists* is provided. These are the people charged with making an orderly market in their selected group of stocks, and who are considered to be the most astute of all traders. The action of these groups can be studied relative to one another and to the public. Perhaps they act differently at market turns. If so, and this difference can be discovered, we may have a good market indicator. There are many who believe this is true.

Take the specialists who buy for their own account if sellers predominate to prevent an undue drop in price. Likewise, they sell from their account to restrain undue upward movement. Since the specialist makes his living this way, it may be argued that he must be very astute and will prepare for what he expects the market to do. That is, if he expects the market to go down, he will be short so he can profit by covering as he buys to support the stock. Likewise, if expecting the market to go up he will reduce his shorts and take on a long position. At any time the specialists will do some short selling to maintain their desired position, the amount of short selling being a relative matter. The ratio of specialist short sales to the total short sales is used to indicate the specialists' evaluation of the market. Some consider a value of 55% about normal with a figure of 45% or less being very bullish and calling a buy signal. At 67% or above a sell signal is indicated.

Such an indicator has often been in the "ball park" in the past but it suffers from the problem already mentioned of not knowing when the turn is expected. For example, a buy started to be indicated at mid-year of 1966 but the actual low of the DJIA occurred about four months later and over 100 points lower; the 1970 low was called only about six weeks early but at over 150 points above the final low; and in 1974 the buys started in earnest at mid-year, then the DJIA fell over 150 points in the next four months. Another way of forming an indicator is to take the ratio of the specialists' short selling to that of the public. This pits those thought to be most astute against the least astute. However, there remains a problem with the specialists' data. Since he has to sell stocks to maintain the orderly market he may either be selling short or merely selling stocks he holds long. This distinction is not reported. It is really the specialists' net short or long position that is important, and this data is not reported. The amount of short covering is also unknown. It may be argued that the specialist is really trying to equalize his position and he is forced to follow the public demand, so is reflecting the public pressures. Perhaps it would be better to build an indicator on the short selling of the public which can be obtained from the difference between the total short sales and Member Short Sales.

If the specialist builds up a net short position to his advantage, then he accumulated these shorts as the market went down having sold at a price higher than the market bottom. He then will profit as the market turns higher when he takes stock from the public to prevent undue upward excesses (covering his shorts). Thus a short position is bullish. Likewise, a decrease in his short selling may also be bullish for it may mean he has reached his desired short position. However, this knowledge does not necessarily mean a market turn to the upside. The earlier he reaches his short position, the greater the profits as he covers at lower and lower prices. If the specialist's crystal ball is really good, then his actions may be taken well ahead of market turns.

THE PUBLIC SECTOR

The public is considered to have no crystal ball and its reaction is more a psychological one. It is not premeditated but more likely to reflect the present attitude. Perhaps one should expect less time lag. The public short selling as a percentage of the short selling or of total volume on the exchange can be used as an indicator. There is another measure of the public short selling and that is in the odd lot statistics. These have the advantage of being reported daily in the financial section of many newspapers as well as in *The Wall Street Journal*. Also reported are the odd lot purchases and sales. If you want to study these further, refer to Drew, Reference 9, who developed the Odd Lot Indicators. They are often misinterpreted in the "financial press" and you should understand Drew's methods before drawing conclusions.

SHORT SALES

At any time, there is some determinable number of shares sold short, which is called the *Short Interest*. The NYS Exchange reports this figure as of the 15th of each month, as does the AMEX. A high short interest is thought to be bullish because it represents more stock that will eventually have to be covered by purchases, so it represents potential buyers. This is, of course, a relative matter and another number is also reported which adjusts for the total trading by taking the ratio of the short interest to the average number of shares traded on the exchange during the preceding month and is termed the *short interest ratio*. A high value is bullish and a low value is bearish. The ratio fluctuates considerably and values of 1.0 and below have represented extremes on the low side while 2.0 and above are extremes on the high side. There are those who attempt to generate market signals based upon this ratio breaking some predetermined level. The wide fluctuations seem to occur regardless of what the market is doing and the extremes often are seen to occur at market turning points when viewed in retrospect, but it is difficult to know at the time when the extreme has been reached. It would appear that this index is more or less responding to a market situation which is already apparent from the price action and has little if any forcasting value.

Similar arguments are advanced for individual stocks. A high and/or increasing short interest is considered bullish because of the buying power it represents. However, as long as the price of the stock falls there is very little incentive to exercise this buying power. When the time comes for the stock to turn upward, then short covering will accentuate the buying pressure but it is not the short interest that turns the price around. If you can determine when the price reversal is likely to occur in a stock, then a high short interest may generate a larger than otherwise price rise.

NEWS EVENTS

When the market is very bearish or very bullish the news media feel compelled to give a daily wrap-up on why the stock market did what it did. Pay little heed to these reports. Regardless of what happened in the market these "news makers" can always explain it. If the market had done the opposite, there would still have been the explanation. If the market does not react, then you can always fall back on the explanation that the market had discounted the news. Of course there are daily market reactions to actual news events, but their effect is soon forgotten by the market. Even major events will not produce permanent effects on the market which will on the average just continue to do its thing—its thing being to go through bullish and bearish cycles and cycles of reaction and recovery.

Long-term influences often gain a general acceptance for the market performance. A good example is in the early part of 1974 when nearly everyone was positive that the market troubles were all due to the three I's. After Impeachment was no longer a problem, Interest rates were falling, and Inflation was being crowded out by Recession; the stock market paid no heed and continued its downward trend. Its cycles were not ready to respond until the New Year. You may say, "Sure, but by then our economy was in bad shape and getting worse, how could we expect the market to recover in view of all of this?" Then when the market did reverse as the economy continued to get much worse, the market was anticipating the recovery. Yes, there are always excuses—in the Spring we had the three I's, but we also were moving down from the top of the major 4½-year cycle. If we had not had the three I's, would the market have continued upward to the 1200 or 1400 on the DJIA as some had predicted? I think not. The cyclic forces are not to be turned off, nor will they be turned off when the cycles turn up. When they do turn up, they will continue up regardless of the current state of the economy, employment, etc., but there will be the proper news to explain things again.

I don't mean to imply that the market has some kind of built-in mechanical cycles that do not respond to outside influences. Unfortunately, no one professes to have a good understanding of the causes of market and economic cycles, other than some seasonal, etc., effects, but nevertheless cyclic phenomena are being discovered in an ever-widening area of the non-physical world. Surely the economy of the country and of the world influences directly, or indirectly, the stock market prices. The economy involves factors which can not change rapidly as well as others which can, and do, change in a matter of months perhaps. It is not too much to expect these factors to exert a varying influence and build up and die off in a cyclic manner. This is all we really need to know. The "news" will be supplied on a day-by-day basis as the effects come to our attention.

ONE-DECISION STOCKS

In the early 1970's you heard a lot about the "one-decision stock." You need to make the one decision—to buy. Buy a growth stock and hold. These stocks were also known as *Glamours*. They looked as if you couldn't miss. Let's take a look at what happened. Some of the outstanding glamours behaved in this manner:

Stock	1970 Low	1972-3 High	1974 Low
Avon	59 ⅛	140	18 ⅝
IBM	175	365	150 ½
Polaroid	51	150	14 ⅛
Winnebago Ind.	2 ½	48	3
Xerox	65 ¼	170	49 ⅜

It was great to see your money double and even more, if in the right stocks at their 1970 lows. It would have been even greater to have reaped your profits at or near the highs of 1972-3. These turning points were due to the prominent 4½-year cycle whose turning point could have been anticipated. The top was not sharp and there was plenty of time to nail down these large profits if you did not keep holding on hoping the market would not go down this time, or at least your glamours would hold up. Well, they didn't and the one-decision stock joined the rest of the stock market myths. If you held on, the chances are you were holding losses by 1974 and they were likely substantial because you probably did not buy at the very low but somewhere considerably higher. You may have collected dividends but not at a very high rate, for the glamours characteristically paid very low dividends—they were growth stocks! Growth stocks are great investments when going up but watch your sell signals. These stocks can go down as fast or faster than they went up.

Then there is the "one-decision stock" you buy for its dividends and hold for your heirs to inherit. American Tel. & Tel. is the outstanding example. Yes, its price is relatively stable, it has paid dividends every year since 1881 and they seem assured and in fact they have consistently increased over the years. However, let's look further at its performance. Its stock sold at 75 in 1964 but did not exceed 65 in the high of 1972-3 and sold as low as 40 in 1974, even though its earnings more or less steadily increased over this period of time. You could have lost nearly half your investment over these ten years though at a slow rate so maybe it hurts less. Its dividends have been good and reached a yield of about 7¾% at the 1974 low, but the average over these ten years is more like half this. The paper loss in stock value was not made up by the total of the dividends paid. In the past 40 years you could not have purchased this stock for less than 17. Perhaps it will never fall this low again, but will it ever again reach its previous high of 75, and if so in how many years? Undoubtedly a good stock—held by the rich, the widows and orphans and yes by a thousand institutions. Is it a stock for you? It is not uncommon to see Am. Tel. & Tel. listed on buy lists for the conservative investor for safety and income. It undoubtedly stands high in this category, but its price is not guaranteed as of anytime in the future. If you want safety and income, maybe a top-grade bond serves your need better. Am. Tel. has a number of outstanding bonds, many with current yield at the end of 1974 of over 8% with maturities ranging up to the year 2005. You could lock in a yield of over 8½% for 30 years if this is what you want. Should you have to sell, your losses would most likely be less than if holding a top-grade common stock. Think it over. There will be times when you hear the same advice from many sources, and well intended, but there may be better alternatives.

Consider this discussion as an example. We may never have the *Glamour Syndrome* again, but probably will as most things go in cycles, but we will most assuredly have similar situations where it seems everyone agrees on what appears to be the "real thing." Watch it! The bubble always explodes!

INSTITUTIONS

The investments of Pension Funds, Trust Funds, Mutual Funds, etc., constitute an ever increasing block of the total available supply of common stocks. The managers of these funds can exert a significant influence on the price of individual stocks. Not only does each of them have to deal in a large number of shares, but they tend to act like sheep—what one buys, the others buy. This causes the prices of "The Favorites" to go up and up, feeding on themselves. Likewise, when one dumps, the others tend to dump. We saw this in the glamour sell-off in 1974.

There have been times when the small investor has been advised to follow the institutions and buy what they are buying for they must be the best informed. They can afford to spend large sums on research and must know more about a company and its prospects than almost anyone else. Market systems have been based on this principle, but can you get out if someone decides to dump, or maybe more to the point, will you? You can at least use stop-loss orders. There are those who recommend avoiding the stocks which have a large following by the institutions for this reason.

There are market systems utilizing studies of large-block trading. *The Wall Street Journal* reports the number of blocks of 10,000 shares or greater which change hands each day. Such blocks must be bought and sold for large portfolios, so provide a measure of institutional activity. Some analyze whether these blocks are exchanged on a rising price or decreasing price and conclude whether institutions are buying or selling. But who is to buy the large lots that one has to sell but another institution? What one considers a sell, another considers a buy at the exchange price. These people must all fall into a single type group.

OFFICIAL PRONOUNCEMENTS

People in high places are prone to emit opinions on the course of the market and the economy, particularly at the extreme conditions. This includes government officials, officers of large institutions, college professors, etc. Even the greatest of these often disagree. Do not pay too much attention to such opinion statements. If you do, you are likely to believe what you want to hear. When evaluating these statements, ask yourself, could this person have taken any other position considering his position? Why did he make the statement? Was he obligated to report to the public or is he merely responding to the media? Are there known facts to support the position? Try to figure out at whom his words are aimed. Keep your head clear, think for yourself, and don't let your emotions get you into a trap.

SELL! SELL! SELL!

Your most difficult market decision is to SELL! Not because sell signals are any more obscure than buy signals but because of the psy-

chological make up of the human mind. It is natural to rush in to buy for
fear of being left behind but to delay selling even though the signals are
clear. You see your stock go down, and you hold on hoping it will come
back, only to see it fall farther. It has been postulated (see "Market Indicators" in Chapter 3) that it is safer to follow a trading strategy than
long-term investing. The trader buys with intention of selling for a quick
profit. He conditions himself to taking losses if the stock does not behave
as he anticipated. The investor tends to put his stocks away and forget
them, when he should be making continuous decisions—the decision to
sell or to hold. I do not mean to decide each day, or even each week, but
preferably when there are significant changes in either the stock or the
market. Even then you may find it difficult. Some suggest reviewing on
some fixed schedule, and some recommend selling a certain percentage of
one's holdings each year. But here psychology enters to encourage you to
do the wrong thing. One tends to sell stocks in which he has a profit,
which may in fact eliminate the most preferable stocks rather than getting
rid of the do-nothing stock perhaps at a large loss. Maybe it would help
some to remember that taking losses can reduce your income tax, while
taking gains will increase these taxes. A good rule, often stated, is to consider whether the stock would be a good buy at its present price. If not,
then sell.

Summary

Think for yourself! Don't blindly accept what you hear or read. Yes,
that includes this book too. Check it out for yourself. Be sure the idea
works for you before adopting it as a part of your strategy. When you find
a technique which works for you, stick with it for much of the success in
investing is having a plan, with established objectives, and following it.
No small part of a "system" is developing the feel for your interpretation
of the market movements. Do explore new ideas but look behind the
"system" and see if it in fact offers anything new.

16

The Mathematical Knowledge
You Need to Make It All Work

This chapter provides the background mathematics that you should be familiar with in order to understand the mathematical procedures discussed in this book. If you are trained in mathematics you may stop at this point. If, however, some operations are a bit hazy in your mind you should become familiar with what is presented here before attempting to understand the mathematical portions of the book. You can use this chapter as a ready reference for points in question, and it may be read independently of the remainder of the book.

COMPUTATIONS

Most of the computations described in this book can be made by hand (pencil and paper methods) together with a few mathematical tables. Slide rule accuracy is satisfactory for most calculations. A few, such as some curve-fitting techniques are only practical with more sophisticated aids. A serious market technician would be well advised to invest in one of the small electronic computers available at very reasonable cost. There are many versions but all have the basic add, subtract, multiply, and divide operation keys. The next most useful operation is a true memory which permits accumulating sums, and storing subproblems for combining with a following subproblem. Next, would be a square root key for it is otherwise a tedious computation or requires use of logarithms or tables. Probably a squaring key and reciprocal key will be included with this combination. Capability of raising a number to any power, finding any root of a number, and the trigonometric functions can be obtained for a reasonable cost and provide a capability for performing all operations contained in this book without reference to the mathematical tables.

NEGATIVE NUMBERS

If positive numbers are used to designate measurement in a given direction, negative numbers designate measurements in the opposite direction. Graphs of a quantity that moves both above and below a zero axis involve negative numbers. Positive numbers are usually used without the plus (+) sign, it being understood. Negative numbers, on the other hand, should always be designated by the minus (−) sign. Use of parentheses, as in accounting practice, to indicate a negative number is to be avoided as parentheses have other uses in pure mathematics.

Remember that subtracting a negative number is the same as adding that number, that is, two negatives make a positive. The same is true for multiplication. The product of a positive and a negative number is negative. The product of two negative numbers is a positive number. It follows that squares of negative numbers are always positive. In some mathematical procedures all numbers are squared to obtain a magnitude value only, independent of their sign. This is basic to the least squares method of curve fitting. When interested in the magnitude only of a number without regard to whether it is positive or negative, we speak of this as its absolute value, and it is designated with vertical bars to either side thus: $|a|$.

EXPONENTS

A number multiplied by itself is said to be squared and is frequently written N^2. That is, 10 times $10 = 10^2$. If multiplied by itself again, it is cubed, or raised to the third power. In general, a number N may be raised to any power n, and expressed as N^n. In this, n is the exponent of N.

Negative exponents are used to express the reciprocal of powers of a number as defined by the relation $N^{-n} = 1/N^n$. Fractional powers express roots of a number. For example, $N^{1/2} = \sqrt{N}$, $N^{1/3} = \sqrt[3]{N}$, etc. The relations involving use of exponents are:

$$a^0 = 1 \qquad\qquad a^x a^y = a^{x+y}$$

$$(ab)^x = a^x b^x \qquad\qquad a^x \div a^y = a^{x-y}$$

$$(a^x)^y = a^{xy} \qquad\qquad (a/b)^x = a^x / b^x$$

Very large or very small numbers are often expressed as a power of 10. That is, the number 3,671,000 can be written 3.671×10^6. The number 0.00058 can be written as 5.8×10^{-4}. Some of the hand-held electronic computers provide a display of this type in order to give several significant figures, even though the actual number is very small, and handle very large numbers, even up to 10^{99}.

FACTORIALS

In many mathematical expressions one finds a group of numbers such as

$$1 \times 2 = 2! = 2$$

$$1 \times 2 \times 3 = 3! = 6$$

$$1 \times 2 \times 3 \times 4 = 4! = 24$$

etc. The expression 4!, for example, is read four factorial and is a shorthand way of expressing the larger number which is in turn the product of a number of successive digits starting with one.

ROOTS

The square root of a number is that number which when multiplied by itself gives the first number. There is a procedure for extracting the square root of any number, but use of a slide rule, tables, computer, or logarithms are practical alternatives. If a is a positive real number, the symbol $\sqrt{a}$ denotes the positive square root of a. There is also a negative square root designated as $-\sqrt{a}$. For example, the two square roots of 9 are 3 and -3, each when multiplied by itself gives 9. In performing calculations one must consider both possibilities.

 Square roots of negative numbers are handled by introducing the relation $i^2 = -1$. The two roots of $x^2 = -1$ are i and $-i$. Thus, the roots of -9 are 3i and $-3i$ or $\pm 3i$.

TRIGONOMETRIC FUNCTIONS

In the right triangle, Figure 16-1, the functions: sine abbreviated to sin, cosine (cos) and tangent (tan) are defined by

$$\sin \theta = \text{side BC/side AC}$$

$$\cos \theta = \text{side AB/side AC}$$

$$\tan \theta = \text{side BC/AB}$$

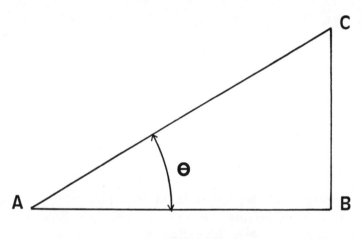

Figure 16-1

When the angle θ^1 is between 0° and 90° the sign of all the functions is positive. However, the angle may be any value up to 360°, and the functions take on various positive and negative values. As a simple aid in determining the algebraic signs and relations between angles in the four quadrants, draw a circle having unit radius (r = 1) as shown in Figure 16-2. Then $\sin \theta = b$, $\cos \theta = a$ and $\tan \theta = b/a$. If conventional positive and negative signs are assigned to the x and y axes drawn through the circle center, the trigonometric functions for all angles between 0° and 360° may be found and their proper sign determined from the signs of the x and y values. This circle representation is all one needs to remember to determine the algebraic signs of the functions in all quadrants, and the relations between functions of angles in the first quadrant and all other angles. Tables are given only for functions of the first quadrant, and it is

---

[1] The symbol θ is the Greek letter Theta.

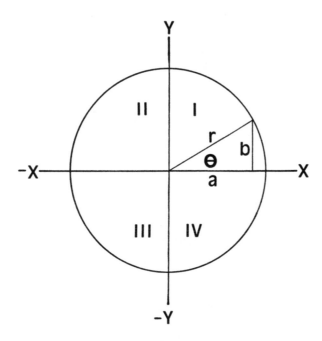

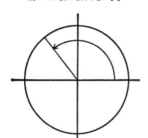

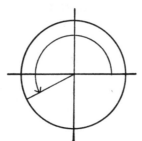

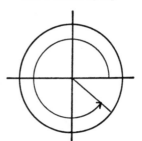

Figure 16-2

frequently necessary to know the functions for greater angles. As noted, the functions will repeat after 360° so if you have an angle greater than 360°, merely subtract multiples of 360° until the result is less than 360° and proceed to find the function of this resulting angle. Angles measured around the circle in a counter-clockwise direction are positive and when measured in a clockwise direction are negative. Thus $-\theta$ is the same as 360° $-\theta$.

Note that all functions are positive in the first quadrant (I). In the second quadrant (II), the sine is positive and the cosine and tangent are negative. In the third quadrant (III) both sine and cosine are negative but the tangent is positive. In quadrant four (IV) the cosine is positive and the sine and tangent are negative.

If the desired function is of an angle between 90° and 360°, subtract either 180° or 360° to give a value between 0° and 90° without regard to sign. Find the function of this angle from the tables and assign the proper algebraic sign as determined from the unit circle for the location of the original angle. See Figure 16-2.

Mathematical handbooks give lists of various trigonometric identities. The ones used in computations in this book may be found in Appendix E.

COMPLEX NUMBERS

If a and b are any two real numbers, a + bi is called a *complex number* and a − bi is its *conjugate* (remember that i is defined by $i^2 = -1$). The product of a complex number by its conjugate is

$$(a+bi)\ (a-bi)=a^2+abi-abi+b^2=a^2+b^2$$

because $\qquad (bi)\ (-bi)=b^2(i)\ (-i)=b^2(-i^2)=b^2$

Every real number corresponds to a unique point on a line with positive numbers to the right of zero and negative numbers to the left of zero.

Complex numbers may be represented by a unique point in a plane. Referring to Figure 16-3, the point P represents a complex number whose real part a is measured along the x axis and whose imaginary part is bi, that is, point P represents the complex number a + bi.

In some computations it is more convenient to express the complex number in trigonometric or polar form. From the right triangle in Figure 16-3

$$a=r \cos \theta \qquad b=r \sin \theta \qquad r^2=a^2+b^2$$

Then $\qquad a+bi=r \cos \theta+ir \sin \theta=r\ (\cos \theta + i \sin \theta).$

To find the roots of a complex number, if n is any positive whole number, DeMoivre's Theorem gives the relation

$$(\cos \theta + i \sin \theta)^n = \cos n\theta + i \sin n\theta.$$

The square root of a complex number must be expressible in the form $R(\cos A + i \sin A)$. Its square would be $R^2(\cos 2A + i \sin 2A)$. Then, to find the square root of a complex number, express it in trigonometric

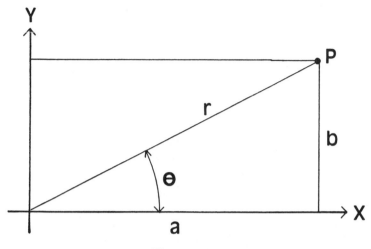

Figure 16-3

form and merely find the square root of its *modulus* ($\sqrt{R^2}$ = R) and divide the angle by two and write down the root. As an example, the square roots of 9 (cos 60° + i sin 60°) = ± 3 (cos 30° + i sin 30°).

There are always three cube roots of any number. The number one has one real root and two complex roots. The roots are 1, $-\frac{1}{2} + \frac{1}{2}\sqrt{3}$ i and $-\frac{1}{2} - \frac{1}{2}\sqrt{3}$ i, or in trigonometric form, cos 0° + i sin 0°, cos 120° + i sin 120° and cos 240° + i sin 240°. To find the cube roots of any complex number, first express it in its trigonometric form. Its root must be expressible in the form R(cos A + i sin A) whose cube is R^3(cos A + i sin A)^3 = R^3(cos 3A + i sin 3A). As an example,

$$\sqrt[3]{8(\cos 45° + i \sin 45°)} = 2(\cos 15° + i \sin 15°)$$

whereR^3 = 8 or R = 2 and 3A = 45° or A = 15°, and since the sine and cosine of an angle are the same as that angle plus any multiple of 360°, cube roots are also

2[cos ⅓ (45°+360°)+i sin ⅓ (45°+360°)]=2 (cos 135° + i sin 135°) and 2 (cos 255° + i sin 255°).

The same result may be obtained by multiplying the first root by the complex cube roots of one. The identity

(cos θ_1 + i sin θ_1) (cos θ_2 + i sin θ_2)=cos (θ_1+θ_2)+ i sin (θ_1+θ_2)

applies.

LOGARITHMS

Use of logarithms will frequently save laborious numerical computations. In the identity $10^2 = 100$, the number 10 is called the *base* and the exponent 2 is called the *logarithm* of the number 100. While any number, greater than 1, may be used as the base, we will restrict ourselves to base 10 logarithms only. We may write $\log_{10} 100 = 2$, read logarithm to base ten of 100 equals 2. The base may be omitted and merely understood. Then $\log 10 = 1$, $\log 1 = 0$, $\log 0.1 = -1$, $\log 0.01 = -2$, etc. The logarithm of a number between 1 and 10 is a fraction, and of a number between 10 and 100 is a number between 1 and 2, etc. The logarithm may be expressed in two parts, an integral portion called the *characteristic* and a fractional portion called the *mantissa*. Tables are made up giving the mantissas. The characteristic is an integer which is added and designates the decimal point. It may be observed that the characteristic is an integer having a value one less than the number of places to the left of the decimal point for numbers greater than one, and for numbers less than one, it is a negative integer having an absolute value one greater than the number of zeros appearing immediately to the right of the decimal point. For example, $\log 30 = 1.47712$, $\log 3 = .47712$ and $\log 0.03 = .47712 - 2$. The last example may also be written as $\log 0.03 = 8.47712 - 10$. There are various other ways of writing the logarithms, but these will suffice.

When using the tables in reverse, that is, finding the number corresponding to a known logarithm, remember to use only the fractional part, then place the decimal point as indicated by the characteristic. The rules for using logarithms are: (1) products of two numbers or more are found by adding their logs and finding the number for this sum; (2) numbers are divided by subtracting the log of the denominator from the log of the numerator to give the log of the quotient; (3) the power of a number is found by multiplying the log of the number by the desired power giving the logarithm of the power; and (4) roots of a number are found by dividing the log of the number by the desired root to give the log of the root.

ALGEBRAIC EQUATIONS

Algebra uses letters to represent variable or unknown quantities along with numerical values. We form algebraic equations when we set one quantity or a group of quantities equal to another group. These equations may be operated on following these rules:

1. If equals are added to equals, the sums are equal.
2. If equals are subtracted from equals, the remainders are equal.
3. If equals are divided by equals, the quotients are equal.
4. If equals are multiplied by equals, the products are equal.
5. The same powers of equal expressions are equal.
6. The same roots of equal expressions are equal.

These rules enable one to solve for an unknown, to eliminate an unknown between certain equations, and to change the form of the expressions.

Certain simple equations may be used to represent stock price movements. An example is the linear equation, or equation of a straight line, $y = ax + b$. When $x = 0$, $y = b$, so the line crosses the y axis at point b, called the y intercept. When $y = 0$, $ax + b = 0$. If b is subtracted from both sides of this equation, $ax + b - b = 0 - b$ or $ax = -b$, then if both sides are divided by a, $x = -b/a$ giving the point of crossing of the x axis. This line may slope in any direction depending on the value and sign of b.

Any linear equation (that is, having only the first power of the unknown x) can be expressed in the form $ax + b = 0$ and is thus called a first-degree equation. An equation of the second degree (of x) can be expressed in the form $ax^2 + bx + c = 0$, and is known as a *quadratic*. It represents a line curving in one direction only. It may be thought of as the sum of two equations. One part, $bx + c$ is a linear, or straight-line part, the other part ax^2. This latter is symmetrical about $x = 0$ since squaring negative values of x gives the same value as the positive values.

The expression $ax^3 + bx^2 + cx + d = 0$ is of degree three and is called a *cubic*. It represents an "S" shape curve, or one curving in one direction, reversing and then curving in the other direction.

In many calculations it becomes necessary to solve equations for the values of x which when substituted in the equation will result in an identity, that is, find the *roots* of x. In $ax + b = 0$, the solution $x = -b/a$ is easily obtained. The second-degree equation $ax^2 + bx + c = 0$ has a solution

$$x = \frac{-b \pm \sqrt{b^2 - 4ac}}{2a}$$

there being two roots given by the $\pm$ values of the radical $\sqrt{b^2 - 4ac}$.

The solution of the cubic equation $x^3 + bx^2 + cx + d = 0$ is more complicated and one proceeds as follows: Find the quantities p, q, R, A and B from

$$p=c-b^2\,3 \qquad q=d-bc/3 + 2b^3/27 \qquad R=(p/3)^3+(q/2)^2$$

$$A=\sqrt[3]{-q\,2+\sqrt{R}} \qquad\qquad B=\sqrt[3]{-q/2-\sqrt{R}}$$

The three roots are then,

$$x_1=A+B-b/3$$

$$x_2=-{}^1\!2(A+B)+i\sqrt{3}(A-B)/2-b/3$$

$$x_3=-\tfrac{1}{2}(A+B)-i\sqrt{3}(A-B)/2-b/3$$

SIMULTANEOUS LINEAR EQUATIONS

We often can derive a system of independent equations in several unknowns. If we have as many equations as unknowns, they can be solved by algebraic combination, to eliminate one unknown at a time until only one remains, then working backward to obtain the values of each unknown one at a time. As a simple example, if we have the two equations

$$x+y = 50 \qquad\qquad (16\text{-}1)$$

$$5x + 2y = 130 \qquad\qquad (16\text{-}2)$$

multiply Equation (16-1) by 5 to give Equation (16-3) and subtract Equation (16-2) thus

$$5x+5y= 250 \qquad\qquad (16\text{-}3)$$

$$\underline{-5x-2y=-130}$$

$$0+3y= 120 \qquad \text{or} \qquad y=120/3=40$$

Substituting the value of $y = 40$ in Equation (16-1) gives $x + 40 = 50$ or $x = 10$. The solution may be checked by substituting the values of x and y

in Equations (16-1) and (16-2). If we have three equations in three unknowns such as

$$2x + y+2z=45 \tag{16-4}$$

$$3x -2y+ z= 5 \tag{16-5}$$

$$2x - y- z= 0 \tag{16-6}$$

the unknown x may be eliminated between Equations (16-4) and (16-5) by multiplying Equation (16-4) by 3 and Equation (16-5) by 2 and subtracting thus,

$$6x+3y+6z= 135$$

$$-6x+4y-2z=-10$$

$$0+7y+4z= 125 \tag{16-7}$$

and from Equations (16-4) and (16-6) by subtracting thus,

$$2x+ y+2z=45$$

$$-2x+ y+ z=0$$

$$0+2y+3z=45 \tag{16-8}$$

Now eliminate y between Equations (16-7) and (16-8) thus,

$$14y+ 8z= 250$$

$$-14y-21z=-315$$

$$0-13z= -65 \qquad \text{or} \qquad z=5$$

Substituting $z = 5$ in Equation (16-8) or (16-7), to obtain y

$$2y+3 \cdot 5=45 \qquad \text{or} \qquad y=15$$

Then, these values in Equation (16-4) give

$$2x+15+2 \cdot 5=45 \qquad \text{or} \qquad x=10$$

THE GAUSS REDUCTION

As the number of unknowns increase, and therefore the number of equations, and when the coefficients become large as well, the above method of solving simultaneous equations becomes tedious and subject to errors. The Gauss Reduction method simplifies the process. The method is first to eliminate the first unknown from all the equations to give a set of equations one less in number. The process is repeated to eliminate the second unknown and reduce the number by one again. This is repeated until only one equation remains with one unknown (the last) whose value is now determined. Then working backwards, the next-to-last unknown is found, etc., until all have been found. As an example, we will solve the set of three equations; (16-4), (16-5) and (16-6), using the Gauss reduction. Refer to the tabulation below as the instructions are given. First, write down

2	1	
1	½	
2	1	
45	45/2	
3	0	
−2	−7/6	1
1	−2/3	4/7
5	−125/6	125/7
2	0	
−1	−1	0
−1	−3/2	13/14
0	−45/2	65/14

the coefficients and right-hand term of each equation in a set of three vertical columns, one above the other. Divide each number in the first (upper) column by the first coefficient of that column to form the first column of a new set written opposite the first. Then divide each number in the next column (corresponding to the second equation) by the first coefficient of that column and subtract the corresponding numbers of the new column above to form the second column of the second set writing it opposite the second column of the first set. This column gives the coefficients and right-hand term of a derived equation in one less unknowns. The same process is carried out with the next (last in this example) column of the first set to form coefficients giving the second equation in one less of the unknowns. The process is repeated with these two sets of coefficients to give a third set of (two) columns as illustrated. The last one (in this example) gives the coefficients of an equation involving only z, that is, $(13/14)z = 65/14$ or $z = 5$. The column just above provides the equation $y + (4/7)z = 125/7$ and with z known to be equal to 5 we can solve for y giving $y = 15$. Proceeding upward, the next equation is $x + \frac{1}{2}y + z = 45/2$ or $x + 15/2 + 5 = 45/2$, giving $x = 10$.

EVALUATING A POLYNOMIAL

The polynomial $y = a + bx + cx^2 + dx^3$ may be written in the form $y = [(dx + c)x + b]x + a$ which can simplify the determination of the values of y for the various values of x. The method may be extended to a polynomial of any degree. In general, starting with the highest power of x, simply multiply the coefficient by x, add the coefficient of the next highest power and multiply the entire quantity by x, etc., until the constant term is reached which is added. If the polynomial is missing some power of x, remember that is the same as a zero coefficient, so zero is added and the quantity is multiplied by x.

SERIES

At times it is convenient to express a quantity as a sum of terms of an infinite series which converges within some reasonable number of terms. The binomial expansion is an example. That is,

$$(x + y)^n = x^n + nx^{n-1}y + \frac{n(n-1)}{2!}x^{n-2}y^2 + \ldots \qquad \text{(if } y^2 < x^2\text{)}$$

This is useful in compound interest computations when the number of times compounded each year becomes large. Take the compound interest formula $A = P(1 + i)^n$ where A is the amount in n years for initial principal P at interest rate i. If compounded t times a year, then the amount of one dollar at the end of one year is $A_1 = (1 + i/t)^t$ and the binomial expression reduces to

$$(1 + i/t)^t = 1 + i + \frac{t(t-1)}{2!}(i/t)^2 + \frac{t(t-1)\,(t-2)}{3!}(i/t)^3 + \ldots$$

The effective annual interest rate is given by the above expression after subtracting one (the \$1 principal). Note when $t = 1$ the expression reduces to i, simple interest, since $t-1=0$ in all following terms.

For daily compounding on a 360 day year, the effective rate would be

$$i+\frac{359 \cdot i^2}{2 \cdot 360}+\frac{359 \cdot 358}{6 \cdot 360^2} \frac{i^3}{} + \ldots$$

If accuracy no greater than three decimal places is required, three terms suffice for ordinary rates, say below 10%.

There are many other series given in mathematical handbooks but in general one has tabulations of values (tables) in which you can merely look up the values to some appropriate accuracy.

DIFFERENTIATION

If we have an equation where y is some function of time t and the variable t changes by an increment such as one day or one week, etc., the value of y will also change by some increment found by subtracting the first value from the second. This increment can be either positive or negative. An increment of t is denoted by the symbol Δt, read delta t, etc.

In a mathematical equation such as

$$y = a + bx \qquad \text{(16-9)}$$

for a straight line, if x takes on an increment, y will take on a corresponding increment and we have

$$y + \Delta y = a + b(x + \Delta x) \qquad \text{(16-10)}$$

If we subtract Equation (16-9) from Equation (16-10) we obtain $\Delta y = b\Delta x$ or the ratio of the increments is $\Delta y / \Delta x = b$. That is, for any increment Δx, y takes on an increment such that the ratio is the constant b. This constant b is known as the slope of the line whose equation is $y = a + bx$.

Taking now a second-degree equation such as $y = x^2$ and as before letting x take on an increment Δx, then subtracting the first equation, we have $y + \Delta y = (x + \Delta x)^2 = x^2 + 2x \Delta x + \Delta x^2$ resulting, after the subtraction, in $\Delta y = 2x \Delta x + \Delta x^2$ or $\Delta y / \Delta x = 2x + \Delta x$. Now as Δx is allowed to become smaller and smaller, Δy likewise becomes smaller and in the limit as Δx approaches zero, the ratio of the increments approaches the value 2x. When Δx approaches the limit zero, the expression is written $dy/dx = 2x$ and is read the derivative of y with respect to x. The process of finding this expression is called *differentiation*. In general, the derivative at a point on a curve is the slope of the line drawn tangent to the curve at that point. We find this useful in locating the maxima and minima of a curve, since the tangent is zero, the line being horizontal, at those points where the curve is rounding over to change direction. Therefore, having the equation of the curve, merely take the derivative and set it equal to zero and solve to find the values of the coordinates where this occurs. The derivative can be zero at points other than reversal points such as when a rising curve flattens out but then proceeds upward instead of turning down. However, this will be apparent from the plot of the equation.

Although the derivative of any expression can be found as illustrated for the simple cases above, tables of derivatives are available in mathematical handbooks. The expressions most likely to be encountered (in stock market analysis) are given in Appendix E.

In some curve-fitting procedures it may be convenient to use the increment as the dependent variable instead of the variable itself. For example, instead of taking the stock price at equal spaced points in time you can use the change in stock price for that increment of time (such as 10 days). This has the effect of minimizing the effect of the longer trends. One should work from a smoothed price curve such as a moving average. The reference time for each increment is the center of the increment, thus if fitting a curve to the smoothed prices, the phase must be referred to this centered value. This procedure is similar to taking the derivative, therefore if you derived a sine curve fit when using the prices, you will get a cosine curve when using the increments.

After taking the derivative of an expression, you may take the derivative of the derivative. This is called the second derivative and is written as d^2y/dx^2. It is read d two of y dx two. The process however, is merely taking the first derivative twice. In the cubic equation, finding the points where the first derivative equals zero locates the reversal points. The second derivative of the cubic set equal to zero and solved for x gives the point of inflection. This is where the curve changes from concave downward to concave upward or vice versa.

SUMS OF POWERS OF THE FIRST n INTEGERS

In making least squares fit of polynomials, it is necessary to find the sum of powers of the independent variable x. When $x = 0$ is placed at the midpoint of the data so that for every n there is a $-n$, all odd powers of x

equal zero. Thus only the sum of the even powers of x have to be found. Formulas are available to give these sums directly[2]. For example, the sum of the squares of x is given for the first n integers as follows

$$\sum_{n=1}^{n} x^2 = 1^2 + 2^2 + 3^2 + \ldots + n^2 = \frac{n(n+1)(2n+1)}{6}$$

but since there is a corresponding negative integer for each positive integer, the sum desired is twice the above or

$$\sum_{-n}^{n} x^2 = \frac{n(n+1)(2n+1)}{3}$$

For example, if n = 10, then

$$\sum_{-10}^{10} x^2 = \frac{10 \cdot 11 \cdot 21}{3} = 770$$

Other even powers are given as follows:

$$\sum_{-n}^{n} x^4 = n(n+1)(2n+1)(3n^2 + 3n - 1)/15$$

$$\sum_{n}^{n} x^6 = n(n+1)(2n+1)(3n^4 + 6n^3 - 3n + 1)/21$$

$$\sum_{-n}^{n} x^8 = n(n+1)(2n+1)(5n^6 + 15n^5 + 5n^4 - 15n^3 - n^2 + 9n - 3)/45$$

---

[2] See Appendix E for formulas for other powers. These and many other mathematical formulas may be found in Weast, Robert C. and Selby, Samuel M. *Handbook of Tables for Mathematics. 3rd ed: The Chemical Rubber Co., 1967.*

APPENDIX A

MOVING AVERAGE ERROR CURVE

A moving average acts as a filter to greatly reduce the amplitude of cyclic price variations whose period is less than the moving average data span while passing less affected those periods much greater than the span. The chart on the following page gives the ratio of the moving average amplitude to the amplitude of the cyclic data in terms of the ratio of the cyclic period to the moving average span (N). These ratios are marked on the curve for various simple fractions.

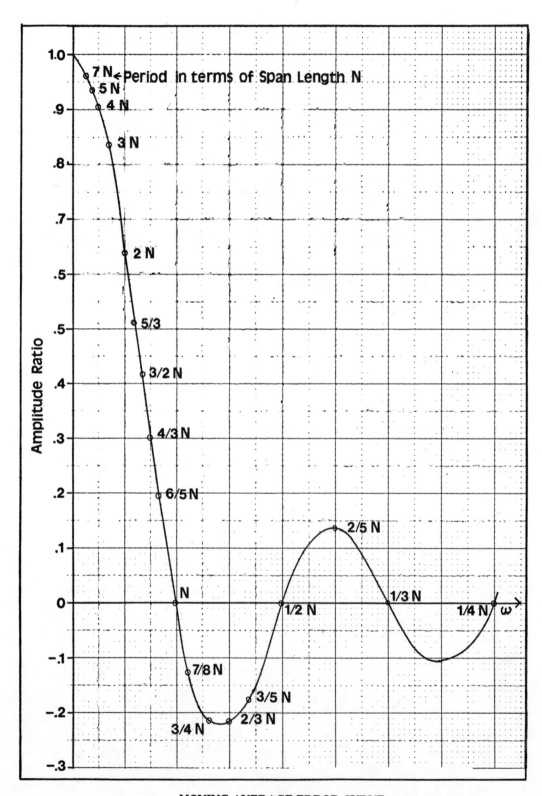

MOVING AVERAGE ERROR CURVE

APPENDIX B

SUMS OF EVEN POWERS OF x

Sums of even powers of x where x takes the values $-n$, $-(n-1)$, ..., $-1, 0, 1, ..., (n-1)$, n. These values are used in making least squares fits to data spans of $2n+1$ where $x = 0$ at the center of the span.

Range of n		Σx^2	Σx^4	Σx^6
-2 to $+2$		10	34	130
-3	3	28	196	1 588
-4	4	60	708	9 780
-5	5	110	1 958	41 030
-6	6	182	4 550	134 342
-7	7	280	9 352	369 640
-8	8	408	17 544	893 928
-9	9	570	30 666	1 956 810
-10	10	770	50 666	3 956 810
-11	11	1 012	79 948	7 499 932
-12	12	1 300	121 420	13 471 900
-13	13	1 638	178 542	23 125 518
-14	14	2 030	255 374	38 184 590
-15	15	2 480	356 624	60 965 840
-16	16	2 992	487 696	94 520 272
-17	17	3 570	654 738	142 795 410
-18	18	4 218	864 690	210 819 858
-19	19	4 940	1 125 332	304 911 620
-20	20	5 740	1 445 332	432 911 620
-21	21	6 622	1 834 294	604 443 862

APPENDIX C

CORRECTION FACTORS FOR PERIOD AND AMPLITUDE

In analyzing stock market data such as plots of prices vs. time, a cyclic trend is often observed. A sine wave may be established which represents the cyclic movement by first making a least squares fit of the cubic equation $y = a + bx + cx^2 + dx^3$. The corresponding sine wave equation will have an indicated period (I.P.) given by I.P. $= 4\sqrt{-b/3d}$. This period should be corrected for span length by the curve of Chart I, where the span length is the length of data span used in making the cubic equation fit.

The phase of the sine wave is established by finding $x_i = -c/3d$, the point of inflection, where the sine is made zero together with a positive or negative sign of the equation which causes the sine to move in the same direction as the data trend.

The indicated amplitude is found by averaging the absolute values of the cubic solution at the two values of x given by $x_i \pm \sqrt{-b/3d}$. This amplitude is in error depending on span length and the ratio of x_i to corrected period found in Chart I. The correction factor is found from the curves of Chart II.

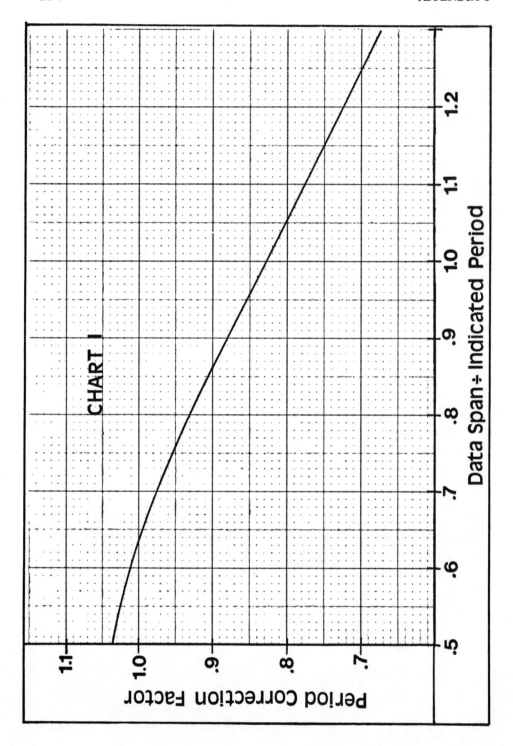

CHART I

Period Correction Factor

Data Span ÷ Indicated Period

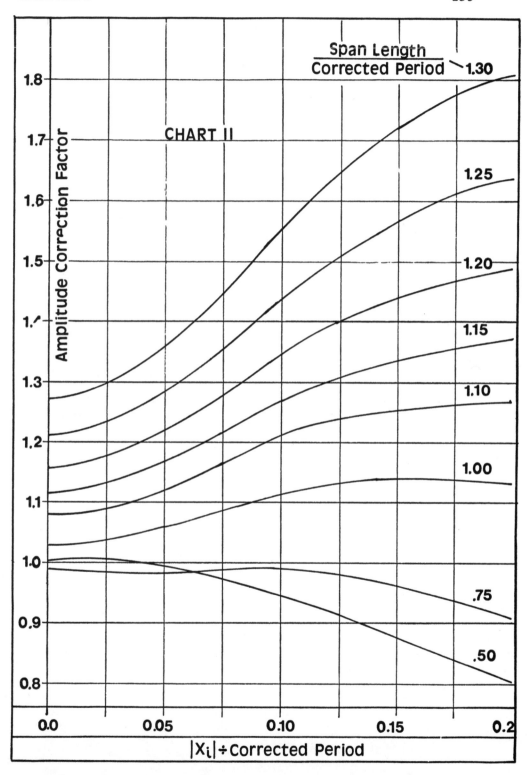

CHART II

APPENDIX D

OPTION VALUES

The empirical equations

$$C = PVA + (P - S)B \qquad\qquad P \geq S \quad (1)$$

$$C = \frac{PVAE}{E + (S - P)/PV} \qquad\qquad P \leq S \quad (2)$$

give the computed value of the call on a stock of price P at a striking price S having D market days to expiration. The values of A, B and E are given for specific values of D in the table on the following page. For other values of D see Chapter 10 giving formulas to compute A, B and E.

The value of V is found for each stock by substituting several combinations of corresponding prices of stock and calls in

$$V = [C+B (S-P)] \div PA$$

and finding their average. See Chapter 10 for criteria in selecting points to give good average values.

D	A	B	E	D	A	B	E
1	0.0	1.0	0.0	95	11.44	0.64	11.31
5	2.89	0.78	1.01	100	11.70	0.64	11.70
10	4.21	0.73	2.11	105	11.95	0.64	12.08
15	5.10	0.70	3.00	110	12.20	0.64	12.45
20	5.80	0.69	3.77	115	12.44	0.64	12.82
25	6.40	0.68	4.47	120	12.68	0.64	13.18
30	6.93	0.67	5.12	125	12.91	0.64	13.54
35	7.41	0.67	5.72	130	13.14	0.64	13.89
40	7.85	0.66	6.29	135	13.36	0.63	14.23
45	8.26	0.66	6.83	140	13.58	0.63	14.57
50	8.65	0.66	7.35	145	13.79	0.63	14.91
55	9.01	0.65	7.84	150	14.00	0.63	15.24
60	9.36	0.65	8.32	155	14.21	0.63	15.56
65	9.69	0.65	8.78	160	14.41	0.63	15.88
70	10.01	0.65	9.23	165	14.61	0.63	16.20
75	10.31	0.65	9.67	170	14.81	0.63	16.51
80	10.61	0.64	10.10	175	15.00	0.63	16.83
85	10.89	0.64	10.51	180	15.19	0.63	17.13
90	11.17	0.64	10.92	185	15.38	0.63	17.44

APPENDIX E

MATHEMATICAL FORMULAS

Mathematical formulas and relations which are encountered in the studies discussed in this book are grouped here for easy reference.

Negative Numbers

$$a-(-b) = a+b \qquad\qquad (-a)(-b) = ab$$

$$a(-b) = -ab \qquad\qquad -a/-b = a/b$$

Exponents

$$a^0 = 1 \qquad\qquad a^x a^y = a^{x+y}$$

$$(ab)^x = a^x b^x \qquad\qquad a^x/a^y = a^{x-y}$$

$$(a^x)^y = a^{xy} \qquad\qquad (a/b)^x = a^x/b^x$$

Complex Numbers

$$i^2 = -1 \qquad\qquad (a+bi)(a-bi) = a^2+b^2$$

Trigonometric Identities

$$\tan\theta = \sin\theta/\cos\theta \qquad\qquad \sin^2\theta + \cos^2\theta = 1 \qquad\cdot$$

$$\sin(180°-\theta) = \sin\theta \qquad\qquad \cos(180°-\theta) = -\cos\theta$$

$$\sin(-\theta) = -\sin\theta \qquad\qquad \cos(-\theta) = \cos\theta$$

Trigonometric Identities *(continued)*

$$\sin(\theta_1 \pm \theta_2) = \sin\theta_1 \cos\theta_2 \pm \cos\theta_1 \sin\theta_2$$

$$\cos(\theta_1 \pm \theta_2) = \cos\theta_1 \cos\theta_2 \mp \sin\theta_1 \sin\theta_2$$

$$\sin\theta_1 \pm \sin\theta_2 = 2\cos\tfrac{1}{2}(\theta_1 \mp \theta_2)\sin\tfrac{1}{2}(\theta_1 \pm \theta_2)$$

$$(\cos\theta + i\sin\theta)^n = \cos n\theta + i\sin n\theta$$

$$\cos(\theta_1 + \theta_2) + i\sin(\theta_1 + \theta_2) = (\cos\theta_1 + i\sin\theta_1)(\cos\theta_2 + i\sin\theta_2)$$

$$2\cos\theta\cos(n\theta) = \cos(n-1)\theta + \cos(n+1)\theta$$

Solution of the Second Degree Equation

$$ax^2 + bx + c = 0 \qquad \text{is} \qquad x = \frac{-b \pm \sqrt{b^2 - 4ac}}{2a}$$

Series

Binomial Expansion

$$(x+y)^n = x^n + nx^{n-1}y + \frac{n(n-1)}{2!}x^{n-2}y^2 + \ldots + \frac{n!x^{n-k}y^k}{(n-k)!k!} + \ldots \quad [y^2 < x^2]$$

Derivatives

$$\frac{dc}{dx} = 0 \qquad\qquad c = \text{a constant} \qquad \frac{dx}{dx} = 1$$

$$\frac{d}{dx}(u+v-w) = \frac{du}{dx} + \frac{dv}{dx} - \frac{dw}{dx} \qquad \frac{d}{dx}(cv) = c\frac{dv}{dx}$$

$$\frac{d}{dx}(uv) = u\frac{dv}{dx} + v\frac{du}{dx} \qquad\qquad \frac{d}{dx}v^n = nv^{n-1}\frac{dv}{dx}$$

$$\frac{d}{dx}\sin v = \cos v\frac{dv}{dx} \qquad\qquad \frac{d}{dx}\cos v = -\sin v\frac{dv}{dx}$$

Sums of Powers of the First n Integers

$$\sum_{n=1}^{n} x = 1+2+3+\ldots+n = \frac{n(n+1)}{2}$$

$$\sum_{n=1}^{n} x^2 = 1^2+2^2+3^2 + \ldots +n^2 = \frac{n(n+1)(2n+1)}{6}$$

$$\sum_{n=1}^{n} x^3 = \frac{n^2(n+1)^2}{4}$$

$$\sum_{n=1}^{n} x^4 = n(n+1)(2n+1)(3n^2+3n-1)/30$$

$$\sum_{n=1}^{n} x^5 = n^2(n+1)^2(2n^2+2n-1)/12$$

$$\sum_{n=1}^{n} x^6 = n(n+1)(2n+1)(3n^4+6n^3-3n+1)/42$$

$$\sum_{n=1}^{n} x^7 = n^2(n+1)^2(3n^4+6n^3-n^2-4n+2)/24$$

$$\sum_{n=1}^{n} x^8 = n(n+1)(2n+1)(5n^6+15n^5+5n^4-15n^3-n^2+9n-3)/90$$

Interest Formulas

Compound interest, where A is the amount in n years for initial principal P at interest rate i, is given by $A = P(1 + i)^i$.

If compounded t times a year, the amount of one dollar at the end of one year is $A_1 = (1 + i/t)^t$.

If compounded daily on a 360-day year, the effective interest rate (accurate to three places) is

$$i+\frac{359\ i^2}{720}+\frac{359\cdot358\ i^3}{6\cdot360^2}+ \ldots$$

When compounded continuously, the effective yearly rate is

$$i+i^2/2+i^3/6+ \ldots$$

Annuity Formulas

The amount of an annuity of unit value per period after (n) periods at interest rate (i) is

$$[(1+i)^n - 1] \div i$$

An annuity whose present value is unity is

$$\frac{i}{1-(1+i)^{-n}}$$

APPENDIX F

REFERENCES

1. Homer, Sidney and Leibowitz, Martin L. *Inside the Yield Book*. Englewood Cliffs, N. J.: Prentice-Hall, Inc., and New York Institute of Finance, 1972.

2. Prime, John H. *Investment Analysis*. Englewood Cliffs, N. J.: Prentice-Hall, Inc., 1967.

3. Hurst, J. M. *The Profit Magic of Stock Transaction Timing*. Englewood Cliffs, N. J.: Prentice-Hall, Inc., 1970.

4. Edwards, Robert D. and Magee, John. *Technical Analysis of Stock Trends*. 5th ed. Springfield: John Magee, Inc., n. d.

5. Lewis, Edward E. *Methods of Statistical Analysis in Economics and Business*. Cambridge: The Riverside Press, 1953.

6. Cummion, John D. *How to get Maximum Leverage from Puts and Calls*. Larchmont, N. Y.: Business Reports, Inc., 1966.

7. Hildebrand, Francis B. *Introduction to Numerical Analysis*. New York: McGraw-Hill Book Co., 1956.

8. Appel, Gerald. *Winning Market Systems*. New York: The Capitalist Reporter, Inc., 1973.

9. Drew, Garfield A. *New Methods for Profit in the Stock Market*. Boston: The Metcalf Press. 1948.

APPENDIX G

MATHEMATICAL TABLES

The mathematical tables of this Appendix are adequate for performing any of the calculations described in this book. The logarithm tables may be used to find powers and roots of numbers and for multiplication and division of larger numbers. The trigonometric tables are given by tenths of a degree for convenience in calculations involving successive integral multiples of angles. The table of squares of the sine and the cosine and their product saves much calculation in trigonometric curve fitting.

In the compound interest formulas discussed in Chapter 2, the expression $(1 + i/t)^{nt}$ may be evaluated using logarithms. Table I gives the logarithms of the quantity in parentheses to eight-place accuracy for specified values for use when the exponent nt is large. After multiplying by nt to obtain the log of the quantity raised to the nt power, the antilogarithms may be found from Table II with sufficient accuracy for practical purposes. For example, the compound amount S of $1 compounded quarterly at 6% for 50 years is found as follows:

$$\log (1 + 0.06/4)^{4 \cdot 50} = \log 1.015^{200} = (0.00\ 646\ 604)^{200} = 1.2932$$

and finding the number corresponding to this logarithm in Table II, the amount $S = \$19.64$.

TABLE I. Logarithms of 1 to 1.199

N	0	1	2	3	4	5	6	7	8	9
1.00	00 000 000	043 408	086 772	130 093	173 371	216 606	259 798	302 947	346 053	389 117
1.01	432 137	475 116	518 051	560 945	603 795	646 604	689 371	732 095	774 778	817 418
1.02	860 017	902 574	945 090	987 563	*029 996	*072 387	*114 736	*157 044	*199 312	*241 537
1.03	01 283 723	325 867	367 970	410 032	452 054	494 035	535 976	577 876	619 735	661 555
1.04	703 334	745 073	786 772	828 431	870 050	911 629	953 168	994 668	*036 123	*077 549
1.05	02 118 930	160 272	201 574	242 837	284 061	325 246	366 392	407 499	448 567	489 596
1.06	530 587	571 538	612 452	653 327	694 163	734 961	775 721	816 442	857 125	897 771
1.07	938 378	978 947	*019 479	*059 972	*100 423	*140 846	*181 227	*221 570	*261 876	*302 145
1.08	03 342 376	382 569	422 726	462 846	502 928	542 974	582 983	622 954	662 890	702 788
1.09	742 650	782 475	822 264	862 016	901 732	941 412	981 055	*020 664	*060 234	*099 769
1.10	04 139 269	178 732	218 160	257 551	296 907	336 228	375 513	414 762	453 976	493 155
1.11	532 298	571 406	610 479	649 517	688 519	727 487	766 420	805 317	844 180	883 009
1.12	921 802	960 561	999 286	*037 976	*076 631	*115 252	*153 839	*192 392	*230 910	*269 394
1.13	05 307 844	346 261	384 643	422 991	461 306	499 586	537 833	576 047	614 226	652 372
1.14	690 485	728 564	766 610	804 623	842 602	880 549	918 460	956 342	994 189	*032 003
1.15	06 069 784	107 532	145 248	182 931	220 581	258 198	295 783	333 336	370 856	408 344
1.16	445 799	483 222	520 613	557 971	595 298	632 593	669 855	707 086	744 284	781 451
1.17	818 586	855 690	892 761	929 801	966 810	*003 787	*040 732	*077 646	*114 529	*151 381
1.18	07 188 201	224 990	261 748	298 475	335 170	371 835	408 469	445 072	481 644	518 186
1.19	554 696	591 176	627 626	664 044	700 433	736 790	773 118	809 415	845 682	881 918

* Since the first two figures will be the same for several lines of the table, they are given in the first line only. The asterisk indicates that the first two numbers of the following line are to be used.

TABLE II. Logarithms*

N	0	1	2	3	4	5	6	7	8	9
10	0000	0043	0086	0128	0170	0212	0253	0294	0334	0374
11	0414	0453	0492	0531	0569	0607	0645	0682	0719	0755
12	0792	0828	0864	0899	0934	0969	1004	1038	1072	1106
13	1139	1173	1206	1239	1271	1303	1335	1367	1399	1430
14	1461	1492	1523	1553	1584	1614	1644	1673	1703	1732
15	1761	1790	1818	1847	1875	1903	1931	1959	1987	2014
16	2041	2068	2095	2122	2148	2175	2201	2227	2253	2279
17	2304	2330	2355	2380	2405	2430	2455	2480	2504	2529
18	2553	2577	2601	2625	2648	2672	2695	2718	2742	2765
19	2788	2810	2833	2856	2878	2900	2923	2945	2967	2989
20	3010	3032	3054	3075	3096	3118	3139	3160	3181	3201
21	3222	3243	3263	3284	3304	3324	3345	3365	3385	3404
22	3424	3444	3464	3483	3502	3522	3541	3560	3579	3598
23	3617	3636	3655	3674	3692	3711	3729	3747	3766	3784
24	3802	3820	3838	3856	3874	3892	3909	3927	3945	3962
25	3979	3997	4014	4031	4048	4065	4082	4099	4116	4133
26	4150	4166	4183	4200	4215	4232	4249	4265	4281	4298
27	4314	4330	4346	4362	4378	4393	4409	4425	4440	4456
28	4472	4487	4502	4518	4533	4548	4564	4579	4594	4609
29	4624	4639	4654	4669	4683	4698	4713	4728	4742	4757
30	4771	4786	4800	4814	4829	4843	4857	4871	4886	4900
31	4914	4928	4942	4955	4969	4983	4997	5011	5024	5038
32	5052	5065	5079	5092	5105	5119	5132	5145	5159	5172
33	5185	5198	5211	5224	5237	5250	5263	5276	5289	5302
34	5315	5328	5340	5353	5366	5378	5391	5403	5416	5428
35	5441	5453	5465	5478	5490	5502	5515	5527	5539	5551
36	5563	5575	5587	5599	5611	5623	5635	5647	5658	5670
37	5682	5694	5705	5717	5729	5740	5752	5763	5775	5786
38	5798	5809	5821	5832	5843	5855	5866	5877	5888	5899
39	5911	5922	5933	5944	5955	5966	5977	5988	5999	6010
40	6021	6031	6042	6053	6064	6075	6085	6096	6107	6117
41	6128	6138	6149	6160	6170	6180	6191	6201	6212	6222
42	6232	6243	6253	6263	6274	6284	6294	6304	6314	6325
43	6335	6345	6355	6365	6375	6385	6395	6405	6415	6425
44	6435	6444	6454	6464	6474	6484	6493	6503	6513	6522
45	6532	6542	6551	6561	6571	6580	6590	6599	6609	6618
46	6628	6637	6646	6656	6665	6675	6684	6693	6702	6712
47	6721	6730	6739	6749	6758	6767	6776	6785	6794	6803
48	6812	6821	6830	6839	6848	6857	6866	6875	6884	6893
49	6902	6911	6920	6928	6937	6946	6955	6964	6972	6981
50	6990	6998	7007	7016	7024	7033	7042	7050	7059	7067
51	7076	7084	7093	7101	7110	7118	7126	7135	7143	7152
52	7160	7168	7177	7185	7193	7202	7210	7218	7226	7235
53	7243	7251	7259	7267	7275	7284	7292	7300	7308	7316
54	7324	7332	7340	7348	7356	7364	7372	7380	7388	7396

* These values are the fractional portion, or mantissa. Add the characteristic for the complete logarithm.

TABLE II Logarithms

N	0	1	2	3	4	5	6	7	8	9
55	7404	7412	7419	7427	7435	7443	7451	7459	7466	7474
56	7482	7490	7497	7505	7513	7520	7528	7536	7543	7551
57	7559	7566	7574	7582	7589	7597	7604	7612	7619	7627
58	7634	7642	7649	7657	7664	7672	7679	7686	7694	7701
59	7709	7716	7723	7731	7738	7745	7752	7760	7767	7774
60	7782	7789	7796	7803	7810	7818	7825	7832	7839	7846
61	7853	7860	7868	7875	7882	7889	7896	7903	7910	7917
62	7924	7931	7938	7945	7952	7959	7966	7973	7980	7987
63	7993	8000	8007	8014	8021	8028	8035	8041	8048	8055
64	8062	8069	8075	8082	8089	8096	8102	8109	8116	8122
65	8129	8136	8142	8149	8156	8162	8169	8176	8182	8189
66	8195	8202	8209	8215	8222	8228	8235	8241	8248	8254
67	8261	8267	8274	8280	8287	8293	8299	8306	8312	8319
68	8325	8331	8338	8344	8351	8357	8363	8370	8376	8382
69	8388	8395	8401	8407	8414	8420	8426	8432	8439	8445
70	8451	8457	8463	8470	8476	8482	8488	8494	8500	8506
71	8513	8519	8525	8531	8537	8543	8549	8555	8561	8567
72	8573	8579	8585	8591	8597	8603	8609	8615	8621	8627
73	8633	8639	8645	8651	8657	8663	8669	8675	8681	8686
74	8692	8698	8704	8710	8716	8722	8727	8733	8739	8745
75	8751	8756	8762	8768	8774	8779	8785	8791	8797	8802
76	8808	8814	8820	8825	8831	8837	8842	8848	8854	8859
77	8865	8871	8876	8882	8887	8893	8899	8904	8910	8915
78	8921	8927	8932	8938	8943	8949	8954	8960	8965	8971
79	8976	8982	8987	8993	8998	9004	9009	9015	9020	9025
80	9031	9036	9042	9047	9053	9058	9063	9069	9074	9079
81	9085	9090	9096	9101	9106	9112	9117	9122	9128	9133
82	9138	9143	9149	9154	9159	9165	9170	9175	9180	9186
83	9191	9196	9201	9206	9212	9217	9222	9227	9232	9238
84	9243	9248	9253	9258	9263	9269	9274	9279	9284	9289
85	9294	9299	9304	9309	9315	9320	9325	9330	9335	9340
86	9345	9350	9355	9360	9365	9370	9375	9380	9385	9390
87	9395	9400	9405	9410	9415	9420	9425	9430	9435	9440
88	9445	9450	9455	9460	9465	9469	9474	9479	9484	9489
89	9494	9499	9504	9509	9513	9518	9523	9528	9533	9538
90	9542	9547	9552	9557	9562	9566	9571	9576	9581	9586
91	9590	9595	9600	9605	9609	9614	9619	9624	9628	9633
92	9638	9643	9647	9652	9657	9661	9666	9671	9675	9680
93	9685	9689	9694	9699	9703	9708	9713	9717	9722	9727
94	9731	9736	9741	9745	9750	9754	9759	9764	9768	9773
95	9777	9782	9786	9791	9795	9800	9805	9809	9814	9818
96	9823	9827	9832	9836	9841	9845	9850	9854	9859	9863
97	9868	9872	9877	9881	9886	9890	9894	9899	9903	9908
98	9912	9917	9921	9926	9930	9934	9939	9943	9948	9952
99	9956	9961	9965	9969	9974	9978	9983	9987	9991	9996

TABLE III. Trigonometric Functions

↓ sin→

Deg.	.0	.1	.2	.3	.4	.5	.6	.7	.8	.9	1.0	
0	.0000	.0017	.0035	.0052	.0070	.0087	.0105	.0122	.0140	.0157	.0175	89
1	.0175	.0192	.0209	.0227	.0244	.0262	.0279	.0297	.0314	.0332	.0349	88
2	.0349	.0366	.0384	.0401	.0419	.0436	.0454	.0471	.0488	.0506	.0523	87
3	.0523	.0541	.0558	.0576	.0593	.0610	.0628	.0645	.0663	.0680	.0698	86
4	.0698	.0715	.0732	.0750	.0767	.0785	.0802	.0819	.0837	.0854	.0872	85
5	.0872	.0889	.0906	.0924	.0941	.0958	.0976	.0993	.1011	.1028	.1045	84
6	.1045	.1063	.1080	.1097	.1115	.1132	.1149	.1167	.1184	.1201	.1219	83
7	.1219	.1236	.1253	.1271	.1288	.1305	.1323	.1340	.1357	.1374	.1392	82
8	.1392	.1409	.1426	.1444	.1461	.1478	.1495	.1513	.1530	.1547	.1564	81
9	.1564	.1582	.1599	.1616	.1633	.1650	.1668	.1685	.1702	.1719	.1736	80
10	.1736	.1754	.1771	.1788	.1805	.1822	.1840	.1857	.1874	.1891	.1908	79
11	.1908	.1925	.1942	.1959	.1977	.1994	.2011	.2028	.2045	.2062	.2079	78
12	.2079	.2096	.2113	.2130	.2147	.2164	.2181	.2198	.2215	.2233	.2250	77
13	.2250	.2267	.2284	.2300	.2317	.2334	.2351	.2368	.2385	.2402	.2419	76
14	.2419	.2436	.2453	.2470	.2487	.2504	.2521	.2538	.2554	.2571	.2588	75
15	.2588	.2605	.2622	.2639	.2656	.2672	.2689	.2706	.2723	.2740	.2756	74
16	.2756	.2773	.2790	.2807	.2823	.2840	.2857	.2874	.2890	.2907	.2924	73
17	.2924	.2940	.2957	.2974	.2990	.3007	.3024	.3040	.3057	.3074	.3090	72
18	.3090	.3107	.3123	.3140	.3156	.3173	.3190	.3206	.3223	.3239	.3256	71
19	.3256	.3272	.3289	.3305	.3322	.3338	.3355	.3371	.3387	.3404	.3420	70
20	.3420	.3437	.3453	.3469	.3486	.3502	.3518	.3535	.3551	.3567	.3584	69
21	.3584	.3600	.3616	.3633	.3649	.3665	.3681	.3697	.3714	.3730	.3746	68
22	.3746	.3762	.3778	.3795	.3811	.3827	.3843	.3859	.3875	.3891	.3907	67
23	.3907	.3923	.3939	.3955	.3971	.3987	.4003	.4019	.4035	.4051	.4067	66
24	.4067	.4083	.4099	.4115	.4131	.4147	.4163	.4179	.4195	.4210	.4226	65
25	.4226	.4242	.4258	.4274	.4289	.4305	.4321	.4337	.4352	.4368	.4384	64
26	.4384	.4399	.4415	.4431	.4446	.4462	.4478	.4493	.4509	.4524	.4540	63
27	.4540	.4555	.4571	.4586	.4602	.4617	.4633	.4648	.4664	.4679	.4695	62
28	.4695	.4710	.4726	.4741	.4756	.4772	.4787	.4802	.4818	.4833	.4848	61
29	.4848	.4863	.4879	.4894	.4909	.4924	.4939	.4955	.4970	.4985	.5000	60
30	.5000	.5015	.5030	.5045	.5060	.5075	.5090	.5105	.5120	.5135	.5150	59
31	.5150	.5165	.5180	.5195	.5210	.5225	.5240	.5255	.5270	.5284	.5299	58
32	.5299	.5314	.5329	.5344	.5358	.5373	.5388	.5402	.5417	.5432	.5446	57
33	.5446	.5461	.5476	.5490	.5505	.5519	.5534	.5548	.5563	.5577	.5592	56
34	.5592	.5606	.5621	.5635	.5650	.5664	.5678	.5693	.5707	.5721	.5736	55
35	.5736	.5750	.5764	.5779	.5793	.5807	.5821	.5835	.5850	.5864	.5878	54
36	.5878	.5892	.5906	.5920	.5934	.5948	.5962	.5976	.5990	.6004	.6018	53
37	.6018	.6032	.6046	.6060	.6074	.6088	.6101	.6115	.6129	.6143	.6157	52
38	.6157	.6170	.6184	.6198	.6211	.6225	.6239	.6252	.6266	.6280	.6293	51
39	.6293	.6307	.6320	.6334	.6347	.6361	.6374	.6388	.6401	.6414	.6428	50
40	.6428	.6441	.6455	.6468	.6481	.6494	.6508	.6521	.6534	.6547	.6561	49
41	.6561	.6574	.6587	.6600	.6613	.6626	.6639	.6652	.6665	.6678	.6691	48
42	.6691	.6704	.6717	.6730	.6743	.6756	.6769	.6782	.6794	.6807	.6820	47
43	.6820	.6833	.6845	.6858	.6871	.6884	.6896	.6909	.6921	.6934	.6947	46
44	.6947	.6959	.6972	.6984	.6997	.7009	.7022	.7034	.7046	.7059	.7071	45
	1.0	.9	.8	.7	.6	.5	.4	.3	.2	.1	.0	Deg.

←cos↑

Trigonometric Functions

↓ sin→

Deg.	.0	.1	.2	.3	.4	.5	.6	.7	.8	.9	1.0	
45	.7071	.7083	.7096	.7108	.7120	.7133	.7145	.7157	.7169	.7181	.7193	44
46	.7193	.7206	.7218	.7230	.7242	.7254	.7266	.7278	.7290	.7302	.7314	43
47	.7314	.7325	.7337	.7349	.7361	.7373	.7385	.7396	.7408	.7420	.7431	42
48	.7431	.7443	.7455	.7466	.7478	.7490	.7501	.7513	.7524	.7536	.7547	41
49	.7547	.7559	.7570	.7581	.7593	.7604	.7615	.7627	.7638	.7649	.7660	40
50	.7660	.7672	.7683	.7694	.7705	.7716	.7727	.7738	.7749	.7760	.7771	39
51	.7771	.7782	.7793	.7804	.7815	.7826	.7837	.7848	.7859	.7869	.7880	38
52	.7880	.7891	.7902	.7912	.7923	.7934	.7944	.7955	.7965	.7976	.7986	37
53	.7986	.7997	.8007	.8018	.8028	.8039	.8049	.8059	.8070	.8080	.8090	36
54	.8090	.8100	.8111	.8121	.8131	.8141	.8151	.8161	.8171	.8181	.8192	35
55	.8192	.8202	.8211	.8221	.8231	.8241	.8251	.8261	.8271	.8281	.8290	34
56	.8290	.8300	.8310	.8320	.8329	.8339	.8348	.8358	.8368	.8377	.8387	33
57	.8387	.8396	.8406	.8415	.8425	.8434	.8443	.8453	.8462	.8471	.8480	32
58	.8480	.8490	.8499	.8508	.8517	.8526	.8536	.8545	.8554	.8563	.8572	31
59	.8572	.8581	.8590	.8599	.8607	.8616	.8625	.8634	.8643	.8652	.8660	30
60	.8660	.8669	.8678	.8686	.8695	.8704	.8712	.8721	.8729	.8738	.8746	29
61	.8746	.8755	.8763	.8771	.8780	.8788	.8796	.8805	.8813	.8821	.8829	28
62	.8829	.8838	.8846	.8854	.8862	.8870	.8878	.8886	.8894	.8902	.8910	27
63	.8910	.8918	.8926	.8934	.8942	.8949	.8957	.8965	.8973	.8980	.8988	26
64	.8988	.8996	.9003	.9011	.9018	.9026	.9033	.9041	.9048	.9056	.9063	25
65	.9063	.9070	.9078	.9085	.9092	.9100	.9107	.9114	.9121	.9128	.9135	24
66	.9135	.9143	.9150	.9157	.9164	.9171	.9178	.9184	.9191	.9198	.9205	23
67	.9205	.9212	.9219	.9225	.9232	.9239	.9245	.9252	.9259	.9265	.9272	22
68	.9272	.9278	.9285	.9291	.9298	.9304	.9311	.9317	.9323	.9330	.9336	21
69	.9336	.9342	.9348	.9354	.9361	.9367	.9373	.9379	.9385	.9391	.9397	20
70	.9397	.9403	.9409	.9415	.9421	.9426	.9432	.9438	.9444	.9449	.9455	19
71	.9455	.9461	.9466	.9472	.9478	.9483	.9489	.9494	.9500	.9505	.9511	18
72	.9511	.9516	.9521	.9527	.9532	.9537	.9542	.9548	.9553	.9558	.9563	17
73	.9563	.9568	.9573	.9578	.9583	.9588	.9593	.9598	.9603	.9608	.9613	16
74	.9613	.9617	.9622	.9627	.9632	.9636	.9641	.9646	.9650	.9655	.9659	15
75	.9659	.9664	.9668	.9673	.9677	.9681	.9686	.9690	.9694	.9699	.9703	14
76	.9703	.9707	.9711	.9715	.9720	.9724	.9728	.9732	.9736	.9740	.9744	13
77	.9744	.9748	.9751	.9755	.9759	.9763	.9767	.9770	.9774	.9778	.9781	12
78	.9781	.9785	.9789	.9792	.9796	.9799	.9803	.9806	.9810	.9813	.9816	11
79	.9816	.9820	.9823	.9826	.9829	.9833	.9836	.9839	.9842	.9845	.9848	10
80	.9848	.9851	.9854	.9857	.9860	.9863	.9866	.9869	.9871	.9874	.9877	9
81	.9877	.9880	.9882	.9885	.9888	.9890	.9893	.9895	.9898	.9900	.9903	8
82	.9903	.9905	.9907	.9910	.9912	.9914	.9917	.9919	.9921	.9923	.9925	7
83	.9925	.9928	.9930	.9932	.9934	.9936	.9938	.9940	.9942	.9943	.9945	6
84	.9945	.9947	.9949	.9951	.9952	.9954	.9956	.9957	.9959	.9960	.9962	5
85	.9962	.9963	.9965	.9966	.9968	.9969	.9971	.9972	.9973	.9974	.9976	4
86	.9976	.9977	.9978	.9979	.9980	.9981	.9982	.9983	.9984	.9985	.9986	3
87	.9986	.9987	.9988	.9989	.9990	.9990	.9991	.9992	.9993	.9993	.9994	2
88	.9994	.9995	.9995	.9996	.9996	.9997	.9997	.9997	.9998	.9998	.9998	1
89	.9998	.9999	.9999	.9999	.9999	1.0000	1.0000	1.0000	1.0000	1.0000	1.0000	0
	1.0	.9	.8	.7	.6	.5	.4	.3	.2	.1	.0	Deg.

←cos↑

Trigonometric Functions

↓ tan→

Deg.	.0	.1	.2	.3	.4	.5	.6	.7	.8	.9	1.0	
0	.0000	.0017	.0035	.0052	.0070	.0087	.0105	.0122	.0140	.0157	.0175	89
1	.0175	.0192	.0209	.0227	.0244	.0262	.0279	.0297	.0314	.0332	.0349	88
2	.0349	.0367	.0384	.0402	.0419	.0437	.0454	.0472	.0489	.0507	.0524	87
3	.0524	.0542	.0559	.0577	.0594	.0612	.0629	.0647	.0664	.0682	.0699	86
4	.0699	.0717	.0734	.0752	.0769	.0787	.0805	.0822	.0840	.0857	.0875	85
5	.0875	.0892	.0910	.0928	.0945	.0963	.0981	.0998	.1016	.1033	.1051	84
6	.1051	.1069	.1086	.1104	.1122	.1139	.1157	.1175	.1192	.1210	.1228	83
7	.1228	.1246	.1263	.1281	.1299	.1317	.1334	.1352	.1370	.1388	.1405	82
8	.1405	.1423	.1441	.1459	.1477	.1495	.1512	.1530	.1548	.1566	.1584	81
9	.1584	.1602	.1620	.1638	.1655	.1673	.1691	.1709	.1727	.1745	.1763	80
10	.1763	.1781	.1799	.1817	.1835	.1853	.1871	.1890	.1908	.1926	.1944	79
11	.1944	.1962	.1980	.1998	.2016	.2035	.2053	.2071	.2089	.2107	.2126	78
12	.2126	.2144	.2162	.2180	.2199	.2217	.2235	.2254	.2272	.2290	.2309	77
13	.2309	.2327	.2345	.2364	.2382	.2401	.2419	.2438	.2456	.2475	.2493	76
14	.2493	.2512	.2530	.2549	.2568	.2586	.2605	.2623	.2642	.2661	.2679	75
15	.2679	.2698	.2717	.2736	.2754	.2773	.2792	.2811	.2830	.2849	.2867	74
16	.2867	.2886	.2905	.2924	.2943	.2962	.2981	.3000	.3019	.3038	.3057	73
17	.3057	.3076	.3096	.3115	.3134	.3153	.3172	.3191	.3211	.3230	.3249	72
18	.3249	.3269	.3288	.3307	.3327	.3346	.3365	.3385	.3404	.3424	.3443	71
19	.3443	.3463	.3482	.3502	.3522	.3541	.3561	.3581	.3600	.3620	.3640	70
20	.3640	.3659	.3679	.3699	.3719	.3739	.3759	.3779	.3799	.3819	.3839	69
21	.3839	.3859	.3879	.3899	.3919	.3939	.3959	.3979	.4000	.4020	.4040	68
22	.4040	.4061	.4081	.4101	.4122	.4142	.4163	.4183	.4204	.4224	.4245	67
23	.4245	.4265	.4286	.4307	.4327	.4348	.4369	.4390	.4411	.4431	.4452	66
24	.4452	.4473	.4494	.4515	.4536	.4557	.4578	.4599	.4621	.4642	.4663	65
25	.4663	.4684	.4706	.4727	.4748	.4770	.4791	.4813	.4834	.4856	.4877	64
26	.4877	.4899	.4921	.4942	.4964	.4986	.5008	.5029	.5051	.5073	.5095	63
27	.5095	.5117	.5139	.5161	.5184	.5206	.5228	.5250	.5272	.5295	.5317	62
28	.5317	.5340	.5362	.5384	.5407	.5430	.5452	.5475	.5498	.5520	.5543	61
29	.5543	.5566	.5589	.5612	.5635	.5658	.5681	.5704	.5727	.5750	.5774	60
30	.5774	.5797	.5820	.5844	.5867	.5890	.5914	.5938	.5961	.5985	.6009	59
31	.6009	.6032	.6056	.6080	.6104	.6128	.6152	.6176	.6200	.6224	.6249	58
32	.6249	.6273	.6297	.6322	.6346	.6371	.6395	.6420	.6445	.6469	.6494	57
33	.6494	.6519	.6544	.6569	.6594	.6619	.6644	.6669	.6694	.6720	.6745	56
34	.6745	.6771	.6796	.6822	.6847	.6873	.6899	.6924	.6950	.6976	.7002	55
35	.7002	.7028	.7054	.7080	.7107	.7133	.7159	.7186	.7212	.7239	.7265	54
36	.7265	.7292	.7319	.7346	.7373	.7400	.7427	.7454	.7481	.7508	.7536	53
37	.7536	.7563	.7590	.7618	.7646	.7673	.7701	.7729	.7757	.7785	.7813	52
38	.7813	.7841	.7869	.7898	.7926	.7954	.7983	.8012	.8040	.8069	.8098	51
39	.8098	.8127	.8156	.8185	.8214	.8243	.8273	.8302	.8332	.8361	.8391	50
40	.8391	.8421	.8451	.8481	.8511	.8541	.8571	.8601	.8632	.8662	.8693	49
41	.8693	.8724	.8754	.8785	.8816	.8847	.8878	.8910	.8941	.8972	.9004	48
42	.9004	.9036	.9067	.9099	.9131	.9163	.9195	.9228	.9260	.9293	.9325	47
43	.9325	.9358	.9391	.9424	.9457	.9490	.9523	.9556	.9590	.9623	.9657	46
44	.9657	.9691	.9725	.9759	.9793	.9827	.9861	.9896	.9930	.9965	1.0000	45
	1.0	.9	.8	.7	.6	.5	.4	.3	.2	.1	.0	Deg.

←cot↑

Trigonometric Functions

↓tan→

Deg.	.0	.1	.2	.3	.4	.5	.6	.7	.8	.9	1.0	
45	1.000	1.003	1.007	1.011	1.014	1.018	1.021	1.025	1.028	1.032	1.036	44
46	1.036	1.039	1.043	1.046	1.050	1.054	1.057	1.061	1.065	1.069	1.072	43
47	1.072	1.076	1.080	1.084	1.087	1.091	1.095	1.099	1.103	1.107	1.111	42
48	1.111	1.115	1.118	1.122	1.126	1.130	1.134	1.138	1.142	1.146	1.150	41
49	1.150	1.154	1.159	1.163	1.167	1.171	1.175	1.179	1.183	1.188	1.192	40
50	1.192	1.196	1.200	1.205	1.209	1.213	1.217	1.222	1.226	1.230	1.235	39
51	1.235	1.239	1.244	1.248	1.253	1.257	1.262	1.266	1.271	1.275	1.280	38
52	1.280	1.285	1.289	1.294	1.299	1.303	1.308	1.313	1.317	1.322	1.327	37
53	1.327	1.332	1.337	1.342	1.347	1.351	1.356	1.361	1.366	1.371	1.376	36
54	1.376	1.381	1.387	1.392	1.397	1.402	1.407	1.412	1.418	1.423	1.428	35
55	1.428	1.433	1.439	1.444	1.450	1.455	1.460	1.466	1.471	1.477	1.483	34
56	1.483	1.488	1.494	1.499	1.505	1.511	1.517	1.522	1.528	1.534	1.540	33
57	1.540	1.546	1.552	1.558	1.564	1.570	1.576	1.582	1.588	1.594	1.600	32
58	1.600	1.607	1.613	1.619	1.625	1.632	1.638	1.645	1.651	1.658	1.664	31
59	1.664	1.671	1.678	1.684	1.691	1.698	1.704	1.711	1.718	1.725	1.732	30
60	1.732	1.739	1.746	1.753	1.760	1.767	1.775	1.782	1.789	1.797	1.804	29
61	1.804	1.811	1.819	1.827	1.834	1.842	1.849	1.857	1.865	1.873	1.881	28
62	1.881	1.889	1.897	1.905	1.913	1.921	1.929	1.937	1.946	1.954	1.963	27
63	1.963	1.971	1.980	1.988	1.997	2.006	2.014	2.023	2.032	2.041	2.050	26
64	2.050	2.059	2.069	2.078	2.087	2.097	2.106	2.116	2.125	2.135	2.145	25
65	2.145	2.154	2.164	2.174	2.184	2.194	2.204	2.215	2.225	2.236	2.246	24
66	2.246	2.257	2.267	2.278	2.289	2.300	2.311	2.322	2.333	2.344	2.356	23
67	2.356	2.367	2.379	2.391	2.402	2.414	2.426	2.438	2.450	2.463	2.475	22
68	2.475	2.488	2.500	2.513	2.526	2.539	2.552	2.565	2.578	2.592	2.605	21
69	2.605	2.619	2.633	2.646	2.660	2.675	2.689	2.703	2.718	2.733	2.747	20
70	2.747	2.762	2.778	2.793	2.808	2.824	2.840	2.856	2.872	2.888	2.904	19
71	2.904	2.921	2.937	2.954	2.971	2.989	3.006	3.024	3.042	3.060	3.078	18
72	3.078	3.096	3.115	3.133	3.152	3.172	3.191	3.211	3.230	3.251	3.271	17
73	3.271	3.291	3.312	3.333	3.354	3.376	3.398	3.420	3.442	3.465	3.487	16
74	3.487	3.511	3.534	3.558	3.582	3.606	3.630	3.655	3.681	3.706	3.732	15
75	3.732	3.758	3.785	3.812	3.839	3.867	3.895	3.923	3.952	3.981	4.011	14
76	4.011	4.041	4.071	4.102	4.134	4.165	4.198	4.230	4.264	4.297	4.331	13
77	4.331	4.366	4.402	4.437	4.474	4.511	4.548	4.586	4.625	4.665	4.705	12
78	4.705	4.745	4.787	4.829	4.872	4.915	4.959	5.005	5.050	5.097	5.145	11
79	5.145	5.193	5.242	5.292	5.343	5.396	5.449	5.503	5.558	5.614	5.671	10
80	5.671	5.730	5.789	5.850	5.912	5.976	6.041	6.107	6.174	6.243	6.314	9
81	6.314	6.386	6.460	6.535	6.612	6.691	6.772	6.855	6.940	7.026	7.115	8
82	7.115	7.207	7.300	7.396	7.495	7.596	7.700	7.806	7.916	8.028	8.144	7
83	8.144	8.264	8.386	8.513	8.643	8.777	8.915	9.058	9.205	9.357	9.514	6
84	9.514	9.677	9.845	10.02	10.20	10.39	10.58	10.78	10.99	11.20	11.43	5
85	11.43	11.66	11.91	12.16	12.43	12.71	13.00	13.30	13.62	13.95	14.30	4
86	14.30	14.67	15.06	15.46	15.89	16.35	16.83	17.34	17.89	18.46	19.08	3
87	19.08	19.74	20.45	21.20	22.02	22.90	23.86	24.90	26.03	27.27	28.64	2
88	28.64	30.14	31.82	33.69	35.80	38.19	40.92	44.07	47.74	52.08	57.29	1
89	57.29	63.66	71.62	81.85	95.49	114.6	143.2	191.0	286.5	573.0	∞	0
	1.0	.9	.8	.7	.6	.5	.4	.3	.2	.1	.0	Deg.

←cot↑

TABLE IV. Square of the Sine and Cosine and Their Product

Deg.	sin²	*sin · cos	cos²	Deg.
0.0	.00000	.00000	1.00000	90.0
.1	.00000	.00175	1.00000	89.9
.2	.00001	.00349	.99999	.8
.3	.00003	.00524	.99997	.7
.4	.00005	.00698	.99995	.6
.5	.00008	.00873	.99992	.5
.6	.00011	.01047	.99989	.4
.7	.00015	.01222	.99985	.3
.8	.00019	.01396	.99981	.2
.9	.00025	.01571	.99975	89.1
1.0	.00030	.01745	.99970	89.0
.1	.00037	.01919	.99963	88.9
.2	.00044	.02094	.99956	.8
.3	.00051	.02268	.99949	.7
.4	.00060	.02442	.99940	.6
.5	.00069	.02617	.99931	.5
.6	.00078	.02791	.99922	.4
.7	.00088	.02965	.99912	.3
.8	.00099	.03140	.99901	.2
.9	.00110	.03314	.99890	88.1
2.0	.00122	.03488	.99878	88.0
.1	.00134	.03662	.99866	87.9
.2	.00147	.03836	.99853	.8
.3	.00161	.04010	.99839	.7
.4	.00175	.04184	.99825	.6
.5	.00190	.04358	.99810	.5
.6	.00206	.04532	.99794	.4
.7	.00222	.04705	.99778	.3
.8	.00239	.04879	.99761	.2
.9	.00256	.05053	.99744	87.1
3.0	.00274	.05226	.99726	87.0
.1	.00292	.05400	.99708	86.9
.2	.00312	.05573	.99688	.8
.3	.00331	.05747	.99669	.7
.4	.00352	.05920	.99648	.6
.5	.00373	.06093	.99627	.5
.6	.00394	.06267	.99606	.4
.7	.00416	.06440	.99584	.3
.8	.00439	.06613	.99561	.2
.9	.00463	.06786	.99537	86.1
4.0	.00487	.06959	.99513	86.0
.1	.00511	.07131	.99489	85.9
.2	.00536	.07304	.99464	.8
.3	.00562	.07477	.99438	.7
.4	.00589	.07649	.99411	.6
.5	.00616	.07822	.99384	.5
.6	.00643	.07994	.99357	.4
.7	.00671	.08166	.99329	.3
.8	.00700	.08338	.99300	.2
4.9	.00730	.08510	.99270	85.1
Deg.	**cos²**	**sin · cos**	**sin²**	**Deg.**

Deg.	sin²	sin · cos	cos²	Deg.
5.0	.00760	.08682	.99240	85.0
.1	.00790	.08854	.99210	84.9
.2	.00821	.09026	.99179	.8
.3	.00853	.09198	.99147	.7
.4	.00886	.09369	.99114	.6
.5	.00919	.09540	.99081	.5
.6	.00952	.09712	.99048	.4
.7	.00986	.09883	.99014	.3
.8	.01021	.10054	.98979	.2
.9	.01057	.10225	.98943	84.1
6.0	.01093	.10396	.98907	84.0
.1	.01129	.10566	.98871	83.9
.2	.01166	.10737	.98834	.8
.3	.01204	.10907	.98796	.7
.4	.01243	.11077	.98757	.6
.5	.01281	.11248	.98719	.5
.6	.01321	.11418	.98679	.4
.7	.01361	.11587	.98639	.3
.8	.01402	.11757	.98598	.2
.9	.01443	.11927	.98557	83.1
7.0	.01485	.12096	.98515	83.0
.1	.01528	.12265	.98472	82.9
.2	.01571	.12434	.98429	.8
.3	.01615	.12603	.98385	.7
.4	.01659	.12772	.98341	.6
.5	.01704	.12941	.98296	.5
.6	.01749	.13109	.98251	.4
.7	.01795	.13278	.98205	.3
.8	.01842	.13446	.98158	.2
.9	.01889	.13614	.98111	82.1
8.0	.01937	.13782	.98063	82.0
.1	.01985	.13950	.98015	81.9
.2	.02034	.14117	.97966	.8
.3	.02084	.14284	.97916	.7
.4	.02134	.14452	.97866	.6
.5	.02185	.14619	.97815	.5
.6	.02236	.14785	.97764	.4
.7	.02288	.14952	.97712	.3
.8	.02340	.15118	.97660	.2
.9	.02394	.15285	.97606	81.1
9.0	.02447	.15451	.97553	81.0
.1	.02501	.15617	.97499	80.9
.2	.02556	.15782	.97444	.8
.3	.02612	.15946	.97388	.7
.4	.02668	.16113	.97332	.6
.5	.02724	.16278	.97276	.5
.6	.02781	.16443	.97219	.4
.7	.02839	.16608	.97161	.3
.8	.02897	.16773	.97103	.2
9.9	.02956	.16937	.97044	80.1
Deg.	**cos²**	**sin · cos**	**sin²**	**Deg.**

* For angles in the second and fourth quadrant, the product of sine and cosine is negative.

TABLE IV (Continued)

Deg.	sin²	sin·cos	cos²	Deg.
10.0	.03015	.17101	.96985	80.0
.1	.03075	.17265	.96925	79.9
.2	.03136	.17429	.96864	.8
.3	.03197	.17592	.96803	.7
.4	.03259	.17755	.96741	.6
.5	.03321	.17918	.96679	.5
.6	.03384	.18081	.96616	.4
.7	.03447	.18244	.96553	.3
.8	.03511	.18406	.96489	.2
.9	.03576	.18568	.96424	79.1
11.0	.03641	.18730	.96359	79.0
.1	.03706	.18892	.96294	78.9
.2	.03773	.19054	.96227	.8
.3	.03839	.19215	.96161	.7
.4	.03907	.19376	.96093	.6
.5	.03975	.19537	.96025	.5
.6	.04043	.19697	.95957	.4
.7	.04112	.19857	.95888	.3
.8	.04182	.20017	.95818	.2
.9	.04252	.20177	.95748	78.1
12.0	.04323	.20337	.95677	78.0
.1	.04394	.20496	.95606	77.9
.2	.04466	.20655	.95534	.8
.3	.04538	.20814	.95462	.7
.4	.04611	.21973	.95389	.6
.5	.04685	.21131	.95315	.5
.6	.04759	.21289	.95241	.4
.7	.04833	.21447	.95167	.3
.8	.04908	.21604	.95092	.2
.9	.04984	.21762	.95016	77.1
13.0	.05060	.21919	.94940	77.0
.1	.05137	.22075	.94863	76.9
.2	.05214	.22232	.94786	.8
.3	.05292	.22388	.94708	.7
.4	.05371	.22544	.94629	.6
.5	.05450	.22700	.94550	.5
.6	.05529	.22855	.94471	.4
.7	.05609	.23010	.94391	.3
.8	.05690	.23165	.94310	.2
.9	.05771	.23319	.94229	76.1
14.0	.05853	.23474	.94147	76.0
.1	.05935	.23628	.94065	75.9
.2	.06018	.23781	.93982	.8
.3	.06101	.23935	.93899	.7
.4	.06185	.24088	.93815	.6
.5	.06269	.24240	.93731	.5
.6	.06354	.24393	.93646	.4
.7	.06439	.24545	.93561	.3
.8	.06525	.24697	.93475	.2
.9	.06612	.24849	.93388	75.1
15.0	.06699	.25000	.93301	75.0
.1	.06786	.25151	.93214	74.9
.2	.06874	.25302	.93126	.8
.3	.06963	.25452	.93037	.7
.4	.07052	.25602	.92948	.6
.5	.07142	.25752	.92858	.5
.6	.07232	.25901	.92768	.4
.7	.07322	.26050	.92678	.3
.8	.07414	.26199	.92586	.2
15.9	.07505	.26348	.92495	74.1

Deg.	sin²	sin·cos	cos²	Deg.
16.0	.07598	.26496	.92402	74.0
.1	.07690	.26644	.92310	73.9
.2	.07784	.26791	.92216	.8
.3	.07877	.26939	.92123	.7
.4	.07972	.27085	.92028	.6
.5	.08066	.27232	.91934	.5
.6	.08162	.27378	.91838	.4
.7	.08258	.27524	.91742	.3
.8	.08354	.27670	.91646	.2
.9	.08451	.27815	.91549	73.1
17.0	.08548	.27960	.91452	73.0
.1	.08646	.28104	.91354	72.9
.2	.08744	.28248	.91256	.8
.3	.08843	.28392	.91157	.7
.4	.08943	.28536	.91057	.6
.5	.09042	.28679	.90958	.5
.6	.09143	.28822	.90857	.4
.7	.09244	.28964	.90756	.3
.8	.09345	.29106	.90655	.2
.9	.09447	.29248	.90553	72.1
18.0	.09549	.29389	.90451	72.0
.1	.09652	.29530	.90348	71.9
.2	.09755	.29671	.90245	.8
.3	.09859	.29811	.90141	.7
.4	.09963	.29951	.90037	.6
.5	.10068	.30091	.89932	.5
.6	.10174	.30230	.89826	.4
.7	.10279	.30369	.89721	.3
.8	.10386	.30507	.89614	.2
.9	.10492	.30645	.89508	71.1
19.0	.10599	.30783	.89401	71.0
.1	.10707	.30920	.89293	70.9
.2	.10815	.31057	.89185	.8
.3	.10924	.31194	.89076	.7
.4	.11033	.31330	.88967	.6
.5	.11143	.31466	.88857	.5
.6	.11253	.31601	.88747	.4
.7	.11363	.31737	.88637	.3
.8	.11474	.31871	.88526	.2
.9	.11586	.32005	.88414	70.1
20.0	.11698	.32139	.88302	70.0
.1	.11810	.32273	.88190	69.9
.2	.11923	.32406	.88077	.8
.3	.12036	.32539	.87964	.7
.4	.12150	.32671	.87850	.6
.5	.12265	.32803	.87735	.5
.6	.12379	.32934	.87621	.4
.7	.12494	.33066	.87506	.3
.8	.12610	.33196	.87390	.2
.9	.12726	.33327	.87274	69.1
21.0	.12843	.33457	.87157	69.0
.1	.12960	.33586	.87040	68.9
.2	.13077	.33715	.86923	.8
.3	.13195	.33844	.86805	.7
.4	.13314	.33972	.86686	.6
.5	.13432	.34100	.86568	.5
.6	.13552	.34227	.86448	.4
.7	.13671	.34354	.86329	.3
.8	.13791	.34481	.86209	.2
21.9	.13912	.34607	.86088	68.1

Deg.	cos²	sin·cos	sin²	Deg.

TABLE IV (Continued)

Deg.	$\sin^2$	sin·cos	$\cos^2$	Deg.	Deg.	$\sin^2$	sin·cos	$\cos^2$	Deg.
22.0	.14033	.34733	.85967	68.0	28.0	.22040	.41452	.77960	62.0
.1	.14154	.34858	.85846	67.9	.1	.22185	.41549	.77815	61.9
.2	.14276	.34983	.85724	.8	.2	.22330	.41646	.77670	.8
.3	.14399	.35108	.85601	.7	.3	.22476	.41742	.77524	.7
.4	.14521	.35232	.85479	.6	.4	.22622	.41838	.77378	.6
.5	.14645	.35355	.85355	.5	.5	.22768	.41934	.77232	.5
.6	.14768	.35479	.85232	.4	.6	.22915	.42028	.77085	.4
.7	.14892	.35601	.85108	.3	.7	.23061	.42123	.76939	.3
.8	.15017	.35724	.84983	.2	.8	.23209	.42216	.76791	.2
.9	.15142	.35846	.84858	67.1	.9	.23356	.42310	.76644	61.1
23.0	.15267	.35967	.84733	67.0	29.0	.23504	.42402	.75496	61.0
.1	.15393	.36088	.84607	66.9	.1	.23652	.42495	.76348	60.9
.2	.15519	.36209	.84481	.8	.2	.23801	.42586	.76199	.8
.3	.15646	.36329	.84354	.7	.3	.23950	.42678	.76050	.7
.4	.15773	.36448	.84227	.6	.4	.24099	.42768	.75901	.6
.5	.15900	.36568	.84100	.5	.5	.24248	.42858	.75752	.5
.6	.16028	.36686	.83972	.4	.6	.24398	.42948	.75602	.4
.7	.16156	.36805	.83844	.3	.7	.24548	.43037	.75452	.3
.8	.16285	.36923	.83715	.2	.8	.24698	.43126	.75302	.2
.9	.16414	.37040	.83586	66.1	.9	.24849	.43214	.75151	60.1
24.0	.16543	.37157	.83457	66.0	30.0	.25000	.43301	.75000	60.0
.1	.16673	.37274	.83327	65.9	.1	.25151	.43338	.74849	59.9
.2	.16804	.37390	.83196	.8	.2	.25303	.43475	.74697	.8
.3	.16934	.37506	.83066	.7	.3	.25455	.43561	.74545	.7
.4	.17066	.37621	.82934	.6	.4	.25607	.43646	.74393	.6
.5	.17197	.37735	.82803	.5	.5	.25760	.43731	.74240	.5
.6	.17329	.37850	.82671	.4	.6	.25912	.43815	.74088	.4
.7	.17461	.37964	.82539	.3	.7	.26065	.43899	.73935	.3
.8	.17594	.38077	.82406	.2	.8	.26219	.43982	.73781	.2
.9	.17727	.38190	.82273	65.1	.9	.26372	.44065	.73628	59.1
25.0	.17861	.38302	.82139	65.0	31.0	.26526	.44147	.73474	59.0
.1	.17995	.38414	.82005	64.9	.1	.26681	.44229	.73319	58.9
.2	.18129	.38526	.81871	.8	.2	.26835	.44310	.73165	.8
.3	.18263	.38637	.81737	.7	.3	.26990	.44391	.73009	.7
.4	.18399	.38747	.81601	.6	.4	.27145	.44471	.72855	.6
.5	.18534	.38857	.81466	.5	.5	.27300	.44550	.72700	.5
.6	.18670	.38967	.81330	.4	.6	.27456	.44629	.72544	.4
.7	.18806	.39076	.81194	.3	.7	.27612	.44708	.72388	.3
.8	.18943	.39185	.81057	.2	.8	.27768	.44786	.72232	.2
.9	.19080	.39293	.80920	64.1	.9	.27925	.44863	.72075	58.1
26.0	.19217	.39401	.80783	64.0	32.0	.28081	.44940	.71919	58.0
.1	.19355	.39508	.80645	63.9	.1	.28238	.45016	.71762	57.9
.2	.19493	.39614	.80507	.8	.2	.28396	.45092	.71604	.8
.3	.19631	.39721	.80369	.7	.3	.28553	.45167	.71447	.7
.4	.19770	.39827	.80230	.6	.4	.28711	.45241	.71289	.6
.5	.19909	.39932	.80091	.5	.5	.28869	.45315	.71131	.5
.6	.20049	.40037	.79951	.4	.6	.29027	.45389	.70973	.4
.7	.20189	.40141	.79811	.3	.7	.29186	.45462	.70814	.3
.8	.20329	.40245	.79671	.2	.8	.29345	.45534	.70655	.2
.9	.20470	.40348	.79530	63.1	.9	.29504	.45606	.70496	57.1
27.0	.20611	.40451	.79389	63.0	33.0	.29663	.45677	.70337	57.0
.1	.20752	.40553	.79248	62.9	.1	.29823	.45748	.70177	56.9
.2	.20894	.40655	.79106	.8	.2	.29983	.45818	.70017	.8
.3	.21035	.40756	.78964	.7	.3	.30143	.45888	.69857	.7
.4	.21178	.40857	.78822	.6	.4	.30303	.45957	.69697	.6
.5	.21321	.40958	.78679	.5	.5	.30463	.46025	.69537	.5
.6	.21464	.41057	.78536	.4	.6	.30624	.46093	.69376	.4
.7	.21608	.41157	.78392	.3	.7	.30785	.46161	.69215	.3
.8	.21752	.41256	.78248	.2	.8	.30946	.46227	.69054	.2
27.9	.21896	.41354	.78104	62.1	33.9	.31108	.46294	.68892	56.1
Deg.	$\cos^2$	sin·cos	$\sin^2$	Deg.	Deg.	$\cos^2$	sin·cos	$\sin^2$	Deg.

254

TABLE IV (Continued)

Deg.	sin²	sin·cos	cos²	Deg.
34.0	.31270	.46359	.68730	56.0
.1	.31432	.46424	.68568	55.9
.2	.31594	.46489	.68406	.8
.3	.31756	.46553	.68244	.7
.4	.31919	.46616	.68081	.6
.5	.32082	.46679	.67918	.5
.6	.32245	.46741	.67755	.4
.7	.32408	.46803	.67592	.3
.8	.32571	.46864	.67429	.2
.9	.32735	.46925	.67265	55.1
35.0	.32899	.46985	.67101	55.0
.1	.33063	.47044	.66937	54.9
.2	.33227	.47103	.66773	.8
.3	.33392	.47161	.66608	.7
.4	.33557	.47219	.66443	.6
.5	.33722	.47276	.66278	.5
.6	.33887	.47332	.66113	.4
.7	.34052	.47388	.65948	.3
.8	.34218	.47444	.65782	.2
.9	.34383	.47499	.65617	54.1
36.0	.34549	.47553	.65451	54.0
.1	.34715	.47606	.65285	53.9
.2	.34882	.47660	.65118	.8
.3	.35048	.47712	.64952	.7
.4	.35215	.47764	.64785	.6
.5	.35381	.47815	.64619	.5
.6	.35548	.47866	.64452	.4
.7	.35716	.47916	.64284	.3
.8	.35883	.47966	.64117	.2
.9	.36050	.48015	.63950	53.1
37.0	.36218	.48063	.63782	53.0
.1	.36386	.48111	.63614	52.9
.2	.36554	.48158	.63446	.8
.3	.36722	.48205	.63278	.7
.4	.36891	.48251	.63109	.6
.5	.37059	.48296	.62941	.5
.6	.37228	.48341	.62772	.4
.7	.37397	.48385	.62603	.3
.8	.37566	.48429	.62434	.2
.9	.37735	.48472	.62265	52.1
38.0	.37904	.48515	.62096	52.0
.1	.38073	.48557	.61927	51.9
.2	.38243	.48598	.61757	.8
.3	.38413	.48639	.61587	.7
.4	.38582	.48679	.61418	.6
.5	.38752	.48719	.61248	.5
.6	.38923	.48757	.61077	.4
.7	.39093	.48796	.60907	.3
.8	.39263	.48834	.60737	.2
.9	.39434	.48871	.60566	51.1
39.0	.39604	.48907	.60396	51.0
.1	.39775	.48943	.60225	50.9
.2	.39946	.48979	.60054	.8
.3	.40117	.49014	.59883	.7
.4	.40288	.49048	.59712	.6
Deg.	**cos²**	**sin·cos**	**sin²**	**Deg.**

Deg.	sin²	sin·cos	cos²	Deg.
39.5	.40460	.49081	.59540	50.5
.6	.40631	.49114	.59369	.4
.7	.40802	.49147	.59198	.3
.8	.40974	.49179	.59026	.2
39.9	.41146	.49210	.58854	50.1
40.0	.41318	.49240	.58682	50.0
.1	.41490	.49270	.58510	49.9
.2	.41662	.49300	.58338	.8
.3	.41834	.49329	.58166	.7
.4	.42006	.49357	.57994	.6
.5	.42178	.49384	.57822	.5
.6	.42351	.49411	.57649	.4
.7	.42523	.49438	.57477	.3
.8	.42696	.49464	.57304	.2
.9	.42869	.49489	.57131	49.1
41.0	.43041	.49513	.56959	49.0
.1	.43214	.49537	.56786	48.9
.2	.43387	.49561	.56613	.8
.3	.43560	.49584	.56440	.7
.4	.43733	.49606	.56267	.6
.5	.43907	.49627	.56093	.5
.6	.44080	.49648	.55920	.4
.7	.44253	.49669	.55747	.3
.8	.44427	.49688	.55573	.2
.9	.44600	.49708	.55400	48.1
42.0	.44774	.49726	.55226	48.0
.1	.44947	.49744	.55053	47.9
.2	.45121	.49761	.54879	.8
.3	.45295	.49778	.54705	.7
.4	.45468	.49794	.54532	.6
.5	.45642	.49810	.54358	.5
.6	.45816	.49825	.54184	.4
.7	.45990	.49839	.54010	.3
.8	.46164	.49853	.53836	.2
.9	.46338	.49866	.53662	47.1
43.0	.46512	.49878	.53488	47.0
.1	.46686	.49890	.53314	46.9
.2	.46860	.49901	.53140	.8
.3	.47035	.49912	.52965	.7
.4	.47209	.49922	.52791	.6
.5	.47383	.49931	.52617	.5
.6	.47558	.49940	.52442	.4
.7	.47732	.49949	.52268	.3
.8	.47906	.49956	.52094	.2
.9	.48081	.49963	.51919	46.1
44.0	.48255	.49970	.51745	46.0
.1	.48429	.49975	.51571	45.9
.2	.48604	.49981	.51396	.8
.3	.48778	.49985	.51222	.7
.4	.48953	.49989	.51047	.6
.5	.49127	.49992	.50873	.5
.6	.49302	.49995	.50698	.4
.7	.49476	.49997	.50524	.3
.8	.49651	.49999	.50349	.2
.9	.49825	.50000	.50175	45.1
45.0	.50000	.50000	.50000	45.0
Deg.	**cos²**	**sin·cos**	**sin²**	**Deg.**

When making a trigonometric fit to a set of data, most of the computational labor is in finding the sum of the products of the functions involved. If making a single frequency fit which is the usual situation for the analysis discussed in this book, a little planning will enable you to utilize the following short table to save most of the calculations. You have a choice of length of data span, the number of data points and the data interval spacing. Normally, a span covering about one cycle is desirable and about ten data points is a good choice. The frequency ω is very easy to calculate and when found may be rounded to the nearest integral degree, its units being in degrees per unit time interval. If the number of degrees does not fall within the 30 to 59 degree range of the tables, merely adjust the data interval until the tables can be used. The data interval may be adjusted using interpolation by reading the points from a graph where the plotted points are connected by a smooth line. Table V gives the indicated sums for the set of N products as ωt varies from zero to $(N-1)\,\omega$ where N is the number of data points. Because of the identity $\sin^2 x + \cos^2 x = 1$, the sum of the $\cos^2 \omega t$ terms is given by $N - \Sigma \sin^2 \omega t$.

TABLE V. $\sum_{t=0}^{N-1} \sin^2 \omega t$ and $\sum_{t=0}^{N-1} \sin \omega t \cdot \cos \omega t$

Deg.	N = 8		N = 9		N = 10	
	$\sum \sin^2$	$\sum \sin \cdot \cos$	$\sum \sin^2$	$\sum \sin \cdot \cos$	$\sum \sin^2$	$\sum \sin \cdot \cos$
30	3.2500	0.4330	4.0000	0.8660	5.0000	0.8660
31	3.2811	0.5417	4.1408	0.8890	5.1163	0.7345
32	3.3414	0.6360	4.2829	0.8707	5.1874	0.5768
33	3.4254	0.7095	4.4145	0.8135	5.2084	0.4090
34	3.5265	0.7578	4.5252	0.7229	5.1798	0.2474
35	3.6372	0.7780	4.6070	0.6070	5.1070	0.1070
36	3.7500	0.7694	4.6545	0.4755	5.0000	0.0000
37	3.8575	0.7330	4.6653	0.3390	4.8715	-0.0655
38	3.9530	0.6717	4.6403	0.2081	4.7358	-0.0858
39	4.0309	0.5896	4.5832	0.0924	4.6076	-0.0621
40	4.0868	0.4924	4.5000	0.0000	4.5000	0.0000
41	4.1181	0.3862	4.3989	-0.0632	4.4234	0.0913
42	4.1236	0.2777	4.2891	-0.0939	4.3845	0.2000
43	4.1041	0.1732	4.1801	-0.0917	4.3862	0.3128
44	4.0617	0.0789	4.0810	-0.0589	4.4265	0.4166
45	4.0000	0.0000	4.0000	0.0000	4.5000	0.5000
46	3.9238	-0.0596	3.9431	0.0783	4.5976	0.5538
47	3.8385	-0.0971	3.9144	0.1679	4.7083	0.5724
48	3.7500	-0.1113	3.9154	0.2603	4.8199	0.5542
49	3.6643	-0.1026	3.9451	0.3468	4.9206	0.5013
50	3.5868	-0.0729	4.0000	0.4195	5.0000	0.4195
51	3.5225	-0.0250	4.0748	0.4722	5.0503	0.3177
52	3.4752	0.0367	4.1626	0.5003	5.0671	0.2064
53	3.4476	0.1074	4.2555	0.5014	5.0494	0.0969
54	3.4410	0.1816	4.3455	0.4755	5.0000	0.0000
55	3.4552	0.2540	4.4251	0.4251	4.9251	-0.0749
56	3.4888	0.3194	4.4876	0.3543	4.8331	-0.1212
57	3.5392	0.3731	4.5283	0.2692	4.7344	-0.1353
58	3.6026	0.4115	4.5441	0.1768	4.6396	-0.1171
59	3.6745	0.4319	4.5342	0.0846	4.5587	-0.0699

TABLE V (Continued)

Deg.	N = 11		N = 12		N = 13	
	$\sum \sin^2$	$\sum \sin \cdot \cos$	$\sum \sin^2$	$\sum \sin \cdot \cos$	$\sum \sin^2$	$\sum \sin \cdot \cos$
30	5.7500	0.4330	6.0000	0.0000	6.0000	0.0000
31	5.7032	0.2421	5.8092	-0.0657	5.8524	0.1377
32	5.6006	0.0844	5.6200	-0.0534	5.7854	0.3182
33	5.4584	-0.0240	5.4611	0.0282	5.8066	0.5038
34	5.2967	-0.0740	5.3553	0.1608	5.9075	0.6580
35	5.1372	-0.0640	5.3158	0.3190	6.0658	0.7521
36	5.0000	0.0000	5.3455	0.4755	6.2500	0.7694
37	4.9016	0.1055	5.4365	0.6043	6.4256	0.7083
38	4.8528	0.2356	5.5720	0.6850	6.5611	0.5810
39	4.8576	0.3709	5.7292	0.7054	6.6337	0.4115
40	4.9132	0.4924	5.8830	0.6634	6.6330	0.2304
41	5.0102	0.5837	6.0099	0.5663	6.5621	0.0690
42	5.1345	0.6330	6.0913	0.4296	6.4368	-0.0459
43	5.2692	0.6342	6.1165	0.2745	6.2819	-0.0971
44	5.3964	0.5877	6.0837	0.1241	6.1269	-0.0793
45	5.5000	0.5000	6.0000	0.0000	6.0000	0.0000
46	5.5675	0.3828	5.8802	-0.0808	5.9234	0.1226
47	5.5914	0.2510	5.7440	-0.1087	5.9095	0.2629
48	5.5699	0.1211	5.6132	-0.0822	5.9587	0.3933
49	5.5074	0.0089	5.5077	-0.0086	6.0600	0.4887
50	5.4132	-0.0729	5.4433	0.0982	6.1933	0.5312
51	5.3003	-0.1153	5.4288	0.2193	6.3333	0.5132
52	5.1840	-0.1150	5.4649	0.3344	6.4539	0.4384
53	5.0795	-0.0741	5.5446	0.4246	6.5337	0.3207
54	5.0000	0.0000	5.6545	0.4755	6.5590	0.1816
55	4.9552	0.0961	5.7766	0.4791	6.5266	0.0461
56	4.9501	0.2001	5.8916	0.4349	6.4438	-0.0624
57	4.9844	0.2977	5.9817	0.3499	6.3272	-0.1256
58	5.0527	0.3753	6.0334	0.2375	6.1988	-0.1341
59	5.1455	0.4225	6.0395	0.1147	6.0827	-0.0887

TABLE V (Continued)

Deg.	N = 14		N = 15		N = 16	
	$\sum \sin^2$	$\sum \sin \cdot \cos$	$\sum \sin^2$	$\sum \sin \cdot \cos$	$\sum \sin^2$	$\sum \sin \cdot \cos$
30	6.2500	0.4330	7.0000	0.8660	8.0000	0.8660
31	6.3175	0.6364	7.2415	0.9014	8.1745	0.6514
32	6.4727	0.7818	7.4715	0.8166	8.2215	0.3836
33	6.6782	0.8383	7.6350	0.6350	8.1350	0.1350
34	6.8882	0.7958	7.6960	0.4018	7.9460	-0.0312
35	7.0582	0.6652	7.6450	0.1728	7.7120	-0.0772
36	7.1545	0.4755	7.5000	0.0000	7.5000	0.0000
37	7.1603	0.2668	7.3006	-0.0806	7.3676	0.1694
38	7.0785	0.0813	7.0979	-0.0565	7.3479	0.3765
39	6.9303	-0.0452	6.9413	0.0587	7.4413	0.5587
40	6.7500	-0.0910	6.8670	0.2304	7.6170	0.6634
41	6.5770	-0.0519	6.8897	0.4117	7.8227	0.6617
42	6.4477	0.0580	7.0000	0.5553	8.0000	0.5553
43	6.3879	0.2107	7.1675	0.6253	8.1006	0.3753
44	6.4077	0.3701	7.3492	0.6048	8.0992	0.1718
45	6.5000	0.5000	7.5000	0.5000	8.0000	0.0000
46	6.6426	0.5720	7.5841	0.3372	7.8341	-0.0958
47	6.8035	0.5708	7.5831	0.1562	7.6501	-0.0938
48	6.9477	0.4973	7.5000	0.0000	7.5000	0.0000
49	7.0451	0.3677	7.3578	-0.0959	7.4248	0.1541
50	7.0764	0.2098	7.1933	-0.1116	7.4433	0.3214
51	7.0366	0.0564	7.0476	-0.0476	7.5476	0.4524
52	6.9365	-0.0613	6.9558	0.0765	7.7058	0.5095
53	6.7990	-0.1208	6.9393	0.2265	7.8723	0.4765
54	6.6545	-0.1123	7.0000	0.3633	8.0000	0.3633
55	6.5342	-0.0408	7.1210	0.4517	8.0540	0.2017
56	6.4632	0.0754	7.2710	0.4694	8.0210	0.0364
57	6.4556	0.2090	7.4124	0.4124	7.9124	-0.0876
58	6.5115	0.3295	7.5103	0.2946	7.7603	-0.1384
59	6.6176	0.4101	7.5416	0.1451	7.6086	-0.1049

Index

261